The Artist Within the Warlord

An Adolf Hitler You've Never Known

Selections from *Ein Anderer Hitler* ("Another Hitler"),
the memoir of architect Hermann Giesler

THE ARTIST WITHIN THE WARLORD
AN ADOLF HITLER YOU'VE NEVER KNOWN

978-0-692-17958-1

First Edition: December 2017
Second Edition: February 2018
Third Edition: August 2018

Copyright 2017 Carolyn Yeager

(Translated from and expanded upon the book *Ein Anderer Hitler*, originally published by Druffel-Verlag A. Lech, 1977.)

All rights reserved.

No part of this publication may be reproduced, stored in a retrieval system or transmitted in any form by any means, electronic, mechanical, photocopy, recording, or otherwise, without prior permission of the publisher, except as provided by U.S.A. copyright law.

Manufactured in the United States of America

About the photographs in this book:
The photographs in this book are almost unanimously from two sources: The German Federal Archive (GFA) and the personal files of Hermann Giesler. GFA photos are uncopyrighted but must retain a domain tag. The Giesler photos are from *Ein Anderer Hitler*, the German-language book from which much of this book was translated.

THE ARTIST WITHIN THE WARLORD
AN ADOLF HITLER YOU'VE NEVER KNOWN

Selections from *Ein Anderer Hitler* ("Another Hitler"),
the memoir of architect Hermann Giesler

Translation and Commentary by

WILHELM KRIESSMANN, PH.D. & CAROLYN YEAGER

TABLE OF CONTENTS

PREFACE 1

INTRODUCTION 3
    Hitler the Artist 4
    Hitler the Military Commander 6
    Who Was Hermann Giesler 7

CHAPTER 1:
    With Adolf Hitler in Paris 9
        An Invitation to Paris 9
        The Importance of the Eiffel Tower 12
        "I Want Peace" 20

CHAPTER 2:
    Fateful Decisions to Invade Poland & Soviet Russia 25
        Hitler's Pact With Stalin 25
        Why Consensus Moves Failed 27
        Russian-Soviet Timing & Tactics 28
        The Political Future of Europe 29
        Stalin & Britain Destabilize the Balkans 30
    From the Translators
        Jozef Beck Refuses to See Reason on Danzig 34
        Jozef Pilsudski: Poland's Nationalist Dreamer 36
        British & Soviet Machinations in the Balkans 38

TABLE OF CONTENTS

CHAPTER 3:
How Adolf Hitler Planned the May 1940 Western Offensive 41
    A Plan for the West in All Its Details 42
    A Plethora of Maps Show Success After Success 45
    The Dunkirk "Miracle" 47
    More Thoughts on Hitler 51
    Keitel & Jodl Explain 52
    Ahead of the Allies: Narvik 54
    May 1940: Giesler's Recollections 55
    From the Translators
    The Controversy: Keitel vs. Halder 58
    The Stunning Victory at Fort Eben-Emael 62

CHAPTER 4:
Why Operation Sea Lion Was Never Launched 67
    August 1942, Fuehrer HQ, Winniza 71
    Lunch at Deutelmoser's Tavern in Munich 74
    Berghof: 1941 76
    From the Translators
    Franco's Lukewarm Commitment to Germany 78
    Why Guernica? The Politics of Propaganda 80
    Barbarossa's Saga 83

CHAPTER 5:
Hitler Strikes First With Operation Barbarossa 85
    Hitler Reveals His Reasoning 85
    Outsmarted by the Russians 89
    From the Translators
    Strategy: Moscow or Kiev? 95
    M-Day: Stalin's Mobilization 99

Table of Contents continued on following pages

TABLE OF CONTENTS

CHAPTER 6:

Inside Hitler's Secret Military Headquarters East, 1942 103
    Wolfsschanze—Winter 1941/42 103
    Hitler Envisions Europe's Future 107
    Werwolf—Summer/Fall 1942 109
    Hitler Needs a Creative Outlet 109

CHAPTER 7:

Hitler Discloses Hidden Treachery at the Front 115
    Hitler Reveals High-Level Sabotage 115
    Hitler's Intended Retirement Home 122
    A Fantastic Storyteller 125

CHAPTER 8:

Valkyrie: The Final Plot Against Adolf Hitler 131
    Giesler Learns of the Bombing 131
    The Kaltenbrunner Reports 134
    Giesler Reflects on the Role of Speer 137
    The People's Court 140
    Giesler Remembers Martin Bormann 141
   From the Translators
    Previous Assassination Attempts 145

CHAPTER 9:

Valkyrie: The Story 147
    Giesler Details the 1944 Attack on Hitler 147
    The Worst of the Treason 155
   From the Translators
    A Day at the Bendlerblock 159

CHAPTER 10:

Valkyrie: The Last Circle 167
    Giesler remembers Telltale Signs of Trouble 167

TABLE OF CONTENTS

CHAPTER 10 (*Continued*):
    Treason in the *Abwehr* & Army Group Center 173
    Treason in the West 178
    From the Translators
    The People's Court 182

CHAPTER 11:
    Methods & Morals of the Traitors 185
    Hitler Critiques the Plot's Lack of Substance 185

CHAPTER 12:
    Jodl Looks Back on Stalingrad; Hitler Faces Surrender 193
    Jodl Talks About Stalingrad 193
    Need for a Corridor 196
    Jodl at Nuremberg 197
    Hitler Seeks a Successor 199
    "We Will Win the War" 201
    From the Translators
    Rudel: The Man Who Might Have Been Fuehrer 207

CHAPTER 13:
    Farewell Berlin 219
    Creative Tasks of the Future 219
    Linz Model Presented to Hitler 221
    Difficulties With Albert Speer 224
    Götterdämmerung at Headquarters 226
    Rudel Gets Personal Attention 229
    After Terrible News, Giesler Bids Farewell 231
    From the Translators
    A Letter from Breker 234
    A Reich of Art & Culture 236

GLOSSARY OF GERMAN WORDS 241
ABOUT THE TRANSLATORS 244

PHOTO: GIESLER PERSONAL FILES

AN AGREEABLE RELATIONSHIP

The special connection that existed between Adolf Hitler and Hermann Giesler (on left) was based on Architecture and National Socialism. Giesler designed a number a important buildings for the Party. Above, they stand on the bank of the Danube, looking across to the city of Linz as they visualize bold renovation ideas for the projected Danube Development of the Banks.

Preface

When I met Wilhelm Kriessmann in July 2008, we were participating on an Internet discussion group of the German World Alliance. I definitely perked up when he mentioned attending the National Socialist Reich Party Congress in Nuremberg in 1938 where he "looked into Hitler's eyes" and "did not see any evil there but still remembers how blue they were." Here was someone who saw the living Adolf Hitler up close?! Wow. I wanted to know more, so to answer all my questions he asked if he could mail me his autobiography which he had written and printed up for his family. "Oh yes," I replied and soon I received in the mail a large 8x11 spiral bound book with text and photos.

That was the beginning of a friendship that continued until 'Willi' quietly passed from this physical world in December 2012 at the age of 93. Willi Kriessmann added so much to my life in those 4 years that I can hardly believe it was so short a time we knew each other. We had a ball doing what we did, which was to write stuff together. I also interviewed him a number of times on the Internet radio program I had started in March 2010, telling about his so interesting life in interesting times and places. Willi had a big personality and amazing vigor for his age, yet a modesty toward his outstanding accomplishments (for example, being one of the few to fly the world's first jet propelled plane, the Arado 234B). I had to talk him into adding to his autobiography the dangerous mission he successfully flew to the besieged Citadel at *Welikije Luki* on the Russian front in 1943 that earned him and his crew the Iron Cross, first class.

Willi introduced me to Hermann Giesler's book *Ein Anderer Hitler.* He had started translating parts of it for me, first completing the entire section headed "With Adolf Hitler in Paris." I worked with him in getting the English to perfectly match the German writing of architect Giesler. We sold this to THE BARNES REVIEW who published it in their Nov-Dec 2008 magazine. By then, Willi was already at work on another section. When we wrapped up this project in 2011, we had the entire last 125 pages of Giesler's 500-page memoir, the section headed *Führer Hauptquartiere.* This makes up the book you are now holding in your hands. It covers the time Giesler spent with Hitler at the various Fuehrer Headquarters between 1940 and 1945.

It is undeniable that an important and unique contribution to the understanding of Adolf Hitler has been achieved by the honest chronicler Hermann Giesler, and it is unfortunate that the respect and appreciation due him is still largely withheld. Although this is not why we undertook it, we came to share the hope that our work of translation and commentary would help to correct that injustice. Thank you, Hermann Giesler!

Finally, to my co-author, I dedicate the publication of this book as a tribute to his life and memory. This is for you, Willi.

—CAROLYN YEAGER
August 2018

Introduction

Through the decades since 1939, Western historians and writers have felt obliged to caricature Adolf Hitler as an embittered egomaniac with a far-fetched goal of world domination. This has never explained the mystique of this man who is arguably the most famous person on the planet today.

Many who knew him and were close to him, some who saw him daily, wrote books telling quite a different tale. Nicolaus von Below, Hitler's *Luftwaffe* adjutant from 1937 to 1945, wrote that Hitler was neither arrogant nor stubborn, but could be persuaded to change his mind if given clear and reasoned arguments (*At Hitler's Side*, 2001). Other writers were Hans Bauer, his personal pilot (*I Flew with the Mighty of the World*, 1957); Rochus Misch, his bodyguard (*The Last Witness*, 2008); Heinz Linge, his valet (*With Hitler to the End*, 2009); two of Hitler's secretaries: Christa Schroeder (*He was my Chief*, 1985) and Traudl Junge (*Until the Final Hour*, 2002). All described an Adolf Hitler who was a considerate, correct and even kind employer, with a calm and agreeable personality, who seldom if ever raised his voice. None of these witnesses had any reason to lie; in fact they had every reason to say otherwise, as they have all been accused of stating falsehoods or being in denial by the gatekeepers of politically correct history.

In addition to the sources that tell of "Hitler the Employer," there is the book published in German in 1977 by Hermann Giesler which reveals a man we can call "Hitler the Artist." *Ein Anderer Hitler* (Another Hitler) is Giesler's memoir of his numerous personal contacts with the Fuehrer concerning sweeping architectural plans for the cities of *Grossdeutschland* (Greater Germany)—Berlin, Munich and Linz—containing intimate insights into the Fuehrer's psychology, decisionmaking, and visionary outlook.

HITLER THE ARTIST

Although Adolf Hitler was an accomplished artist and had an impressive knowledge and self-taught ability for architecture, the general public has been deceived into believing that Hitler was an itinerant house painter and a poorly schooled man who used "gangster" tactics and a gift for persuasive speech to "seize power" at the highest level of German government, and from there ruled a passive people with dictatorial methods. All untrue. In fact, Hitler was a man of wide-ranging knowledge and culture.

A watercolor sketch by young Adolf Hitler of the Karlskirche in Vienna. There are an estimated 723 Hitler paintings and sketches known to exist, though how many more may be in the hands of unknown private collectors is a mystery.

Adolf Hitler attended his first opera—a performance of Richard Wagner's *Lohengrin* in his hometown of Linz—at age 12 and was a passionate opera- and theatergoer from then on. At that age he also decided he would become an artist—a painter—and began his stubborn resistance to his father's plan to turn him into a civil servant. Hitler's great interest in architecture also emerged at an early age—in his teens he would walk through the city of Linz with his friend August Kubizek, pointing out the public buildings that needed to be "redone" and describe exactly how he would do it. Later, although he had only studied architecture

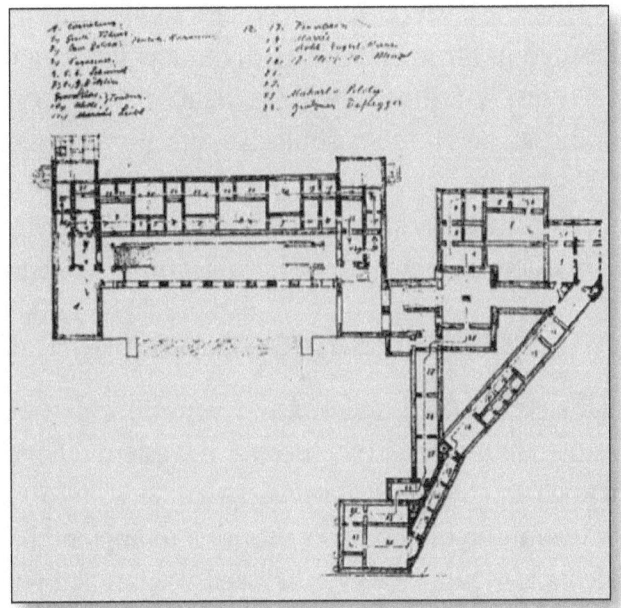

Hitler's 1925 sketchbook included his plan of a proposed German National Art Museum. At the top he wrote the names of his most highly regarded artists and the room number where their works were to be displayed.

on his own in books, he could discuss the subject on an equal footing with professional architects (who always expressed amazement at the depth and exactitude of his knowledge).

Giesler's Hitler is one who can't bear to live without spending time with other artists at regular intervals, and whose favorite relaxation was to spend an evening drawing architectural designs for the rebuilding projects of German cities. When among creative people, Hitler was always happier—he felt in his element. He insisted on keeping theater, opera and symphony performances going for as long as possible during the war years, not wanting the German people to get used to doing without what he considered the necessary cultural side of life. Art museums and galleries also remained open. He saw to it that traveling exhibitions and symphonies, the best the cities had to offer, went on tour to the smallest towns and villages. He ordered that the upper level of German artists not be drafted, as their lives were too valuable to the entire *Volk* to be lost.

To Adolf Hitler, a great nation produced a high culture and that is how he measured it. But he was also fully aware that in order to enjoy the gifts of culture, you must first have bread in your stomach. Thus, Hitler the politician and military strategist were also necessary roles that he took on. During the war years, the time of Giesler's close contact with the Fuehrer, the trustworthy architect became the unexpected "confidant" of the military leader beset with problems, worries and disloyalties.

HITLER THE MILITARY COMMANDER

We meet the Hitler who pondered and came up with the operational plan that resulted in the decisively successful Western Offensive of 1940 before Gen. Erich von Manstein proposed a similar solution to him. This swift victory led him to offer a peace proposal to England based on that victory, which Churchill, however, refused. We are shown Hitler the strategist of the Soviet invasion, Operation Barbarossa, with its huge early victories, and also Hitler who, as the victim of treason by his own military commanders, felt but could not comprehend this treason until too late.

There is Hitler and Valkyrie, with all the details of this final assassination plot given to Giesler at Hitler's order, as well as Hitler's thoughts and reflections afterward. We learn of Hitler's disgust at discovering the treason by his own generals, especially those in charge of the telephone switchboard at Fuehrer headquarters by which they transmitted *Wehrmacht* military orders to the Soviet Union via the Lucy spy ring in Switzerland, thereby bringing defeat on their own armies and directly causing the death of hundreds of thousands of their fellow soldiers and officers. Finally, we see Hitler facing defeat with dignity, even though retaining hope and determination to the very end.

In these selections, you will discover that Giesler's account of Hitler during these years is internally consistent, and it fits with other's accounts of what was transpiring where and when he was present. We can trust Giesler, just as Hitler trusted him. He shows us a believable, three-dimensional person, a human being of varying moods, a persuasive leader, a soldier, a friend, and not least, a fellow artist. ♦

WHO WAS HERMANN GIESLER?

Hermann Giesler was born in 1898 into a family of architects. He volunteered for the German Army in 1915, became a lieutenant in the Pioneers and ended as a WWI pilot. He completed his architectural study at the Munich Academy of Applied Art after the war. Giesler was impressed by Oswald Spengler, whom he met in 1919 at a symposium at the Munich City Hall. In 1923 he married and had two sons. Beginning in 1930, he worked as an independent architect, winning several awards. He joined the NSDAP well before 1933. In 1937 he gained a professorship, received the Grand Prix and gold medal for his architectural designs at the World Exhibition in Paris, and was assigned in 1938 to the overall design of Germany's exhibits at the 1942 World Exhibition in Rome.

That year (1938), Adolf Hitler asked him to plan Munich's architectural renovation, as well as to design and build his private residence in Munich. Later on, Giesler was put in charge of planning Hitler's pet project, the city of Linz. He worked on plans and a large model for the Danube Development of the Banks, and on designs for the cultural center which Hitler regarded with particular interest. When war broke out, he was promoted to *generalbaurat* and given the task of construction for war-related building projects in the Balticum (Lithuania/ Latvia/Estonia). In 1942-44 he was chief of the Organization Todt Group North and from 1944-45, chief of OT Group VI (Bavaria, Upper and Lower Austria). Giesler later wrote about the friction between himself and Hitler's "other" architect, Albert Speer, during 1940-42. It started with Speer's dominant control of building-material, labor and construction and ended with Speer going behind Giesler's back to take over the Linz project. Giesler called Speer "the Cesar Borgia of the 20th century." Giesler became a POW of the U.S. in 1945, and was interned for two years. He was prosecuted as a war criminal, receiving a life sentence at hard labor. Considered sufficiently "denazified" by 1952, he was released, after which he started his own business. In 1977, he published his memoir about his architectural and personal relationship with Hitler. He died in 1987. ✦

Hitler and his entourage enter the Paris Opera House while it was still dark outside. Though a guardian walked ahead, Hitler led the way through the opulent interior, confidently pointing out significant features and especially admiring the proportions. When they stepped outside again it was bright day and they had their first view of the famous façade.

CHAPTER 1

WITH ADOLF HITLER IN PARIS

Translators' Introduction: There is no better way to become acquainted with the real personality of the Fuehrer—his alert mind, thoughtfulness, and his artist nature—than Giesler's account of the Paris visit on the eve of the armistice between France and Germany. After the decisive German victory of the Battle of France, Hitler was eager to see the architecturally rich capitol. He shared this sightseeing tour with his favorite architects and sculptor, along with adjutants and officers of the just-completed campaign. Giesler's detailed description of this remarkable day leaves us in no doubt that Hitler's knowledge of architecture was vast, his taste cultured, and his mind open to learning.

AN INVITATION TO PARIS

From the beginning of the war, I and my architect and engineer co-workers were entrusted with the planning and management of construction for the armament industry. On the morning of June 22, 1940 I was on my way to the construction site "Wespe" when a police unit stopped me southeast of Vienna and directed me to drive to the Vienna airport. From there, a JU 52 courier airplane flew me to an airfield in southern Belgium where a cross country vehicle brought me to a small village with only a few very simple houses: Bruly de Peche, north of Sedan—Adolf Hitler's headquarters. In a little while I stood in front of him.

"All right, Giesler, at that time you could not know it, but I was sure of my strategic concept, the necessary tactical details, and my confidence in the fighting power of the German forces. Out of it, the carefully planned timetable developed. Naturally, I remembered that during the winter I invited you to go with me to Paris; I've asked Breker and Speer[1] to come along. With my artists, I want to look at Paris. We will take off early in the morning."

That evening, in a simple hut, I shared a modest dinner on two long primitive tables with Hitler, the leading military staff and the adjutants. Remembering those evenings at Bruly de Peche, I have to say there was no triumphant attitude, no loud voices–only serious dignity. The faces of the responsible leaders still wore the stress of the past weeks. I considered myself unworthy of the reward of sitting with them.

The next morning, June 23rd, the Fuehrer airplane landed in darkness at the Paris airport. Open vehicles were waiting, amongst them a car for the Chief (what we called Adolf Hitler), with Kempka at the wheel. Speer, Breker and I rode in his car, along with the SS adjutant Schaub and an orderly, for the journey thru Paris. The former military attaché in Paris who knew the city well, Col. Speidel, drove ahead of us as pilot and silent mentor.

With our dimmed lights we could only see the contours of the buildings. We passed barricades—the guards stepped out and saluted; one could sense armistice was not completely at work. Adolf Hitler was sitting in front of me and I recalled the past winter evening when he talked about Paris, his confidence that he would see the city soon. Now his wish was being realized. But he did not arrive in Paris as the Supreme Commander of the German *Wehrmacht*—he arrived as the *Bauherr* (construction boss) of German cities which he already visualized with their new faces. He came here to compare architecture, to experience the atmosphere of the city in the company of his two architects and one sculptor, even though escorted by a military entourage—soldiers which surely had earned the privilege to see the capital of France with him.

I had the impression that the itinerary was carefully planned. Our first destination was the Imperial Opera House, designed by the architect Garnier. Since Hitler wanted to see the façade in bright sunlight, we immediately went inside to the brightly lit rooms. Though a guardian walked ahead of us, Adolf Hitler led the way, pointing out the significant features of the building.

It might be that the contrast from the simple atmosphere of the Fuehrer headquarters in the small village of Bruly to this magnificent display of the past Empire increased the impression it made. Up to this day, I only knew of the Opera façade and was surprised by the clear concept of the basic plan, impressed by the arrangement of the spacious rooms: the entry halls, the generous staircase, the foyers and the splenderous, gleaming, gold inner theater. We were standing in the middle loge. Adolf Hitler was fascinated—wonderful, exceptionally beautiful proportions, and what festivity! It was a theater with a special character, regardless of its splendor of the *Belle Epoque* and a stylish eclecticism of a certain overabundant baroque. Hitler repeated that its main importance remains within these beautiful proportions. "I would like to see the reception room, the salon of the president behind the proscenium box," said Hitler. "According to Garnier's plan, it must be around here." A bit of uncertainty took place before the guard remembered that after a renovation the room was removed. Hitler remarked, "The democratic republic doesn't even favor its president with his own reception salon."

We returned through the splendid foyers, stopped at the sculptures of the French *Coryphaei*, still appreciating the view. We went back to the staircase with the elegantly rising steps conforming to the wide frocks of the ladies of the Empire era, stepped down it and out into the bright day where we had a first view of the famous façade in daylight. Then to the Madeleine, which did not impress Hitler much. Now began the journey to the important squares and streets.

Slowly, in a wide circle, we drove around the fountains and the Luxor obelisks at the place de la Concord. Adolf Hitler stood up in his car to get an all around view. He looked across the large square toward the Tuilleries to the Louvre, then across the Seine River to the building of the Chambre des Deputes. At the beginning of the Champs-Élysées, he asked to stop. Looking at the walls of the Admiralty, he could now see, through the short street space of the rue Royal, the column gable of the Madeleine—now really effective.

Adolf Hitler took his time to absorb all this—then a short signal with his hand and we drove slowly along the slightly rising Champs-Élysées towards the Etoile with its all-dominating Arc de Triomphe. Critically checking this, his eyes looked at the road construction, which he could see through the tree-lined streets around the Round Point. Hitler told me later: "Having learned a lot from what I saw, I always compare it with my plans. The Arc de Triomphe benefited by the soft, long rise of the Champs-Élysées—otherwise it would be too small in scale for this large, important street space. Our disposition of the street axis from the Party monument to the new railway station in Munich is correct." He then drew that street plan. He thinks dividing the street with a strong median strip provides a powerful direction, profile and scale—something missing a bit at the Champs-Élysées, that so important street of the world. The architecture along the street is individually designed but by no means convincing.

And the etoile, I asked? Now, one can call the 10 or 12 streets or avenues radiating from it a star, or the other way around: those 12 are storming toward it, tearing the space into burgher sections. As long as the tree crowns are leafed out that might be alright; otherwise the wedge-shaped buildings look too weak. Did not an architect from Cologne build it? "Yes, I think Hittorf, or something similar."

THE IMPORTANCE OF THE EIFFEL TOWER

Continuing with Paris, we drove on from the Etoile to the Embarcadero, viewing the giant of the 19th century, the Eiffel Tower, across the Seine from the large terrace of the Palais Chailot. Beyond it, the Mars field stretched out wide, with the Ecole militair at its end.

Adolf Hitler told me that he considers the Eiffel Tower not only as the beginning of a new standard of buildings, but also as the start of an engineering type of tectonics. "This tower is not only synonymous with Paris and the world exhibition at that time, but it stands, if not yet, as an example of classicism, and yet for the beginning of a new epoch." He means the epoch of a new technology with completely changed targets and dimensions (*Groessenordnungen*), at that time unknown. What follows are wide-spanned bridges, buildings with large vertical dimensions which because of exact engineering calculations could now be used as static structures. But only through coordination between engineers, artists and architects could he see the possibility of proper creativity. Classicism, which we have to aim at, can only be reached by tectonics which conform with new materials—steel and reinforced concrete indeed being proprietary.

On our further drive across the Seine to the Ecole militaire we stopped at a monument of a French general of the 1914-18 war with an inscription insulting German soldiers—very tasteless. Hitler got angry, waited for the accompanying car to stop, turned to the military men and ordered they see to it that it is blown up. Honoring Col. General Keitel, who traveled with us, we visited the *Cour d'honneur de l'Ecole militaire*. Then we arrived at the highlight of our trip—at least for me.

In the dome of the Invalides, Adolf Hitler stood for a long time at the rim of the crypt with his head bent and stared down at Napoleon's sarcophagus. I stood at his left side, not by coincidence, but because he pulled me to his side. Quietly he said to me, "Giesler, you will build my grave site, we'll talk about it later."

Quiet and thoughtful, he left the dome; we remained a few steps behind him. Outside the gate, Hitler turned around: "Bormann, I want the Herzog of Reichsstadt to be brought back to Paris."

***

Translators' Note: The Herzog, Napoleon's son with his second wife, the Austrian Princess Marie Luise, was kept in Vienna and educated there. He died in 1832 at the age of twenty-one at the Schoenbrunn palace in Vienna and was buried at the Habsburg tomb, the *Kapuziner Gruft*. The restoration of the body of the Herzog von Reichsstadt from its burial place in Austria to the crypt of his father in Paris is one of the little-known and seldom spoken of actions undertaken by Adolf Hitler to show his respect for the French people and culture.

***

We drove on and stopped for a short while at a well-proportioned city palais, the future German embassy. Adolf Hitler gave orders for its careful renovation with the assistance of French conservators. At the Panthéon at the top of the Latin Quarter, Adolf Hitler was very disappointed;

HITLER VISITS NAPOLEON'S CRYPT

Wearing a light-colored dust coat (*Staubmantel*) covering his field gray uniform and having removed his military cap out of respect, Adolf Hitler stands quietly at the rim of the crypt silently gazing down upon Napoleon Bonaparte's empire-style sarcophagus in the Dome des Invalides, Paris, on the morning of June 23, 1940. He is accompanied by his equally respectful military and cultural entourage. What thoughts were going through his mind as he contemplated the fate of one of Europe's greatest conquerors, a man he was known to admire? Does he see Moscow burning and the horrible retreat across the Beresina? We know he had thoughts of his own legacy—and his own death—for he turned to Giesler and said to him, "You will build my gravesite." Later that same day, he told Giesler, "At the *dome des Invalides*, I really absorbed only Napoleon's sarcophagus at the open ronda of the crypt. I kept strangely under the spell—everything else was for me meaningless." [PHOTO: GIESLER PERSONAL FILES] leaving the building abruptly, he shook his head and heaved a sigh: "My God, it does not deserve its name, if you think about the Roman Pantheon with its classical interior, the unique lighting from the wide open ceiling—it combines dignity with solemnity. And then you look at that"—and he pointed back—"more than somber even on this bright summer day." As we returned to our car, a few women spotted us, crying out: *c'est lui*—that's he.

Bypassing the Sorbonne and Cluny across the Seine to the Ile de la Cite, driving slowly without a stop, we saw the Notre Dame. A back and forth talk between Hitler and Breker began about the name and the use of a building. Hitler pointed toward a building with a cupola: "Isn't that the so-called Tribunal of the Chamber of Commerce?" Breker said No, and since he lived many years in Paris he was sure about it. When we came closer it was obvious Hitler had already recognized the building from a distance by its form and location. Below the gable one could read: Tribunal de Commerce.

Crossing the Pont d'Arcole of the second Seinearm, we drove to the square in front of the Hotel de Ville to the rue de Rivoli and further to the place des Vosges. The queen Maria de Medici ordered that square arrangement, remembering her Florence. Because of the dense tree lines, the original space idea is no longer recognizable. The way the place des Vosges presented itself did not impress Hitler. After a short look at what he could still recognize, we moved on.

Hitler commented on the rue de Rivoli:

> Its kilometer-long uniform façade is just right and is effective because, at the opposite side, the Louvre and the adjoining Tuilleries Gardens require that quiet and even form. All the more of a surprise, then, is the disruption of the small square with the Jeanne d'Arc monument.

We turned around and drove through the rue Castiglioni to the place Vendome, with its famous column on this magnificently shaped square, then the rue de la Paix to the place de l'Opera, with a lofty view of the

HITLER & HIS ARTISTS

Adolf Hitler and his entourage step resolutely through the gates of the *dome des Invalides* into the early Parisian morning after viewing Napoleon's burial site. Immediately behind Hitler are his "artists," (left to right) sculptor Arno Breker and architects Hermann Giesler and Albert Speer, wearing military coats and caps. Behind them are the "soldiers that had earned the privilege to see the capital of France with him." [PHOTO: GIESLER PERSONAL FILES] vivid, although a bit theatrical, facade of the Opera, now in bright light. Hitler admired that city-planning connection. "Certainly," he said to me later, "it is very decorative, partly too rich, but naturally corresponding to the style taste of that epoch. Planning our architecture, we will aim at a classicism of stricter, sharper forms, according to our character. What I have seen in Paris forces me to compare the performance of the German architecture of the same period: Gilly, Schinkel, Klenze, Hansen and Semper, and Siccardsburg with his Vienna Opera—I have the impression they can hold their place. Not to mention the great creations of the baroque architects like Lukas Hildebrandt, Fischer von Erlach, Balthasar Neumann, Prandtauer and others. What the Germans miss is continuity and persistence in their architectural aims, but this is still recognizable in the Germany of the Middle Ages with cathedrals and domes of the city communities, and the baroque buildings of the royal houses."

Approaching the Montmartre, Hitler barely looked at the Sacre Coeur. From the elevated terrace in front of the church, he wanted to see down across the part of Paris he had just visited, with its streets and squares. He wanted to get an impression of the relief effect of the buildings within the city spaces—how a certain order wins control over the jumble of buildings—how decisively the impressive buildings establish a strong order within their set scale: the Notre Dame and the Arc de Triomphe, the big squares, the great street axes, the Hausmann-avenues.

Adolf Hitler believed that as far as he could view the concentration of Paris from the Sacre Coeur terrace, the monuments and places stood out only weakly from the monotony of living quarters and functional buildings. The great cohesion from the Louvre to the Etoile, the Ile de France with the Notre Dame, the flowing of the Seine to the Eiffel tower is just barely maintained. Actually, only this tower, meant and built for an exhibition, maintains—regardless of its filigree transparency seen from here—its reputation. What he means is that the Tower justifies its existence in this city only by the deliberately planned vertical tendency—an astonishing feature for that epoch. Naturally, for the city of Paris it meant a symbolic novelty, a city with such a deep historical tradition from the Romans to the very significant eras of the kings, the revolution,

HITLER & BREKER AT THE EIFFEL TOWER

Hitler with Sculptor Arno Breker in front of the Eiffel Tower on the morning of June 23, 1940. The Fuehrer was a great admirer of French culture and commented rather extensively to Giesler his sense of the architectural importance of the famous Paris landmark.

GERMAN FEDERAL ARCHIVES

the empire, the buildings of the republic after Napoleon III; they are all meaningless, of no importance for the overall structure of the city—with the exception of the Eiffel Tower.

Adolf Hitler turned toward us—Speer, Breker and me: "For you a tough time begins, work and pressure, the forming of cities and monuments which are put into your trust. As far as I am able, and can afford the time, I will lighten your work! Bormann will assist me. Look after my artists and keep away from them everything that might obstruct their work."[2] And then again to us: "Put everything on Bormann's broad shoulders. He will stand by you."

We drove to the airport; the sight-seeing excursion to Paris was over. The aircraft circled above the center of Paris. Fascinated, Adolf Hitler looked down: the center of this city is just magnanimous. But its streets and squares were deserted, I remarked, and only with the people and the traffic is Paris vivid, only then these streets and squares have their justification. I saw it that way in 1937 during the world exhibit. Yes, he can imagine it.

By early afternoon we were back in the village of Bruly de Peche. Messages were handed to Hitler, he read them standing outside. Among them was a wire from the former Kaiser Wilhelm II: "What a turn around by God's providence." These were exactly the same words his grandfather used, sending a telegram to the Kaiserin. But Wilhelm II forgets the strong belief behind deeds for Germany, the endurance, the unshakeable optimism, the trouble to build party and state, and above all the sacrifice necessary to make that providence possible.

That evening I walked with Adolf Hitler up and down in front of his dwelling, a farmer's house. We talked about every detail of our trip through Paris. Some of his impressions and judgments I have already mentioned: The Place Vendome with its column—a renaissance of the Roman Trajan and Marcus-Aurelius Column. Fischer von Erlach integrated it into his unconventional composition of the *Karlskirche* (Charles Church) in Vienna, he said, and this column made it possible for the street to enlarge into a square with powerful uniform facades. Hitler said:

Similar to Rome, you could read off the historical eras all over that city. Every epoch was manifested in its buildings. The remnants of the Roman founding that only archaeologists and historians can recognize. The middle ages, however, represent themselves powerfully in Notre Dame, not only a monument of her time but also of her mighty institution, the Church. The epoch of the worldly power, of the kings and the nobility, we drove by this morning at the Louvre and the Palais. The Revolution—she first tore down the sign of the hated system, the Bastille. For the Empire, for Napoleon I, the Arc de Triomphe symbolizes; for Napoleon III, the work of Hausmann and, strangely, the Opera.

Then nothing more? Oh yes, something decisive—a genius engineer designs a gigantic tower. Is it beautiful? It does not matter, it mirrors his epoch. The occasion was significant—first the World Exhibition, then it stands for the Revolution. A hundred years after 1789, that Tower points to a new time—the time of industrial development. It is a monument of technology that sets its own rule, tectonics unknown up to that date, the building material steel—and thus a new method is recognized.

I was fascinated by this short analysis and explanation of the Eiffel tower as a symbol, not just for Paris, but of the new era. It indicates how strongly he felt that history, men and institutions influenced art and architecture and shaped cities. After 30 years, I'm only able to reproduce a sense of the content, but not the fascination which was surely rooted in the happenings and personalities of that day.

"I WANT PEACE"

Adolf Hitler was quiet for a while before he said with a low voice: "At the *dome des Invalides*, I really absorbed only Napoleon's sarcophagus at the open Ronda of the crypt. I kept strangely under the spell—everything else was for me meaningless."

After a while, he reasoned why he wanted his gravesite in Munich, why I should build it and in what form he wanted it to be built. It surprised me, but still, as a National Socialist, that reasoning made a lot of sense. That he discussed that on the day of the victorious finale of the French battle was certainly caused by the view of Napoleon's gravesite. But this thought suggested that he was thinking about that for a long time.

Silently we walked up and down the narrow path through the forest. Then Adolf Hitler stopped and said with great emphasis:

> I want peace—and I will do anything to make peace! It is not too late yet. I will go to the limit of the possible as long as the sacrifice and dignity of the German nation allows it. I know of better things than waging war! If I merely think about the loss of German blood—the best always fall, the bravest and the ones willing to be sacrificed; their task should be to exemplify the nation.
>
> I do not need to make a name by warmongering like Churchill. I would like to make my name as a steward of the German people. I want to secure its unity and Lebensraum, to achieve National Socialism and shape the environment—add to it the new rebuilding of the German cities according to modern knowledge. I would like that the people will be happy there and be proud of their town, their lebensraum, and nation.

After awhile he said the peace should be signed in Muenster.[3] "I have my reasons for that—it would mean an historical caesura. When I now return to Munich, I have to take the necessary steps for the beginning of the rebuilding of the city—a forward-looking planning in all areas of a city-wide development." I, and also Speer, would receive orders from him to start immediately with reconstruction. That naturally includes especially the central railway station and the Autobahn circle—they are the prerequisite of further rebuilding of the city. Dr. Todt will receive the order to make the necessary steel available. Then he repeated again: "I will Peace," and changed the subject.

At the time of Nov. 8, 1939, Hitler was worried because of a strange event. I experienced it personally.[4] He asked himself at that time if it was

Bruly de Pesche. Hitler spent the month of June 1940 at his secret military headquarters for the Western Campaign, named *Wolfsschlucht*. In this photo, Hitler walks outside the community meeting hall in the company of *Reichsmarschall* Hermann Goering, just as he walked with Giesler after the Paris trip.

only careless talking and leaking at high military levels, or high treason. No, he is certain it was high treason, and that high treason has been repeated: the deadline, day and hour of the *Weseruebung*[5] for securing our Northern flank has been transmitted to the government of Denmark and Norway. "No, listen," he said, "also betrayed was the beginning of the battle of France, May 10th." I was alarmed and wanted to ask . . . "No questions, don't talk about it!"

We all joined for the late dinner at the community barrack. June 23rd ended and the armistice began. The trumpet signals, *Das Ganze halt* (All hold), arrived out of the night from different distances. The windows were open. Separate from us, Adolf Hitler stood alone folding his hands. He looked into the darkness. When long after the signal he returned to us, he had tears in his eyes. Quietly, with his typical loose move, he said goodbye to us. He lifted his bent arm, the hand upwards-opened, like a greeting of friendship.

* * *

Translators' Note: Who cannot be moved by the poignant and revelatory picture that emerges during this Paris visit of an Adolf Hitler whose deep awareness of history and far-reaching understanding of the role of art and architecture in the lives of peoples and nations, causes him naturally to prefer peace to war? Here is a man who wants to build and beautify, not tear down and degrade, with always his faith in his people, the German people, and his concern for Europe as a whole as his motivation and inspiration.

On the tail of a decisive victory, he wanted to make peace, and build a united, anti-communist Europe. It was not to be. The new Europe was instead built on the ashes and rubble of his Germany, and he has been condemned as the destroyer, when he really wanted to be a great builder. ◆

CHAPTER NOTES:

1 Arno Breker was Hitler's favorite sculptor, and Albert Speer his most important architect.

2 *Reichsleiter* Martin Bormann was responsible to execute all of Hitler's orders in the civil sector.

3 The Westfalian peace treaty marking the end of the destructive Thirty Years War was signed in Muenster. Was Hitler comparing the past nearly thirty turbulent years since 1914, and hoping to end it in the same way?

4 Hitler got the message while at Giesler's office that the military plans for the attack in the West had been betrayed to the Allies. He had to change his plans and postpone it twice, to Spring 1940. *Ein Anderer Hitler*, Hermann Giesler, page 411: "I ordered the attack for middle November. Then that mysterious betrayal of the planned start of the attack deadline. . . ."

5 *Weseruebung* was the code name for the Denmark/Norway invasion.

GERMAN-SOVIET NON-AGGRESSION PACT

Foreign Minister V. Molotov signs the German-Soviet non-aggression pact; German Foreign Minister Joachim von Ribbentropp stands behind him, next to Stalin. The pact laid out the detailed plans of the "Great Partition of Poland." After 18 days of fierce fighting by the Germans, the Russians simply marched in from the east and met the German officers at the Brest-Litovsk fortress, where the 1918 peace treaty between the Kaiser and the Bolsheviks was signed. Border and map corrections were the only military agendas on the table. The Soviets then collected the remnants of the badly beaten Polish army and led 10,000 officers and common soldiers east into a dark and deadly future. Right away, hundreds of freight cars filled with goods began rolling in both directions.

PHOTO: GERMAN FEDERAL ARCHIVES

CHAPTER 2

FATEFUL DECISIONS TO INVADE POLAND & SOVIET RUSSIA

Translators' Introduction: Hitler would often review out loud his previous decisions concerning important matters of state when working together with Giesler on city building plans. It was Hitler's style to think out loud; to speak his thoughts, rather than to write them. So it was that in Fall 1944 at *Wolfsschanze* (Hitler's main military headquarters on the Eastern front), after the Valkyrie assassination attempt, Hitler spoke to Giesler about what led to his fateful decision to invade Poland in 1939, and the equally fateful decision to invade the Soviet Union two years later. Giesler's account speaks for itself, but we have added three short articles of historical background intended to assist the reader with a fuller understanding of the challenges Hitler faced.

HITLER'S PACT WITH STALIN

The themes of my evening and late night talks with Adolf Hitler in the fall of 1944 resulted from my job as a city builder. The involvement with those problems helped Hitler to relax and, at the same time, gave him the opportunity to determine the future form of those cities from an unusual observation post. His interpretations, ideas and suggestions were significant and were integrated into my planning.

However, those evening talks were not always confined to city building, architecture and technical matters. Sometimes those themes were pushed aside by heavy burdens of military or political events. A dissonant *Lage* (military planning meeting) could also lead Hitler to reactions and reflections expressed very frankly, thus turning me into his confidant.

One evening he talked about the beginning of the war, indicating what thoughts had moved him in August 1939 to the pact with Stalin. He wanted to prevent the menacing encirclement of Germany, and saw that agreement as a last chance to peacefully solve the Danzig and corridor problems.[1]

For years, he said, he tried hard to win Poland over for a fateful European union. It made good sense that Poland should participate in a defense wall against Bolshevism. Every Polish division, he went on, would mean strengthening the military power against not only a possible, but now already significantly obvious, onslaught of Bolshevism against Europe. But the people responsible for Versailles were able to masterfully drive a nearly invincible wedge between Germany and Poland. "Danzig and the corridor!" Their democratically lined cloak of self-determination would have been removed whenever they felt there was need to do so.[2]

That Poland had to have free access to the Baltic Sea was for Hitler self-evident. He therefore tried to reach a settlement along that line, and defuse a poisonous tension in their relationship. It was by no means in our interest to share borders with Soviet Russia—and when he signed an agreement with Marshal [Jozef] Pilsudski,[3] he saw some value in that. But Pilsudski's admonition to his people[4] collapsed under the promises and chauvinistic agitation of the Allies. Up to March 1939, he hoped to reach a settlement with Poland or even sign a friendship pact, but Chamberlain's Guarantee Declaration deemed that hopeless. Poland was in the West's camp. He saw an agreement with Russia as the only chance to avoid encirclement by the Western Powers.

England's diplomats had already tried to strengthen the encirclement by adding Russia's power. He became aware that the Polish problems, now already an open threat, could no longer be solved without Russia. Still, he tried once more to come to a sensible solution. His offer to the Polish government was not only magnanimous, but reached the utmost limit Germany could bear. Only he could make such an offer, serving peace with an honest heart, adverse to the legitimate interests of the German people.

But the Poles stirred the warmongers and persisted in keeping the injustices of Versailles alive. They felt protected by the senseless Guarantee Declaration of England and France. Today, Hitler is convinced that Stalin was part of those warmongers. Icily calculating, Stalin was driving a devilish double game—a binding treaty with us, while at the same time winking at the Western Powers.

WHY CONSENSUS MOVES FAILED

Our treaty with Stalin[5] did not motivate the Poles to yield to a peaceful settlement of the Danzig and corridor problem. Also, because of the continued provocations and persecutions of the German minorities in the part of Poland added by the dictates of Versailles, the now unavoidable war could not have been localized by that German-Russian agreement.

Already at that time, he felt the currents of reaction as real—not only of military, but also those with diplomatic and church connections. But it didn't dawn on him to what villainy that scum out of the German population might be capable. The scope of the malicious behavior, combined with the foolishness and total misjudging of the actual world situation, appeared only later—revealed by the assassination.[6]

Until the last massive snub[7] by the Polish leadership at the end of August 1939, he couldn't imagine that they would let it come to a fight. Sober deliberations would have led the Poles to the following conclusions:

1) The German claim for Danzig is justified because Danzig is a German city.

2) The settlement of the corridor question is necessary and the request for a plebiscite[8] is correct.

3) The alternative offer of the plebiscite for a final and peaceful settlement represents the utmost limits of what can be expected from Germany.

4) After the signing of the German-Russian treaty, Poland's military situation was hopeless.

5) England's Guarantee Declaration did not change anything, nor did any additional far-reaching assurances by England and France. Between the two power blocs of Germany and Russia, Poland would be smashed in a few weeks.

Something else countered those facts and encouraged the Poles in their attitude. Either an English perfidy, which made the Poles risk a war, or the English hint of an assured regime collapse: the removal of the war threat by a reactionary clique within Germany, followed by a putsch.

A multitude of wishful thinking might just explain the following . . .

The (German) reactionary: "If you remain tough, we will get rid of him."

The English: "That's how we finish Germany and the Nazis, we use the Poles."

And the Poles: "Yes, if that's so, in a few weeks we are in Berlin."

When England and France declared war in September 1939, Poland was not their concern. The Guarantee Declarations gave them the goal they were after: a war among the European nations, which complies exactly with Lenin's prophecy. As the war against Poland was now inevitable, Stalin used it to clear the Soviet's west border—after we conquered Poland, Stalin effortlessly finished the rest and then liquidated over 10,000 Polish officers and leaders at the Katyn forest.

RUSSIAN-SOVIET TIMING AND TACTICS

The reports of Polish brutality against the German minorities in the Corridor and the border areas had affected Hitler terribly. Partly before and partly after the beginning of the battles, they were rounded up and beaten to death. More German minorities (*Volksdeutsche*) were beaten and tortured to death than German soldiers died during the regular fighting. That had influenced his attitude toward the Poles.

Hitler then talked again about the German-Russian agreement. That treaty protected our back; we were able to win time. But Stalin, too, needed to gain time when he signed the pact with us. By its Guarantee Declaration, England made any rational and peaceful settlement impossible and wanted war. Stalin, too, drove toward war without being involved right away. Unrest within Europe and Germany's weakness was his goal—and on that his very smart chess moves were aimed at getting us deeply involved in the war and Russia would take the advantage.

Those are the old Czarist, now Lenin-Stalin, political aims: by the partition of Poland, the Soviets gained their Western fore field. While we were tied down with our forces in the West, they annexed the Baltic States, occupied Bessarabia and Northern Bukovina; they were not squeamish, they turned spheres of interest into annexations.

After the French campaign, Stalin certainly expected long-lasting battles; he assumed we would attack England and England thought we would go against Russia. Stalin laid in wait, time was with him, and that "time" was the gigantic Russian-Asiatic continent. We did not have any of that—neither time nor space. And both are decisively interconnected.

Stalin—no, Russia, since Peter the Great—wanted still more territory. Russia wants the Balkans as a "sphere of interest" naturally, like the Baltic states. Russia intends Bulgaria as "a sphere of interest"—it would give her access to the Aegean Sea. She wants bases at the Dardanelles.

Stalin's demands now went from Finland to the Aegean Sea, as a basis for the Bolshevik world revolution—or were those the Old Russian imperialist aims of Peter the Great? Had Hitler agreed to what Molotov demanded in the name of Stalin, he would have betrayed Europe.

THE POLITICAL FUTURE OF EUROPE

The destiny of the Occident (*Abendland*) was at stake—Spengler prophesied in the 1920s its disintegration and decline. He (Hitler) considered it his task to win over the German people, the whole of Europe even, for a strong, social revolution. He planned to ruin Lenin's, and Lenin's successors, quite openly-announced intent to "bolshevize" Europe with the support of Asia. He wanted to avoid the Occident sinking into various types of Marxism. A social reconstruction can only happen within the framework of a nation, a people's union *(Volksgemeinschaft)*, and not by means of an international, splitting-and-class-struggling Marxism. A socialism based on Marxism divides the nation completely, meaning it destroys the only possible carrier of social thinking.

We have seen where this divide leads: to the party pettiness of Social Democrats, Independents and all the way to the Communists. But exactly the same applies to the errors of Liberalism. Neither can be the expression of our century; it would be a relapse worse than during the rule of the Bourbons. Only the synthesis of nation and socialism is meaningful for us and our century.

STALIN & BRITAIN DESTABILIZE THE BALKANS

Adolf Hitler continued to talk. He said: "Behind Stalin's cold, hard demands, expressed by Molotov during his visit to Berlin in (November) 1940, stood an increasingly obvious military threat at our Eastern border—the Eastern border of Europe. At first, 150 Russian divisions faced a thin veil of German forces. Stalin's marching armies could have cut us off at any time from raw materials necessary for carrying on the war. By that, he was in a favorable situation to wait and re-arm and negotiate with the Western powers."

Had we still been bitterly involved in a fight with England, Stalin's price would have been even higher—a price Hitler was not willing to pay. It was different with the Allies—any price, which the rest of Europe would have to pay, would have been accepted by the Western gangsters. In their blindness, they recognized only one goal: Germany's destruction—the French with Richelieu's ideas, the British with their balance of power policy,[9] the rest with senseless hate!

When we did not attack England—because good sense and European responsibility forbade it—Stalin started trying to dissolve the Balkan states. He tried to ignite a putsch that would create a chaotic situation in Romania; the conditions favored him because Italy plunged the Balkans into restlessness. New warfare areas were to be developed to split our strengths.

When (Hitler) tried hard to win over the Balkans for a common Europe—or at least to calm it down, neutralize it—the Italians attacked Greece without letting us know. A senseless adventure! He was confronted with that madness when he arrived in Florence after the disappointing meetings at Hendaye and Montoire.[10]

The Italians couldn't even hold on to their own Cyrenaica! Their attack on Greece was unsuccessful not because of unfavorable weather, but more so because of the courageous defense of the Greeks. Naturally, one also has to consider that the Italian attack was brought on by the deliberate snub and break of neutrality by Greece.

A typical English infamy lurked behind all that: to expand the war, to create a new war theater and distract from their island empire, England landed troops in Crete and, at the same time, on Greek territory—nearly 70,000 soldiers of their elite units.

At first, he (Hitler) thought the decision (Mussolini's) to attack Greece had its roots in the reminiscing of their Roman empire, but today he knows of the intentions of the sly Ciano.[11] He never trusted him and is convinced the fateful decision the Duce made was influenced by his cunning nepotist. He now must have feared that Yugoslavia, pressed by England and Russia, would take over the role Czechoslovakia once played. He was relieved when he was able to sign the treaty in the spring of 1941, hoping he could protect his Southern flank.

It turned out differently—a few days later the putsch occurred in Belgrade. Here again, although hidden, the combined effort of the English and Russian leadership stage managed that revolt. The Yugoslavian government was toppled and its forces were mobilized against Germany.

As it became necessary in 1940 to protect our Northern flank all the way up to the North Cape for reasons of the raw material situation, he now has to secure the Southern flank, against his intentions, for the same reason. The Balkan became a new war theater for us—a new front emerged. Troops and forces were tied up; casualties of men and materiel occurred; valuable—yes, very decisive—time elapsed. We would experience that bitterly.

In the meantime, a threatening readiness of Russian divisions and armies at the German and Romanian east borders took place. No hesitation was possible. Our preventive stroke met battle-ready armies of the Soviets. Our attack did not surprise the Russian leadership.[12] On the contrary, we were surprised by the deeply-stacked Russian forces, the strength of their artillery, and especially their incredible mass of tanks: the robust, battle-proven T-34s.

With that attack, not only the two-front war, which he tried to avoid, but an all-sided battle began. He always expressed the opinion that we never should have allowed ourselves to be involved in such a situation. The Napoleonic Russian campaign stood, menacing and terrorizing, in front of his eyes: "Do not doubt that I carefully considered all phases and events Napoleon had to experience in Russia," Hitler said. "Why then, still, our attack? We were condemned to that struggle; it was our fate. What we still could decide on our own was when to attack. But even the choice of our most favorable moment did not depend on our decision.

"Especially after the development at the Balkans and the Russian threat, there was no hope left to attack the English island; to strike England and Gibraltar was blocked for us. Suez would have made sense only in connection with Gibraltar.

"Time was against us. By all means, we had to try to avoid an extended war. When England staked all its hopes on the Red Army, for us only one possibility remained: to eliminate that Red Army and force the Western Powers into peace, before America's interference, with all its consequences, occurred. In order to avoid a multiple-front war, that Red Army had to be conquered within a foreseeable time."

Another viewpoint had influenced his decision: it was equally important for Germany and Europe's future to confront the Bolshevik threat. We could not confine ourselves to the defense of merely the German territory. Only by a preventive stroke could we succeed in carrying the campaign into the vast regions of Russia.

There was no doubt that it would be a struggle to exist or not to exist. That struggle could only be fought by a solid unity and the hard, unshakable will of the German people (*Volk*). "I repeat what I said at the beginning of the war," Hitler continued. "If we acquire that solidarity, then our strong will, our unity should overcome any peril. But in that, the solidarity, I misjudged. I underestimated the reactionaries. The bearers of that treason never recognized the meaning and destiny of that battle for Germany and for Europe." ◆

CHAPTER NOTES:
1 The Danzig Corridor was Hitler's demand for a "land bridge" (actually a narrow passageway) through Polish territory to connect Germany with its landlocked province of East Prussia.
2 Wilson's "14 Points" called for self-determination of peoples living in disputed territories, but this was not applied to Germans.
3 Marshal Jozef Pilsudski signed a 10-year peace pact with Hitler in 1934—the German-Polish Pact of Nonaggression. Pilsudski was an ethnic Lithuanian from an aristocratic, polonized family. As a young man, he was involved in radical socialist politics against the czarist authorities, even carrying out bank and train raids to fund a revolutionary army. After 1918, he fought against Russian Bolsheviks and became a leader of the newly formed Poland. He died in 1935.
4 To keep the door open for talks with Hitler's Germany.
5 Molotov-Ribbentrop non-aggression pact of Aug. 23, 1939.
6 The failed 1944 "Valkyrie plot."
7 The Polish ambassador, Lipski, did not meet the ultimatum that Hitler had set. Lipski was acting by order of his minister of foreign affairs, Col. Beck, who was backed up by the British government.
8 A direct vote of the entire electorate to determine their preference of rule—German or Polish.
9 Cardinal Richelieu wanted France as the dominant power in Europe. Britain's "balance of power" policy wanted to prevent any single mainland nation gaining control over Europe.
10 Hitler met General Franco in Hendaye in order to persuade him to join Germany in the war, or at least to support him in the effort to take Gibraltar. Franco stalled, which made Hitler very upset and disappointed. His meeting with Marshal Petain at Montoire stabilized the relationship with the Vichy government.
11 Conte Galeazo Ciano was Mussolini's son-in-law, and was later charged with, and hanged for, high treason.
12 Even though he was presented with the exact timing of the invasion from different sources, such as the famous spy Richard Sorge in Tokyo and British intelligence, the suspicious Stalin would not believe it and adjust his attack plans.

Jozef Beck Refuses to See Reason on Danzig

Hermann Giesler points out in his memoirs that: "Until the last massive snub by the Polish leadership at the end of August 1939, [Hitler] couldn't imagine that they would let it come to a fight."

***

The photo above shows Adolf Hitler and Polish Foreign Minister Jozef Beck in 1937 when relations were still fairly good. By August 1939, Beck was ignoring Hitler's requests to talk about their common borders and Hitler's main concern that could wait no longer—Danzig. The Germans, on August 29, made a new offer to negotiate with Poland. British Foreign Secretary Lord Halifax encouraged the Hitler government to believe that the Poles were willing to talk, when he knew they were not.

On the 28th, Beck had informed the British he would not negotiate without an explicit statement from Hitler that Germany had abandoned Danzig once and for all, and that she would never again seek to improve her transit communications to East Prussia through the Polish Corridor. This was not relayed to the Germans. A note given from Hitler's government to the British ambassador to Germany, Sir Nevile Henderson, at 7:15 p.m. on August 29, stated that Hitler wished the British Government to advise Poland to send an emissary to Berlin on the following day, Wednesday, August 30. He emphasized that urgency was required by the pressure of events, and he expected the arrival of a representative from Poland not later than midnight on August 30. Hitler assured Henderson that he would negotiate with Poland on a basis of full equality. Henderson assured Hal-

Above left, Nevile Henderson. Right, Foreign Secretary Halifax.

ifax that the terms would be moderate. Henderson also urged Polish Ambassador to Germany Jozef Lipski, before midnight on August 29, that his country could and should send a special envoy to Berlin the following day.

Lipski informed Beck, but by the afternoon of August 30, the general Polish mobilization notices had been posted throughout Poland and Beck had issued an "Orwellian" communique' stating that Poland had supported all efforts for peace by Allies or neutrals, but their efforts had brought no reaction from Germany! Still, Hitler, Goering and Ribbentrop continued to hope that the Poles would yet send an emissary to Berlin— and waited even into the morning of the 31st.

After receiving Lipski's message, Beck called in Britain's Ambassador to Poland, Hugh Kennard, who was extremely anti-German, as was his boss Halifax. Kennard did not advise Beck to stop the Polish mobilization scheduled for that morning, August 30, and went so far as to advise him to reject Hitler's offer, even though his own government had dishonestly assured Germany two days before that Poland was prepared to negotiate.

As it turned out, Beck had sent instructions to Lipski shortly before noon to accept no proposals and enter into no negotiations with the German government. This became known when the telegram was intercepted and decoded by Goering's special investigation office. Thus, saying his conscience was now clear as he had done his best for months under trying circumstances, Hitler issued the final invasion order in the early afternoon of August 31. The Polish refusal to discuss a settlement with Germany on any terms, and the insult of no reply from either Britain or Poland to Hitler's final offer, was the "massive snub." ♦

MARSHAL JOZEF PILSUDSKI: POLAND'S NATIONALIST DREAMER

HERMANN GIESLER REMARKED: "It was by no means in [Germany's] interest to share borders with Soviet Russia—and when [Hitler] signed an agreement with Marshal Pilsudski, he saw some value in that. But Pilsudski's admonition to his people collapsed under the promises and chauvinistic agitation of the Allies."

* * *

Marshal Jozef Pilsudski (left), in 1930 five years before his death, had a vision of a heroic Poland. He insisted not only on complete Polish independence, but that Poland should be recognized as equal to the Great Powers as the leading state representing Eastern Europe. From 1914 until 1939, his ideas were the defining influence on the development of Poland, even though Pilsudski was of Lithuanian descent.

Pilsudski saw World War I as an opportunity to gain territory for a new Polish Republic. In 1917, he switched from support of Germany to support of the Western Allies, demanding a completely independent Polish national army and severance from all ties that made Poland dependent on the Central Powers.

Poles were ecstatic over Germany's final surrender and at the peace process their demands were exorbitant. While they didn't get all they asked for, they did get more than they had any right to, making an enduring peace in the border areas between Germany and Poland unlikely. Between 1918 and 1924, Polish oppression of ethnic Germans in the former West Prussia drove 400,000 of them to the extreme step of leaving behind their historic home and crossing the new border farther west into the now smaller Germany. At the same time the new Polish Republic drifted under its democratic regimes, with no economic progress. In May 1926, the more authoritarian-minded Pilsudski ordered a *coup d'etat* on the existing regime and after a short civil war, took control but with no broad base of popular support.

PHOTO: GERMAN FEDERAL ARCHIVES

Above, Pilsudski (center) with Gen. Gustav Orlicz-Dreszer (right) on Poniatowski Bridge in Warsaw, during the May *coup d'etat*, 1926. In keeping with his desire to maintain Poland's independence, Pilsudski signed a Soviet-Polish Non-Aggression Pact in 1932 and a German-Polish Non-Aggression Pact in January 1934 with Adolf Hitler (referred to in the quote above). Hitler wanted a German-Polish alliance against the Soviet Union, but Pilsudski declined, preferring to be prepared for potential war with either Germany or the Soviet Union, while keeping alive the friendship with France and England as support. However, he did advise that the door always be kept open for talks with Germany, advice his personally appointed successors (Beck, Edward Rydz-Smigly) didn't follow.

At right, an official governmental photo of Rydz-Smigly as a marshall of Poland. First published in *Gazeta Polska* in 1937. ✦

WIKIPEDIA

PHOTO: GERMAN FEDERAL ARCHIVES

BRITISH & SOVIET MACHINATIONS ACROSS THE BALKANS

HERMANN GIESLER TELLS US: "[A] few days later the putsch occurred in Belgrade. Here again, although hidden, the combined effort of the English and Russian leadership stage-managed that revolt."

* * *

Yugoslavia's anti-Soviet regent Prince Paul rides with Adolf Hitler in March 1941 (above) when he agreed to join the Tripartite Pact (Berlin-Rome-Tokyo). The Balkans now seemed secure since Bulgaria also signed, and Hungary and Romania were already partners. Hitler was aware of the danger of military operations by the west via a thrust from the Mediterranean toward Greece, Albania or Trieste. Two days after Yugoslavia's formal signing of the pact in Vienna on March 25, Paul's regime was toppled in a military coup led by Serbian General Dusan Simovic, but initiated and planned by British officers, and certainly with the encouragement and knowledge (if not active help) of the Soviets.

Deploying the Waffen SS *Leibstandarte* Adolf Hitler Division from the Russian front and *Gebirgsjaeger* mountain divisions from Austria, Hitler attacked both Yugoslavia and Greece hard on April 6. Simovic and the newly installed pro-British King Peter fled the country, ending up in England in June. On April 10, the nation of Croatia seceded from Yugoslavia and allied itself with Germany. Yugoslavia capitulated on April 17. The British invasion troops fled to Crete, to Cyprus and finally to Egypt.

On June 2, Greece collapsed after a tough battle in which Austrian mountain battalions played a decisive role. Three or four *Gebirgsjaeger* divisions accomplished a remarkable feat, first by arriving there so quickly, and then

by successfully climbing around behind the Thermopylae Pass in the rocky Greek hills, carrying their equipment (guns, ammunition, food) on mules and small horses, with some motorized vehicles. Along with a shortage of water in the great heat, they met heavy resistance from the Greek army. Gen. Ferdinand Schoerner, shown above, a Bavarian from Munich and the last chief of the German army in 1945, commanded the 4th *Gebirgsjaeger* division and became the "Conqueror of the Acropolis."

It was a complete victory for the Axis forces, but it delayed the invasion of the Soviet Union, which may have been a fatal stroke in that war. ✦

King Peter II (center) with two of his ministers, Prime Minister of Yugoslavia Gen. Simovic (left) and Court Minister M. Knezevic (right) arriving in England.

PHOTOS: GERMAN FEDERAL ARCHIVES

CHAPTER 3

HOW ADOLF HITLER PLANNED THE MAY 1940 WESTERN OFFENSIVE

Translators' Introduction: Was Hitler, on his own, capable of coming up with the audacious military strategy that conquered France, Belgium, the Netherlands, Denmark and Norway in two months time? This is the firm conviction of his top commanders, Wilhelm Keitel and Alfred Jodl. When the invasion start date had to be changed several times,[1] Hitler had the opportunity to develop his own idea of a thrust across the Maas River at Sedan instead of the old WW1-type plan presented to him by Halder. When Giesler was at headquarters in Fall 1942, Hitler gives him map-by-map explanations for his strategic decisions. Following this, Hitler explains his thinking on another historically controversial military decision: not to capture or destroy the remaining British forces at Dunkirk.

FACING PAGE: Germany's 1940 west offensive—which Hitler planned himself—was one of innovative brilliance. His use of new military tactics—combining stuka bombers, fast-moving tank divisions, surprise glider units and commandoes—paid off. The new style of warfare was named "blitzkrieg," or "lightning war," and rightfully so. Within two months, German troops had taken control of a huge amount of territory from Narvik in northern Norway to Brest and Lyons in central France, with Belgium, Netherlands and Denmark in between. All these nations had believed they had sufficient military prowess to ward off an attack from a major military power or that they had constructed or possessed impregnable physical defenses.

A PLAN FOR THE WEST IN ALL ITS DETAILS

It was a large collection of maps bound in leather: The France War Campaign in Its Chronological Sequence. One day it was placed on Adolf Hitler's work desk. The Armed Forces Adjutancy had told me the volumes were prepared as a military-historical documentation, and its first edition was presented to Hitler at Winniza.[2]

Hitler, as a preamble for his giving me a review of the campaign that surprised the world, explained to me that he had already requested from the chief of the general staff (Franz Halder[3]), before the end of the Polish campaign, a presentation of the strategic dispositions for an offensive campaign in the west. He said, "First, I did not trust the peace; second, an offensive in the west had to be thought through and prepared in all its details; and finally, the timing—the most important factor. We were permanently under time pressure and still are; the time, she stays as a powerful ally with the enemy, more relentless than the past winter with its premature snow, ice and shattering cold."

Pensive, he added, "From my youth on, like a premonition, I never liked snow or ice. Already, long before the French campaign, I told you that the chief of staff presented me in September 1939 with the rehashed Schlieffen plan[4]—not, however, in detail. How it happened—I mean, the arrogance of a presentation of shallow nothingness, of repetitions of the thought processes of the honorable Gen. Schlieffen, which was still, in its operational principle, part of the 19th century and not accounting for the possibilities of modern weapons, tanks and air force!"

Hitler was silent, remembering. After a while, he said:

"I looked at the chief of the general staff and was convinced that any further words, or even a critical analysis, would lead to nothing, would end in emptiness—he is not able to think in all dimensions whatsoever, yet he is convinced he is of a unique military capacity. He is lacking in ideas, novelty, imagination, daring and, above all, in the charisma that is normally characteristic of a military leader.

"But how much time remained to change that 'strategy according to

Schlieffen,' and those meticulously compiled tactical detail plans by radically new offensive thinking? In the short time available, one could only reinforce tank units and motorized divisions in front of Luxembourg, and thus at that attack section emphasize the offensive thrust in the direction of Neuchateau and Sedan.

"I gave the order to attack at middle of November 1939. Then that mysterious betrayal of the start of the offensive happened. Its discovery was relayed to me at your office, on November 8th.[5] I immediately called the offensive off. It was not easy, we lost time. But on the other hand, the assassination attempt against me[6] did not succeed, and the decision to call off the attack turned out later to be correct because of the very unfavorable weather conditions.

"The traitor, up till now, has not been found.[7] Camouflaged, he sits in a high military position; all offensive deadlines have so far been betrayed! What hatred against me, and National Socialism, lies behind that revolting and cowardly treason—without any hesitation German soldiers are sacrificed.

"A decision in the west in 1939 was not possible anymore. We lost time, valuable time, but I used that time to deal with the strategy of the French campaign and to thoroughly study the tactical details that derived from it."

We walked over to the maps and Hitler opened the volume. First was a map surveying the area from the Mediterranean to the North Sea, marked with the military forces as of September 1939.

"I was now dealing on my own with the strategic possibilities, keeping completely to myself. My idea was: If I act as if I was attacking *'a la* Schlieffen,' and thus fooled them thoroughly"—with one hand he outlined an area—"and begin with an energetic thrust, here, where they would not expect it at all"—his index finger pointed down to Sedan—"what will then be the consequence? Slowly, my ideas became focused. I could see the sequence of the surprise attacks, everything firmed up. But still I kept it to myself; I didn't talk to anyone about my deliberations.

"I requested all supportive material and checked it out thoroughly. I surveyed the Maginot fortifications as far as they were known to us and marked on our general staff maps. Then I had relief maps and aerial photos set before me, but from all sections, not only from the area of my planned thrusts. Furthermore, I dealt with the entire road system and its pass-through volume, and checked the possibility of camouflaging the readiness positions.

"Gradually, I felt sure, and now I committed my *Wehrmacht* adjutants[8] to absolute secrecy so that they could assist me.

"Slowly, I gained the conviction that is eminently necessary to feel that 'this is the way and no other.'

"In December 1939, the offensive plan moved from a mere idea into a more concrete stage. Great strategy takes place not only on an intellectual level, but according to its own laws, similar to city building and architecture—I am nearly tempted to say, it is artwork.

"Should that strategy lead to a complete success, should it be achieved, it will be by a logical interconnecting of all tactical details, which have to be sensible and carefully planned. These tactical details must be completely integrated and subordinated to one great strategic idea. They are, at the same time, both the foundation and structure. Naturally, precautionary preparations had to be planned in order to meet all possible unknowns. Furthermore, to reach the great goal, surprise is necessary.

"Now I had to deal with the details and the respective tactics of attack; I took my time and did it thoroughly. From maps we went to sand box exercises. I still kept the circle of the insiders small, and according to my later experiences my precautions were absolutely correct.

"Beginning January 1940, that strategy was solidly cemented by all tactical detail planning.

"Now I took Keitel and Jodl[9] into my confidence—no, I did not win them over for my plans right away. They disapproved and raised objections, like: Would it not be wiser to go northward around the Maginot fortifications?

"Just that is what the adversaries expect and make preparations for, I told them. My offensive plans were too bold, too daring. Naturally it was risky; not only the front-thrust but also the flanks from south, west and even from the east were in danger, in case the divisions following the first thrust are not able to secure the breakthrough area in time. They didn't make it easy for me to convince them.

"The blocking barrier of Maginot? Well, I was sure about that. The Czech barrier forts, directed against us then and built by French engineers similar to the Maginot bunkers—not only did I have a close look at those, but they were for me useful objects for shooting trials. The results met my expectations—the bunkers were cleanly penetrated by direct shots of 8.8 special shells. Also, by Stuka attacks I would either eliminate them or keep them down.

"Around the middle of February, the newly nominated commanding generals, among them Manstein, reported in. [Gen. Rudolf] Schmundt made me aware of him, indicating that his ideas about the war strategy in the west were nearly the same as mine.

"After he reported in, I gave Manstein the opportunity to present his thoughts about the west offensive. Yes, it was as Schmundt told me.

"Manstein was the only general who found the way to the same basic plan of operation; my thinking was thus confirmed. I still kept silent though—the fewer who knew about it, the more surprising the thrust would be. It would not have been prudent to let Manstein know how far advanced beyond the basic strategic concept the tactical details had already been worked out."

A PLETHORA OF MAPS SHOW SUCCESS AFTER SUCCESS

During his talk, Hitler had turned over map after map covering the months of the "*drole de guerre*" (funny war) until May 1940. On the map you could notice the markings of the takeoff positions for the attack.

"I don't want to get involved now with all the details, like the rapid taking over of crossings, bridges, and barriers. Once they were situated close to the border, I engaged raiding commandos—partly even on bicycles—so they could quickly and silently run over the enemy positions.

"Most important was the storming of Eben-Emael (see page 62), the impenetrable, modern barrier fort. It could be taken without heavy losses only by a surprise raid, by coordinating the attack from the air and the ground. Gliders should silently land on top of the fort and drop off the commandos. Airplanes with parachute troops, and gliders with raiding commandos, will engage as tactical considerations at the time require it. Whenever possible, airfields behind the enemy lines will be captured that way.

"Believe me, Giesler, all these attacks I discussed, and exercised on a model, with officers and flying personnel, pioneers, parachutists and infantries—and we succeeded totally."

Hitler opened the next map: it showed the attack that took place on the morning of May 10 with the markings for the first-day targets. Following that were maps with sections of the different divisions, then a second map series marking the success by the individual panzer and battle groups.

Drawn on a larger scale could be seen the hard battle for Sedan. That was the energetic thrust the enemy did not expect—then the breakthrough and the advance of the panzers, secured at their flanks by the forward pushing divisions. Now, map after map followed, sometimes two for one day, graphically reporting the battle success of the panzer thrust along the east side of the Somme to Abbeville. He wanted to catch and cut off the French-English motorized forces, which, in all probability, would cross the French border to enter Belgium.

"My biggest worry was securing the flanks; counterattacks from the south and southwest, energetically executed, would have grown to a serious threat. Logically, at the same time, the 'Schlieffen attack' had to be seriously carried out in order to draw the main forces of the enemy, the motorized units, into Belgian territory. The deception succeeded; the mass of the enemy forces moved into those battle areas, as I imagined they would, and were cordoned off. The frontal attack of our divisions also showed total success and forced Holland and Belgium to surrender. The operation, later called *Sichelschnitt* [the sickle-cut plan], became a decisive success. But the total defeat of the Western Allies was not yet won."

THE DUNKIRK "MIRACLE"

"The opponent was actually decisively beaten in the north sector. Pressed from the east and south by our fast-moving troops, cut off toward the west, only the sea remained as the last open flight path. The mass of those primarily English forces was concentrated around Dunkirk, on the Flemish plains, which I remembered well from my world war time. Oh, I know, my Dunkirk decision was described as a big mistake, not only by the circle of the so-smart general staff—those 'know-it-alls' and those with their so-Christian feelings thought it was my biggest stupidity not to have completely destroyed the already-beaten British forces.

"Various considerations kept me from doing so.

"First, the military reasons: The Flemish lowlands restrict tank operations basically to the roads. Long, drawn-out battles, with our own losses and the possible high breakdown of our tanks, were to be expected. For further necessary operations toward the west and south, into France proper, I could not sacrifice one tank. But above all, we must not waste our strength and lose time. The enemy had been shocked; now everything had to be done stroke by stroke.

"After listening to Rundstedt, my inner circle of military advisers also shared that opinion. It was absolutely necessary to continue the attack to the west and south without any hesitation before the enemy succeeds in building up a strong defense along the Somme and the Aisne. Our follow-up thrust already met with strong resistance there. It also had to be assumed the English would send additional troops, assisted by the artillery support of their battleships, across the channel—they could not let France down as they did Poland!

"We had to attack toward the west—Paris and northern France had to be taken very fast, to make it impossible for the English to land additional troops. We also had to direct an offensive toward the south, with a thrust behind the French fortifications. We had to enforce a final decision and thus bring the French campaign to a quick finish because there was another reason of a military-political kind. I did not remain orientated to only one side: for a long time I was listening, worried, toward the east.

"And did not a slight possibility of peace still exist, even though a vague one, which I might have obstructed by a pitiless defeat of the Dunkirk army?"

Hitler was deliberating on rational grounds as he was so often doing in the past years; he did not think only as a German—he thought as a European. He truly thought in a sense of a higher humanity, which he wanted to be realized within ethnically based unified societies (*Volksgemeinschaften*).

That he judged the possibility of peace higher, there is in my eyes one proof: On June 24, 1940, at his headquarters Bruly de Peche, he gave orders for peacetime tasks,[10] issuing a decree on the 25th giving authority to Speer and me to begin the restructuring of German cities.

Later, I was once more reminded of the "mistake" of Dunkirk. If I remember correctly, it was in August 1943 after the devastating air attacks in Hamburg. In an adjoining room, Hitler gave orders to an adjutant. A pile of photographs was lying on a table; I picked them up.

They were horrible testimonials of the effect the phosphor-hail had on women and children by that terrible terror attack at Hamburg with over 40,000 civilian deaths.

When Hitler returned to the workroom, he saw the photographs in my hand. With a quiet, but very resolute voice he said: "Let it go, Giesler; don't look at the pictures anymore. After a while, I had to rethink: it didn't agree with my character to step on the one who lies on the ground. I was mistaken—magnanimity will not be recognized. They repay my sparing them at Dunkirk with bombs and phosphorus on women and children whose men and husbands were fighting for Europe. What you see there is destructive brutality"—he pointed to the photographs—"again and again one tries not to believe this; now I know—no mercy!"

Those words were for me proof that his decisions at that time came from ethical ideas of war, rather than only military and political reasons.

I thought back to fall 1942 at Winniza. Upset and pondering, I had arrived there late at night or early morning and could not sleep. After

CHAPTER 3 | 49

BLITZKRIEG: German panzers make the "big thrust" into Belgium along the narrow roads of the Eifel border region in May 1940. PHOTO: GERMAN FEDERAL ARCHIVES

Hitler talked with me, the explanation for his mistrust and chilly attitude toward the generals was evident. It was not commonly so because, contrary to that, he kept the front officers and fighting troops in high esteem—and of whom he said: "They know what is at stake."

It dawned on me why he so thoroughly explained, with the map documents, his strategic and tactical decisions and the way the French campaign was won. It was not based on the fact that the first example of that documentation was now set on the table; it was not just the explanation of his carefully planned campaign. No doubt, by reviewing, he wanted to assure himself that his strategic idea, his tactical dispositions were correct and had led to a surprisingly rapid success. His explanations were by no means arrogant. Deeds, courage and self-sacrifice of the soldiers and commanders always took first place, above all events.

He said to me, "Only with such soldiers and officers could I dare to plan such an audacious performance." He followed with the remark, "The strategy for the Russian campaign was deliberated exactly the same way."

For a while he was silent, and then he continued, "When I recognized,

50 | THE ARTIST WITHIN THE WARLORD

after the talks with Molotov, that no other possibilities existed—I had the choice: fight or give up and betray Europe. I decided to fight. It was the hardest decision of my life."

***

Translators' Commentary: A lot of consternation and wild speculation among military historians has centered about the Dunkirk operation of May 26 to June 4, 1940. Hitler's description of these fateful days strongly supports the belief that it was primarily political considerations that led him to the decision to hold the panzers which were ready to encircle and defeat close to a half-million soldiers of the British expedition corps. We know of Hitler's aversion—at least at that time—to fighting the Brits tooth and nail.

He thought his already obvious victory in the west should convince England to enter into peace negotiations and discussions of a new order in Europe together with Germany. Thoughts of himself as a European, not only a German, military leader were in his mind—thoughts very different, as we know, from those of Churchill and his sinister advisers and dark *Hintermaenner* who wanted war.

The decision to hold the panzer corps at Dunkirk was discussed at the OKW and agreed to by von Rundstedt and his chief of staff—Manstein's successor—Gen. [Georg] von Sodenstern. Hitler, Keitel, Jodl and Rundstedt had two military considerations in mind leading to this decision:

1) The rapid thrust of the panzers had driven men and material to the utmost limits—rest and repair were necessary. On May 23, Panzerkorps Kleist reported close to 50% of their panzers lost. The flat environment of Dunkirk demanded full strength of the panzer corps. Rundstedt gave the halt order and overruled OKH, and Brauchitsch and Halder's further advance.

2) The southern flank of Army Group A was partly wide open. Even though the sickle movement of the two Army groups cut the Allied forces in half, there were still formidable French forces, tanks and motorized divisions assembled south and west of the Somme and Aisne to be reckoned with.

It is also known that Goering assured Hitler that the *Luftwaffe*, if called, would be able to devastate the grounded British expeditionary corps. As it turned out, bad weather grounded the *Reichsmarschall's* bombers for days, allowing 338,000 British soldiers to escape across the channel. England was saved, but thousands of weapons and vehicles were left at the beaches.

German panzers and infantry crossed the Somme and Marne after a short, hard-fought battle and took Paris. In a forest clearing at Compiegne, in the same railway car the German delegation signed the armistice in 1918, the French general [Charles] Huntziger signed the new armistice of June 22, 1940.

***

MORE THOUGHTS ON HITLER

I asked myself: Why does Hitler reveal all these problems and thoughts to me? Apart from the fact that his loneliness urged him to talk, he knew I was not only a National Socialist and follower he could trust, but, in addition, close to him as his architect.

He also recognized that I understood his goals—even more, he sensed that I saw him as a far-forward thinker who was already planning and fighting for the next generation. The joint work on city building conceptions and their architectural details created trust; he accepted and respected me. During those hours of mutual planning, he saw himself bound to peace, and his real mission as forming a new social order of the German people and their environment. He found the answer to the challenge of the time, the challenge of the technique, and the challenge of the new social order. In those hours, he was lifted up; I was more to him than his architect.

As always, I attended lunch. Hitler was pensive; our discussion was restricted to my impressions of the Danube bank design in Budapest. Right on the first day of our joint lunch and dinner, I asked to be served the same food as he was having. Hitler mentioned that I could order the mess-menu—it would not disturb him at all.

"No," I replied, "I'm not pretending. I really want to get acquainted with your diet, and for the orderlies it is simpler to serve." So I spooned the 'roasted semolina soup' and forked the potato pancakes with vegetables. At that lunch, they served milk-rice, and with it ground chocolate in a small cup, as dessert. I sprinkled some over the milk-rice. Hitler criticized, "That's too little—it is a rare pleasure," and then poured nearly everything out of the cup over my rice.

"I am not allowed too much of it," he remarked. I could see that by his small rice portion. It was rather surprising how little nourishment he needed.

After dinner he said, "Giesler, you are not only exhausted, but you also have not had enough sleep. I can see it. You will now take a walk, naturally with company—with Professor Brandt—and then go to the sauna, and you will sleep well. I'm very busy with military discussions and deadlines; no planning talks today. I'll see you at tea time, late evening after the Lage."

During the walk, I talked with Karl Brandt, of whom I think highly, about Hitler's loneliness and his great burden. "If I am already worn out after hours in my small professional work here, and the talks with him, think then about the continuous demands made on him."

"No," Brandt interrupted me, "you have to look at it differently, Giesler. It's obvious that you are tired out by the nightly discussions with the chief, but also obvious that, for him, it means complete relaxation. He gains distance and new energy for decisionmaking. That's why you're so important here now."

KEITEL & JODL EXPLAIN

I had dinner at the casino barracks and had a chance to talk to Field Marshal Keitel, with Gen. Jodl present—naturally about the French campaign. I wanted to hear his assessment.

"Well, when I think about the past, it gives me confidence," Keitel said. "He rarely talks about it. He was probably inspired by the map collection.

"What he presented to you, based on the maps, I can only add it was

Adolf Hitler explains his western strategy to Keitel (center) and Jodl.

his idea, in all details his work. He alone was the commander of the French campaign."

Keitel continued, "When he explained, in January 1940, his concept about the western campaign, worked out to all strategic details, I was startled by his audacity, even though I had to acknowledge the brilliant strategy." Jodl nodded, agreeing, and remarked, "We were pretty much perplexed when he put it on our table, complete with all details!"

"For his attack solution, he first won Jodl over, when I still could not accept it," Keitel added. "I asked myself: would we succeed in deceiving the Allies to such an extent that they would thrust their motorized army and tank units into the Belgian-Holland region, in order to block the 'Schlieffen-Wing'? Would they consider the breakthrough at Sedan as a tactical, space-limited attack only? Could the flanks for the panzer thrust to the coast be secured at all? I never would have had the courage for such an audacious operation.

"Gen. Schmundt said later that Manstein had the same thoughts. His ideas were not accepted and were refused by the chief of the General Staff (Halder). I found that out in January and arranged that Manstein could present his ideas to the Fuehrer. That was possible when he reported to the Fuhrer after his nomination to a commanding general (*Kommandierenden General*) in middle February 1940.

"At that time, the Fuhrer had already planned and committed down to tactical details beyond the strategic operations—up to the commandos he needed for Eben-Emael. With an incomparable insistence, he pushed through his strategic ideas and all tactical measurements. When Manstein presented his ideas for an offensive campaign, he could by that time only confirm what the Fuhrer had intended."

Field Marshal Keitel and Gen. Jodl were hanged at Nuremberg[11]; Gen. Schmundt became a victim of the July 20 assassination attack. But the field marshal confirmed what I heard from him in Winniza in the notes he left. The courageous, inspired strategy of the western campaign was explicitly and absolutely Hitler's work; he alone was the chief commander of the French campaign.

AHEAD OF THE ALLIES: NARVIK

Translators' Introduction: During the preparations for the West Offensive, alarming reports of naval and troop concentrations in East Anglia arrived at Hitler's headquarters from Adm. Canaris's *Abwehr*. Chief of Operations Jodl and Col. Gen. Nikolaus von Falkernhorst were certain this meant the British were preparing to invade Norway and realized the great danger of being cut off from the vital supply of Swedish iron ore, and an encirclement from the north. Hitler reacted swiftly, ordering the invasion of Denmark and Norway under the code name *Weseruebung* on April 9, 1940. Hermann Giesler reports about the tremendous tension and pressure being felt at headquarters in Berlin.

CHAPTER 3 | 55

German *Gebirgsjagers* in the mountains around Narvik.

MAY 1940: GIESLER'S RECOLLECTIONS

During the decisive battle in Norway, especially around Narvik, I was Adolf Hitler's guest for lunch and dinner at the Reichs Chancellery. After the evening military meeting, Hitler returned to the "Bismarck" living quarters; he wanted to talk until the reports arrived. He was restless, under tension, and had been worried for hours.

His greatest worry is the battle for Narvik; that's why he is restless. The battle group Dietl[12] is too weak to resist the massive enemy forces still being strengthened by the English fleet and ample supply.

By his order our soldiers are involved in a desperate fight against that superior power—and we cannot help them. Any supply possibilities by sea are prevented by the English; a land bridge is impossible. How long will they be able to hold on? To stay in Narvik is of utmost importance.

"Do you understand how I feel? I question myself, is it time for the battle group to move into Swedish territory and surrender? Gen. Jodl pleads for continued fighting. I now recognize, remembering my own time as a soldier, it is easier to fight than to be responsible for the battle.

Well, Giesler, let's walk up and down until new reports arrive."

Messages arrived continuously; very hard fights around Narvik—fights against English and Norwegian forces in the valleys north and south of Trondheim. One question was in Hitler's mind: Where is the Norwegian king; did they succeed in capturing him?

Then the decisive message came in: The keep-on-fighting, hang-on-tough paid off. We succeeded. The king, who was with his troops in the north, offered to surrender; he may have recognized that further resistance of his troops was senseless. The German forces pushed forward . The fighting against the English-French expeditionary corps continued, but the success of that bold Norway operation was assured.

Now Hitler had to face a new, burdensome responsibility: the battle against the West. "Giesler, we beat the English by only a few hours. A dangerous threat for Germany from the north could have occurred." ✦

CHAPTER NOTES:

1 One had to do with captured staff officers of *Luftwaffe* Gen. Felmy (chief of Luftflotte 2) who were ordered to a place in the Rhine Valley—they were supposed to go by train, but they got hold of a small four-seater plane—ran into foggy weather and emergency-landed in Dutch territory. One staff officer tried to burn, and then swallow, the documents they were carrying, but was not successful. They were delivered to the Dutch General Staff and, because the secrecy was breached, the attack had to be postponed. Felmy was replaced because of this incident.

2 The location in Ukraine of Hitler's headquarters *Werwolf*. Winniza is the German spelling used by the translators; the English spelling is Vinnitsa; Ukrainian is Vinnytsya.

3 Halder, Franz, *Kriegstagebuch 1939-1942*, three vols., Stuttgart Kohlhammer, 1962-64.

4 Halder was the chief of the general staff at that time. Schlieffen's plan in WWI was to make the right wing of the German forces strong and fast moving. However, they stopped at the Marne River and didn't move on; and never captured Paris.

5 See Chapter 1 of this book.

6 Referring to the Nov. 8, 1939 bomb explosion at the Buergerbraeukeller in Munich, which Hitler attended, but left early.

7 It was Hans Oster, who passed the date of the invasion of Netherlands to the Dutch attaché in Berlin.

8 Schmundt from the *Wehrmacht* (Armed Forces), von Puttkammer from the navy, von Below from the *Luftwaffe*, Engle from the army, Schaub from the party.

9 Chief of Staff OKW Wilhelm Keitel and his assistant Chief of Operations OKW Alfred Jodl.

10 At the time of the German-French armistice, Hitler visited Paris with architects Giesler and Speer. Hitler told them, "For you a tough time begins, work and pressure, the forming of cities and monuments which are put into your trust."

11 Though Keitel and Jodl pleaded not guilty, the Nuremberg court found them both guilty on all charges, and shamefully hanged them on Oct. 16, 1946, though they had requested to be executed by a firing squad, which was the only honorable method for officers. Jodl's last words were reportedly "My farewell to you, my Germany"; Keitel's were "I follow now my sons—all for Germany!" In 1953, Jodl was found, posthumously, "not guilty" of the main charges against him by a German court, and the verdict was declared "a mistake."

12 Col. Gen. Eduard Dietl commanded part of the Third Mountain Division in Narvik. His troops were landed by German destroyers that got involved in a disastrous naval battle in which all were sunk or scuttled, after which 2500 stranded navy men joined the Mountaineers. They withdrew into the hills, were cut off and partially supplied by air drops, but managed to retake the town.

The Controversy: Keitel vs. Halder

WHO WAS THE PLANNER of Germany's initially successful operations in the west? You would think this would be common knowledge, but there is considerable controversy about it.

BY WILHELM KRIESSMANN, PH.D.

Reviewing his book *History of the German General Staff* in the newspaper *Die Welt* of Jan. 27, 1971, Walter Goerlltz says that Col. Gen. Franz Halder, chief of the German general staff from 1938 to 1942, was the author of the campaign in the west. Goerlitz's review is titled "The portrait of the chief of staff who planned the west offensive." Gen. Walter Warlimont also thinks he knows for sure who the planner was. He calls the chief of the general staff the "original planner of the successful operations"[1] and means by that, Halder.

Adolf Hitler first learned of Gen. Erich von Manstein's parallel plans on Feb. 17, 1940, when not only the strategy but also the tactical details like strength, team line-up, weapons and time schedule for the Eben-Emael commandos were already laid down. Warlimont's report can only be seen as an effort to falsify history. On another page, Warlimont contradicts that by reflecting ". . . [O]ne was fully aware that the merits for the great victory in France were the least of Hitler and his staff. The brain was Gen. von Manstein."[2]

The Manstein strategy, which the general defended parallel to Hitler's plan, was always ignored by Halder and never pierced the filter at the OKH (Supreme Command Army) before Feb. 17, 1940. Gen. von Manstein confirmed that explicitly when he wrote: "Gen. Warlimont, deputy of Jodl, and the first General Staff officer Gen. von Lossberg, told me at the same time that the OKH never approached Hitler with our ideas. For us, a rather disturbing situation. . . ."[3] Later he wrote: ". . . Hitler

Colonel General Franz Halder (left), chief of the general staff, gave the impression that the daring strategy for the offensive in the west was his plan, but according to Hitler and Keitel (center) what Halder offered was the warmed-over WWI "Schlieffen Plan." Gen. Erich von Manstein (right) surprised Hitler by coming up with a similar plan for a sneak attack through Sedan. Manstein said his ideas were blocked from reaching Hitler by Halder.

PHOTOS: WIKIPEDIA

declared to me, that he will never let me forget that I was the only one before the western campaign who said to him that by the thrust through Sedan one could not only win a battle but could and must accomplish the final decision in the west."[4]

Manstein also acknowledged that on Nov. 12, 1939, to their utmost surprise, Army Group A received a teleprint with Hitler's detailed orders finalized along the lines of von Manstein's strategy. He wrote "[M]aybe Hitler came to that thought by himself. He had an eye for tactical possibilities and pondered a lot over maps. He could have recognized one could cross the Maas the easiest way at Sedan, when further down the panzer of the 4th army would have it much tougher. He could have seen the Maas crossing near Sedan as a favorable place." (*Verlorene Seige*, p. 106)

However, Halder wanted the occasion to be seen as follows: "... [T]he fierce argument of different opinions were decided by Hitler's binding order that preparation for the German attack had to be focused through

THE ARTIST WITHIN THE WARLORD

May 14, 1940 1st Panzer Regiment crosses pontoon bridge over the Meuse at Floing, near Sedan [Army film office, Spandau-Ruhleben]

the Belgian provinces of Limburg and Brabant and had to be executed at the earliest possible time. It was a poor copy of the Schlieffen plan, whose weakness has been seen in World War I.

"The OKH was fighting that plan and prepared to shift the center of the attack, within a short time, to the Ardennes, in accordance with its own considerations. But Hitler also had no confidence. Uncertain as he was, he gave his ear to the whisperings of a person in the high command staff at the west front with whom he had a personal relationship. [The OKH] correctly pointed out that there existed a weak spot at the French border fortifications north of Charleville. That command staff suggested to take advantage of this weak spot, surround the Maginot line by an attack in a southerly direction, and thus prevent an expected threat...."[5]

Against that, we have Keitel's notes:

"A few days later—it must have been before October (1939)—Halder was called to visit Hitler in order to present his Operation Plan West. Jodl and I were present. Hitler interrupted his report with different questions and held back his final reaction when Halder had to hand over the plan and marked maps to him.

"Shortly after Halder left, Hitler said to us something like: 'Hey, that's the old Schlieffen Plan with the strong wing movement toward the Atlantic Coast. One does not perform such operations twice and go unpunished. I am of a quite different opinion and will tell (you and Jodl) that in a few days, and will discuss it with OKH.'

"I don't want to deal here with operational questions deriving from that. This much I'd like to say—that it was Hitler who personally requested, as his solution, the thrust with panzer forces over Sedan to the Atlantic Coast at Abbeville.

"I expressed my reservations that the brilliant operation might fail if the French Panzer Army would not do us the favor to immediately attack our north wing through Belgium, but would hold back when they recognized Hitler's plan of the breakthrough. Jodl, as well as Hitler, did not agree with my fear.

"I'd also like to mention that Hitler told me at a later date, with obvious joy, that he had a personal discussion with von Manstein about this operational question—that he was the only general of the army who arrived at the same solution. That satisfied him highly."[6]   ◆

ENDNOTES:
    1 Walter Warlimont, *Inside Hitler's Headquarter 1939-1945*, Frankfurt 1962, p 26.
    2 Warlimont, p 116.
    3 Erich von Manstein, *Verlorene Siege (Lost Victories)*, Munich, 1976, p 110.
    4 Manstein, p 615.
    5 Franz Halder, *Hitler als Feldherr (Hitler as Warlord)*, Munich, 1949, pp 28-9.
    6 *Generalfeldmarschall Keitel, Verbrecher oder Offizier (Field Marshal Keitel: criminal or officer?)*, Walter Goerlitz, Editor-Publisher, Goettigen, 1961, pp 226-7.

The Stunning Victory at Fort Eben-Emael

The Belgian fort of Eben-Emael, at the border of Germany, Belgium and Holland, was located at a commanding position overlooking the Maas River and three bridges spanning the Albert Canal. It presented a major obstacle preventing troops from advancing into Belgium and Holland from Germany.

The fort drew the early attention of Hitler as he began to plan for the May 1940 campaign in the west. In late 1939, he arranged for special commandos of parachute troops (*Fallschirmjaeger*) and airborne units (*Luftlandetruppen*)—using glider planes because of their silence, and with brand new weapons and explosives (*Haftladung*)—to train under top secrecy at the similar border fortifications in Czechoslovakia.

The assault on the fort Eben-Emael was part of the much larger campaign, *Fall Gelb*, of combined airborne troops, parachute troops, Stukas and transport aircraft (400 Ju 52 transporters) against bridges, airfields and fortresses in Belgium and Holland. On May 9, 1940 these forces were gathered around Cologne. The force tasked with assaulting the fort and capturing the three bridges was named *Sturmabteilung Koch* (Assault Detachment Koch) after the leader of the force, Hauptmann (Capt.) Walter Koch.

Hauptmann Koch divided his force into four assault groups. Group Granite, under First Lt. Rudolf Witzig, was to assault and capture Fort Eben-Emael from above. The other three groups were to capture the bridges. Eleven gliders carrying the 85 men of Group Granite, rope-towed by Ju 52s, left an airfield near Bonn at 4:30 a.m., May 10, with the task to land on top of the fort and assault the cupolas and casemates with the new "hollow explosives," flamethrowers and automatic weapons.

Absolute radio silence was enforced; the Ju 52 pilots were guided by vertical searchlights toward the Belgian border and released the gliders at 7,000 ft., about 20 miles before the target. Witzig's glider was hit by a

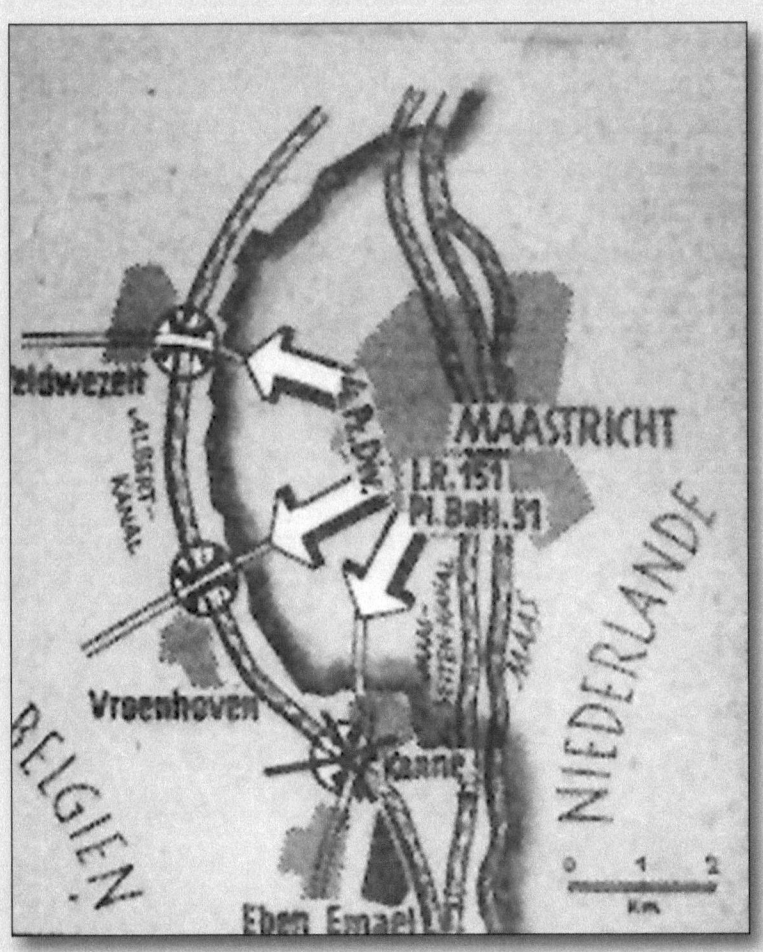
Positions of the strategic objectives.

snapping towline, forcing it to land in Germany; another glider released too early. Thus undermanned, only nine gliders landed on the roof of Eben-Emael, where the troops quickly emerged and began attaching explosive charges to emplacements housing the artillery pieces. Each glider troop had its own objective. Some of the larger guns were more difficult to destroy, and troops from two gliders, and sometimes even more than that, had to join together to finally disable them.

The fighting in the major part of the fort was fierce, and Stuka bombers had to be called in to quell some pockets of resistance. Entrances and exits located by the airborne troops were destroyed with explosives to seal them off.

In the meantime, Witzig had quickly called up another glider and, after flying through anti-aircraft fire, landed on top of the fortress and participated in the fighting. Group Granite was not relieved by the 51st Engineer Battalion until 7 a.m. May 11 because the Belgian engineers managed to destroy some bridges over the Maas River, which the Ger-

The German target map of Eben Emael showing objectives. Nos. 9, 12, 18 and 26 are casemates, each with three 75-mm guns. Nos. 23, 24, and 31 are retractable rotating armored cupolas with two 75-mm guns and two 120-mm guns. Nos. 15 and 16 were dummies. Nos. 13 and 19 are machine-gun bunkers. Nos. 3, 4, 6, 17, 23, 30 and 35 are anti-tank, searchlight and machine-gun emplacements in walls overlooking the canal and ditch. No. 29 is Flak position. Nos. 2 and 25 are billets.

mans had to repair before crossing. Under great pressure, Group Granite suffered six killed and 19 wounded. But the defenders suffered 60 killed and 40 wounded, and surrendered shortly after noon, at 12:30, on May 11, with an estimated 1,000 Belgian soldiers taken into captivity.

The three bridges across the Albert Canal were successfully captured by the three glider groups under the command of Capt. Koch. As a result of these successes, the armored division of the 18th Army was able to enter the heart of Belgium. Both Koch and Witzig were awarded the Knights Cross.

Gen. Kurt Student, commander of the *Fallshirmjaegertruppen* and advisor to Hitler on Eben-Emael, wrote of the operation, and the efforts of Group Granite in particular, that, "It was a deed of exemplary daring and decisive significance. . . . I have studied the history of the last war and the battles on all fronts. But I have not been able to find anything among the host of brilliant actions—undertaken by friend or foe— that could be said to compare with the success achieved by Koch's assault group." (Volkmar Kuhn, *German Paratroops in World War II*, Ian Allen, Ltd., 1978. Page 36)—W.K. & C.Y. ✦

GEN. KURT STUDENT

SPECIAL INNOVATIONS

During the planning of Operation Sea Lion, the Germans developed an amphibious, armored tank to provide support to infantry. The Tauchpanzer III was a modified version of the Panzer III, with a crew of 5, weighing 22 tons, armed with a 37mm gun and two machine guns, and was deployed from a landing craft around a mile offshore. Instead of floating, the Tauchpanzer III drove on the seabed. A rubber hose supplied the engine and crew with air and gave the waterproofed tank a maximum diving depth of 15 meters (49 ft). One hundred sixty-eight were produced.

PHOTO: GERMAN FEDERAL ARCHIVES

CHAPTER 4

WHY OPERATION SEA LION WAS NEVER LAUNCHED

Translators' Introduction: Prior to his speech in the Reichstag in which he appealed again for peace with England, Hitler had issued his Directive #16 on July 16, 1940 for Germany's armed forces to plan and prepare for an amphibious operation against her. In this chapter, we give the details of that plan and Giesler explains, in the Fuehrer's own words from the vantage point of 1942, the doubts he had from the beginning about such an operation. Giesler then recalls a conversation with Hitler in October 1940 regarding French Marshal Petain, Francisco Franco of Spain and Rudolf Hess. Finally, Giesler remembers the day in February 1941 at the Berghof when he learned that Hitler had made his decision to go ahead with the invasion of the Soviet Union, and had relayed that decision to his generals at a meeting that had just ended.

***

Translators' Commentary: Not quite four weeks after the new president of the defeated Republic of France, Marshal Henri Philippe Petain, signed the armistice with Germany, Adolf Hitler spoke to the Reichstag and the German nation. It was July 19, 1940, when the Reichstag deputies were assembled at the Kroll Opera House in Berlin, joined by all government ministers and the top brass of the *Wehrmacht*.

"I have summoned you to this meeting in the midst of our tremendous struggle for the freedom and the future of the German nation," Hitler began. "I have done so . . . with the intention of appealing, once more and for the last time, to common sense in general."

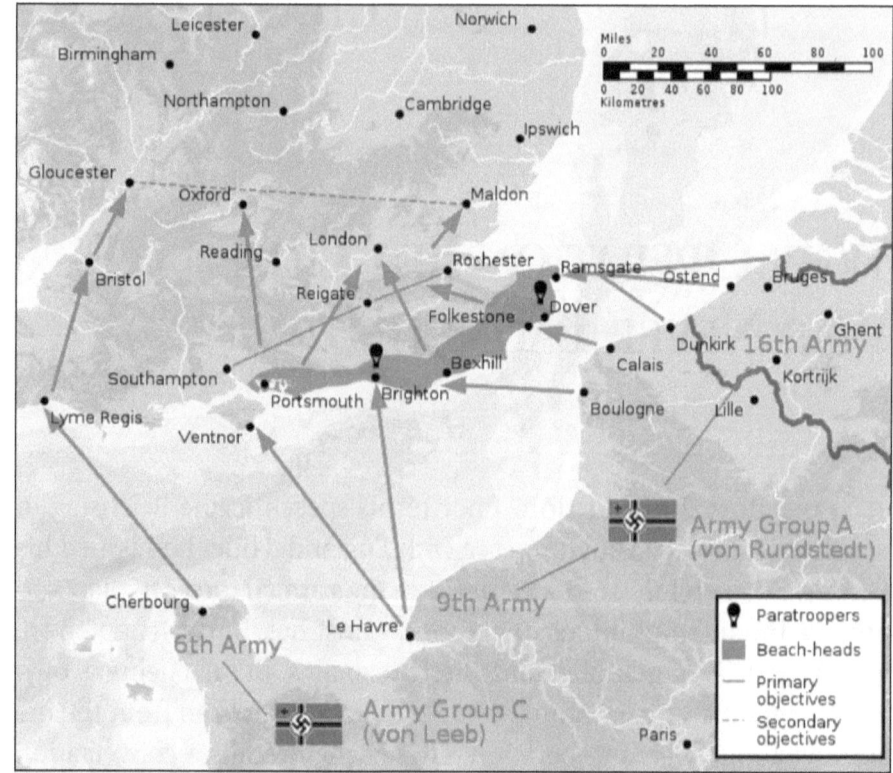

PLAN OF ATTACK

For Operation Sea Lion, OKH (*Oberkommando des Heeres*—Army Supreme Command) came up with a bold, massive offensive across a wide stretch of southern England: three Army groups with a total of 36 divisions, including six tank and two airborne. Hitler intervened and demanded a revised plan, which resulted in the invasion force being cut down to 26 divisions. As shown in the map above, a first wave of six divisions of General Busch's 16th Army (from Army Group A) was to assemble in the ports of Rotterdam, Antwerp, Dunkirk and Calais, going ashore between Folkstone and Dover. Two divisions of General Strauss's 9th army were to assemble at the harbor of Boulogne and landing between Eastbourne and Bexhill. Three divisions of Field Marshal Walther von Reichenau's 6th Army would assemble at Le Havre, invading the shores at Brighton. As an important condition, the navy requested absolute control of the airspace by the *Luftwaffe*.

He described his political, social and economic goals and how they had succeeded since his *Machtuebernahme* [taking office] in 1933. Raising his voice slightly, he said, "The program of the National Socialist Movement, besides freeing the Reich from the fetters of a small substratum of Jewish-capitalist and pluto-democratic profiteers, proclaimed to the world our resolution to shake off the shackles of the Versailles Dictate."

Toward the end of his speech, showing visible emotion, he proclaimed, "From France and England, I never demanded anything but peace ... because my intention was not to make war, but to build a new social and cultural state. ... At this hour I feel obligated before my conscience to once more appeal to common sense in England. ... I don't see any reason to continue this senseless fight."

England's answer was Churchill's cynically uttered, "I don't propose to say anything in reply to Herr Hitler's speech, not being on speaking terms with him." The British prime minister and his controllers wanted war and the destruction of Germany.

Prior to this speech, Hitler had issued on July 16 his Directive No. 16. It began: "Concerning preparations for an amphibious operation against England. Since England, in spite of her hopeless military situation, still shows no sign of coming to an agreement, I have decided to prepare, and if necessary carry out, a landing operation against her."

He then outlined his strategy in broad strokes and requested plans from all three of his Armed Forces Commanders in Chief (*Heer, Kriegsmarine, Luftwaffe*) by early August.

At a meeting at his Berghof residence on July 31 with Field Marshal Walther von Brauchitsch (CiC army) and Grand Admiral Erich Raeder (CiC navy), Hitler requested detailed position papers for the operation after listening to their ideas. Already at that time, he told them he would start the campaign against Russia if Operation Sea Lion [the contingency plan to invade England] were not executed, revealing he was aware of the serious problems confronting a possible invasion.

The OKH (*Oberkommando des Heeres*, or Army Supreme Command) came up with a bold, massive offensive across a wide stretch of southern England that would tie up large enemy forces. Three army groups (Army

Group A under von Rundstedt; B under Strauss and C under von Reichenau) with a total of 36 divisions, including six tank and two airborne, would invade the southeast coast, a 200-km-long area between Ramsgate, the Isle of Wight and Lyme Bay. Three waves, the first one with six divisions (16th, 9th and 6th Army), supported by 650 tanks (280 submerging amphibious) should attack on "D-Day" between September 19 and 21, not to be confused with the Allied D-Day, of course.

OKM (*Oberkommando der Marine*—Navy Supreme Command) followed with its operational plan. They requested a smaller attack area— no Lyme Bay—and concentrating between Folkstone and Eastbourne. With a strength differential of 1:10 for the German navy to the Royal Navy, they could not give enough protection at the far western end, since large naval units were unable to operate in the small English Channel-Strait of Dover. The navy proposed to make a flotilla of 10 destroyers and 20 torpedo boats available for the west side; 30 Schnell-boats[1] and 21 submarines for the east side; large minefields on the flanks; and to fake naval operations with a battleship, cruisers and troop transporters out of German North Sea ports and the south coast of Norway.

The navy also requested absolute control of the airspace by the *Luftwaffe*. There were some obvious military basics missing—for instance, time and space for unloading troops from ships to landing boats or vehicles.

Hitler intervened and demanded a revised plan to be worked out by the operations department of OKH. The invasion force was cut down to 26 divisions. A first wave of six divisions of Gen. Busch's 16th Army (from Army Group A) was to assemble in the ports of Rotterdam, Antwerp, Dunkirk and Calais, going ashore between Folkstone and Dover. Two divisions of Gen. Strauss's 9th Army were to assemble at the harbor of Boulogne and landing between Eastbourne and Bexhill. Three divisions of Field Marshal Walther von Reichenau's 6th Army would assemble at Le Havre, invading the shores at Brighton.

In the meantime, from August 13th—"Eagle Day"—Luftflotte 2 and Luftflotte 3 of Germany's *Luftwaffe* tried to gain control over the island's skies. It seemed to work, as they strafed and bombed airfields and communications, until the "Ultra" machine deciphered the wireless orders of the Luftflotte and enabled the British Command to quickly assemble Spitfires and Hurricanes for fierce counter-attacks. When *Reichsmarschall* Goering ordered reprisal attacks against British cities for the terror bombing of German cities, the goal of airspace supremacy was lost.

On Sept. 17, 1940, the Fuehrer Headquarters, recognizing these problems, postponed Operation Sea Lion and it never took place. Hitler turned his attention to the east.

What follow are Giesler's recollections.

* * *

AUGUST 1942, FUEHRER HQ, WINNIZA

"Why didn't I give the order to attack England? I had various reasons," Hitler said. We were having our nightly tea at Winniza. It was not clear to me what Hitler was drinking most of the time. Once he said to me, "Chamomile tea with honey tastes very good, sometimes peppermint tea or rose hips . . . also tea of mixed flower blossoms. And quite delicious is a boiled apple served in a glass."

I chose black tea with oat cookies; from time to time, he took one.

For sure, he let the preparations for the attack go ahead; he had his reasons. Operation Sea Lion sounded very promising, but he was by no means sure about it. The forces for the attack had already begun their exercises; ships were concentrated; offensive operation plans had to be worked out.

"But I wanted peace! Was it not possible that our offensive preparations would have been detected by reconnaissance, eagerly reported via the Vatican, Switzerland, Sweden and Portugal to England, and possibly contribute to willingness for peace? But soon I recognized the hate was stronger; they preferred 'blood, sweat and tears.' The powers in the dark—incomprehensible—did not mind; it was not their blood or their suffering. This war was satisfying their hate and drive for profit and power; Churchill was only the order taker."

The offensive toward the west had never been his goal; he wanted to avoid it, and an attack on England seemed to him senseless. What losses would have occurred by such an attack across the channel! Fall was approaching, with its unruly seas; most of the transport ships were not seaworthy. At first, he only felt a slight apprehension about it, but then he saw a threat—the very busy diplomatic activity of the enemy. Their target: a renewed effort at encirclement. But for the time being he left that aside.

"Let's assume we attack England and the attack succeeds, under great sacrifices. What then? We would not possess the English government, the Royal House, the fleet—they moved away to Canada. The war in the west would continue, but not to our advantage, and in any case with an enormous tie-down of our forces. The occupation of England would not relieve the situation in Norway and France.

"And how would we feed the island when we ourselves are just making it, with restrictions? Then, our forces would bleed to death on the way to England and in England itself, while the Russians rolled over the Balkans, as they did in the Baltic with Estonia, Latvia and Lithuania. First they declare it a 'sphere of interest,' then comes military occupation, and finally the Bolshevization, and with it, gaining military and economic strength.

"But not only that, the Russian could cut off our supplies and block important raw materials at the Balkans, above all oil. No, he would have us in his hand, dictating. We should even be glad he would not attack us right away. That would depend on how much our forces were weakened by our attack of England."

Those were his considerations at that time.

Why was England not ready for peace? Churchill has said only one word: "Russia."

Already, long before (just after the French campaign had ended), it was clear to him that, depending on the war and political world situation at the time, Russia will act—either by its Bolshevik idea of a world revolution or by a nationalistic Russian idea of expansion towards the West, Europe. Both would come to the same result in the end. It's a problem of greatest importance, not only for Europe but more so for the whole world. It lurks on the horizon like a threatening cloud before a thunderstorm.

Certainly the Russians were not yet quite ready, but the threat was already obvious. The deployment against us had already begun, first diplomatically, followed very soon by military preparations. Now he knew it would not take long for blackmail to enter. He anticipated far ahead of what Molotov presented.

Stalin would naturally have preferred us to attack England, to weaken and entangle ourselves according to Lenin's prophecies. Not only common sense but European thinking spoke against an invasion of England.

More and more, threatening signals appeared—danger from the east. Not only the decision for Germany, but one for the whole world rested with us. Churchill and Roosevelt, warmongering figures visible in the darkness, bet on the Russian card. To forestall them with our attack was the only possibility; first to ward off the Russian-Bolshevik danger, second to secure food and raw materials, and third to not only take the Russian card out of the hands of the West, but to make it obvious that, by Germany securing its food and raw material, a continuing of the war would be senseless.

For sure, individual operations in the west, like Gibraltar, would have been possible and could have shown significant results, but only on our own, without drawing Spain into the war. He has been advised against this. He had talked to me about his disappointments after negotiating with Franco. He naturally wanted to attack Gibraltar from the land side. He by no means intended to draw Spain into the war. Ally with Spain? Never.

We were burdened enough by the Italians. Spain would draw us into war fronts of neither military, nor, above all, of any economic interest. That's one side of the coin. The other is that we would have had to help them; we could not allow them to get beaten, even in battles picked by them for which we saw no need.

Specifically, he was thinking about the very senseless attack on Greece—he could not prevent it.[2] He had told me that on his visit in Florence he faced a *fait accompli*—an expanding war, followed by restlessness at the Balkans and the consequence: Yugoslavia.[3]

All in all, a loss—a tiedown of forces. We lost time, unrecoverable time, over two months time. We missed the original assault time window for reaching the targets he had set. That lost time was a gain for the Russians; they threatened our border by putting 175 divisions into readiness.

A neutral Italy, mobilized and ready for action, could have helped us and been useful to them, too. Already in 1940, when we had taken Paris, Hitler had prophesied to me that we would not be able to hold back the Italians; they wanted to have a part in it. They lessened our victory and the possibility of peace. If they really wished to fight, they should have taken Malta.

After pondering in silence, he said with a slow voice: "Yes, now I face the most difficult decision of my life. What will happen if I push open the door to the east?" Hitler was quiet again for a while, then, "Enough for today, Giesler. I'll see you tomorrow for lunch."

LUNCH AT DEUTELMOSER'S TAVERN IN MUNICH

Alone, I had time to think and ponder also. I recalled the 26th or 27th of October, 1940, when I had been asked to the "Osteria Bavaria" for lunch. After the meetings with Franco and Petain, Hitler came to Munich at midmorning, before meeting later on with Mussolini in Florence. Deutelmoser, the owner of the inn, was always highly honored when Hitler chose his small, simple restaurant for lunch. I was amused every time at the stir-up in the kitchen. But Deutelmoser was cool and collected when he served the potato soup and the turnip salad with the air of serving treasures.

After lunch, I was sitting alone with Hitler at the table. He talked about his trip and said of Petain:

"A soldier, honorable and dignified, he fully met my idea of a French marshal, but he is already too old to plan into the future. Well, now to Franco—it may well be that my disappointment influenced my judgment. Our discussion remained without results. Franco has no personality; he is absolutely average. Without the Jesuits, who in my opinion not only advise but direct him, he would be insignificant. He is certainly

Oct. 24, 1940: French President Marshal Petain meets Adolf Hitler at Montoire in front of Hitler's interpreter Paul Schmidt with Foreign Minister Ribbentrop.

PHOTO: GERMAN FEDERAL ARCHIVES

clever in his way, but so are traders."

He believes if he had already recognized Franco's political aims and his character in 1936, his sympathies would have been with those who stood up against the feudal system and the clerics. But those revolutionaries were led by communists, and once they get their foot in the door there is no turning them out again. A socialism that suits Spain, yes; a Spanish-Communistic state as a satellite of the Soviets, no. It was a European task to prevent it and in that he agreed with the Duce. Thus, we had to intervene with help. It would then have been up to Franco to start a new social order with his Falangists.

Hitler looked around, met the eyes of the guests with a smile and a gesture of greeting. "What might I expect in Florence? I have an unpleasant feeling," he said, facing me again with a completely changed look.

At his request, I gave him a short report about the status of the Munich city planning and the steps I initiated for the construction of the Autobahn ring and the new railway system. I also asked him if he thinks that, for the time being, all constructions and plans for (NSDAP) party buildings should be set aside. "Absolutely"; he meant preference has to be given to plans serving city rebuilding and community purposes.

It was certainly the word "party" that turned his thoughts.

He worries a great deal about Rudolf Hess. He knows he can talk about it with me: Hess's nearly occult, airy behavior, his hypochondria and what he is doing for it. He (Hitler) is certainly not against homeopaths and alternative medical practitioners, but strongly against all those Hess trusts with his confidence. He should by all means find the confidence of a physician with rank. Hitler is really worried, not only because of Hess's position and tasks, but simply because he is sincerely fond of him. "That I keep him in such high esteem, that I feel an obligation, well, he is the 'Faithful' since the beginning of the National Socialist struggle."

Hitler stood up, waved his hand to his guard commando, saying goodbye, to travel toward new disappointment and trouble. When he arrived in Florence, Mussolini told him he issued the order to attack Greece. That was now the second extension of the war and war theaters, totally undesired and useless, idiotic.

Hitler expressed it once to me as a fallback of two millennia, and its origin lay in the historically based myth about the Roman empire. He explained that the turbulence in the Balkans, cleverly stirred up by the English, surely led to Yugoslavia's breakaway and the Balkan campaign, causing losses and tying up divisions and airplanes necessary for the offensive against Russia, and above all using up time, precious time.

BERGHOF: 1941

"The most difficult decision of my life," Hitler told me at the end of our nightly talk in his work room at the Winniza headquarters. A memory appeared like a picture in front of my eyes: around February 1941, on an afternoon at the Berghof, after a discussion with my construction staff for Obersalzberg (*Bauleitung Obersalzberg*), I arrived at the large living room of the Berghof for the usual walk to the tea pavilion.

The military talks were just finished. Hitler stood with a few generals at the marble table in front of the big window and gave some orders to his adjutant. Dr. Todt, who participated at the talks, stood with me toward the back of the large room. He pointed to the scene and said quietly, "They know about the decision—Russia. It will be tough. Who knows what is waiting for us behind that border? What is already known to us is threatening enough. But look, here the Fuehrer stands, concentrated, collected, and in the background the Untersberg. You know the saga: For 1,000 years the hope of Germans has been connected with this mountain—isn't that strange?"

Yes, it was a striking picture, somber and impressive. I looked at Hitler's profile as some generals and SS officers were facing him with serious, tight expressions. In the background, the view through the large window looked over the deeply snowed-in landscape of the Berchtesgadener Land. The Untersberg alone stood high above the dark forests, its red, precipitous rocks now white, illumined by the last sunrays of the day.

In the evening we were sitting around the fireplace; Hitler was silent, focused inward. We talked quietly. Around midnight, Hitler asked Martin Bormann for something. Then, to our complete surprise, the powerful, fateful-sounding melodies of Liszt's *Les Preludes* swept through the large hall, lit only by the flames of the fireplace. ✦

CHAPTER NOTES:
1 Schnell-boats (in German, *Schnellboote* or *S-boote*—meaning "fast boats") were heavily armed coastal craft often referred to by the Royal Navy as E-boats. Faster and better armed than the Royal Navy MTBs and PT-boats, they became the most effective inshore attack craft of World War II. All German Schnell-boats carried two separate torpedo tubes. In total 249 Schnell-boats were built for the *Kriegsmarine*, with a total of 157 being lost or scuttled. The United States, UK and Russia divided up the surviving boats between them.

2 Benito Mussolini, impressed by Hitler's success, wanted to do his own war and started the attack on Greece without informing Hitler. This can be attributed to jealousy, combined with imperial pride, on Mussolini's part.

3 Giesler is referring to the putsch in Yugoslavia that forced the redirection of German forces to the Balkans just before the planned invasion of the Soviet Union. Guided by the British secret service and probably supported by the Russian air force, Serbian Gen. Simovic overthrew the pro-Hitler regency of Prince Paul and installed a pro-British military government.

Franco's Lukewarm Commitment to Germany

Adolf Hitler remembered his meeting with Generalissimo Francisco Franco at Hendaye as one of his worst experiences. They met at this French town on the Spanish border in October 1940. Hitler was upset for two reasons:

First, the general's growing hesitancy to support Hitler's "Operation Felix," the plan to take Gibraltar and extend the operation into Spanish Morocco. Franco did not want Spain to join the war. Unbelievable as it sounds, Franco was advised to take up that attitude by Hitler's chief of the *Abwehr*, Adm. Wilhelm Canaris, who was an expert for Spanish affairs and twice visited Madrid in 1940.[1]

Second, Hitler was angered by Franco's outrageous demands for Germany to supply raw materials, armaments, machinery and even foodstuff with which to fight the war. Franco knew well enough Germany could never fulfill this request. That devious move was also suggested by Canaris. The meeting ended with the signing of a worthless document of mutual cooperation. Hitler reportedly stated about this meeting: "I would rather have my teeth pulled than meet with Franco again."[2]

Franco's Jesuit conscience must have pestered him, however. He could not but remember the decisive help given to him by Adolf Hitler during his life-and-death struggle with the Red Republic from 1936-39, which resulted in unfa-

Left, Francisco Franco.

Francisco Franco, center, greets Adolf Hitler in Hendaye, Oct. 23, 1940. Franco did not repay in kind the substantial aid that had been extended to him from Germany and Italy during his civil war of 1936-39.   PHOTO: GERMAN FEDERAL ARCHIVES

vorable publicity such as the "Guernica myth" being leveled against "the fascists," including Germany. He did permit Spanish military forces to join Germany's war in Russia. The Blue Division (*Division Azul*) under the command of Gen. Agustin Munoz-Grandez fought with distinction for two years at the Leningrad front. ◆

ENDNOTES:

1 John H. Walter, *The Unseen War in Europe*, p. 155. 1996, Random House, New York.

2 Published in *The Journal of Art, History and Literature*, from Count Ciano's transcript of Hitler's October 28 meeting with Mussolini, written a few days after Hendaye. Ciano was Mussolini's son-in-law.

Why Guernica?
The Politics of Propaganda

By Carolyn Yeager

Every year, tens of thousands of museum-goers in Spain view the most famous anti-war painting in the world: *Guernica* by Spanish-born Pablo Picasso. But does what really happened to this small town justify its becoming a worldwide symbol for "terror bombing"? Or is it another instance of leftist international manipulation?

When we look more closely at the record of the events, we find that manipulation is indeed what happened—the story of Guernica became a propaganda tool of the Communists with the aid of a world-class artist like Picasso. If it was truly about terrorizing a population, Picasso should have created a Dresden, Hamburg, Nagasaki or Hiroshima masterpiece instead.

The bombing raid carried out by the German Legion Condor on April 26, 1937, as allied support for Franco's Nationalist forces, was not a planned terror act or "test," yet that idea continues to be repeated today.

From an article[1] based on interviews of participants and surviving documents of the *Luftwaffe*—specifically an unpublished history of the Legion Condor from the year 1940—by Alfred de Zayas, published in the *Journal of the Bundeswehr* in 1974, we learn the following:

• Guernica was on the front line and not an open city. It was heavily defended by 12 battalions of Basques and a number of Cantabrian troops. An armament factory was inside the city and other Red Army facilities were in the immediate vicinity.

• An air attack at the bridge and road crossing east of Guernica was ordered. All Condor orders were strict that cities must be spared, and

Museum visitors view Picasso's famous propaganda painting "Guernica." The Spanish Republican (Red) government commissioned Picasso to create a large mural they could display at international expositions in 1937. They also put the painting on a world tour, which brought their version of the war to world attention. A copy in tapestry form, commissioned by Nelson Rockefeller in 1955, hangs in the United Nations at the entrance to the Security Council room. [PHOTO: WIKIPEDIA]

most especially churches. (Knowing this, the "Rojas" [Reds] stored ammunition in churches, blowing them up when they couldn't get it out.) Only in special cases were military targets in cities permitted to be attacked.

• Nine aircraft dropped a total of 7,950 kg of bombs, but no hits at the bridge were observed, because visibility was very poor. The reason for the poor visibility was fire and smoke from the blasting and setting of fires by the Reds, and possibly the international brigades, ahead of the air attack. The relatively primitive targeting devices used at that time were also responsible for non-military objects being hit.

Because the city was wrapped in fire and smoke, the enemy press was able to blame specifically the German squadron for the destruction of Guernica.

The erroneous story that Hermann Goering admitted that Guernica was a "testing ground" for the effects of terror bombing was traced by de Zayas to a Chinese Central News Agency in Taiwan, whose New York office denied issuing any such report. Other original reports said the city was destroyed by arson, not by air attacks.[2]

What Goering did say at the IMT in Nuremberg in 1946 is that transport, bomber and fighter planes were sent "to Spain" (no mention of Guernica) to test materiel under warlike conditions. De Zayas lists several otherwise reliable authors who have repeated the terror lie in their histories.[3]

Deaths were also greatly exaggerated. Originally claiming over 1,000, it's now accepted there were only around 200 civilian deaths—not a large number compared to WW II death tolls. The Condor orders can be seen at the military archives at Freiberg. ◆

ENDNOTES:

1 *Guernica im Lichte neuerer Untersuchungen* ("Guernica in Light of the Latest Research"), by Alfred Maurice de Zayas, Wehrforschung (WF), June 1974. De Zayas is a distinguished author, researcher and expert on international human rights.

2 The anti-Franco monarchist Antonio Ansaldo wrote in his memoirs that shortly after the attack he was in Guernica and believed at that time the city was destroyed by arson. Later he read about Goering's alleged confession in a French newspaper story and changed his belief.

3 Hugh Thomas, *The Spanish Civil War*; John Killen, *History of the Luftwaffe*; Vincente Talon, *Arde Guernica*; Pedro de Basaldus, *En defensa de la liberdad*; and Alberto de Onainda, *Hombre de Paz en la Guerra*.

Barbarossa's Saga

At the time of the crusades, the German Kaiser and Holy Roman Emperor Frederick I, called Barbarossa ("Red Beard"), left to fight in the Holy Land. During the 3rd Crusade in 1190, the emperor died tragically by drowning in the River Saleph, in Asia Minor.

Soon, however, rumors that he was not dead, but would return, began to circulate and developed into the Barbarossa saga. The enchanted Frederick was said to still live with his whole court in the Kyffhäuser, a mountain in Thuringia, or in the Untersberg, straddling the border between Berchtesgaden and Salzberg.

One version of the legend has it that the emperor is seated in the mountain at a table with his golden crown on his head; his beard grows around the table and has circled it twice. When the time comes, Barbarossa will step out from the mountain and again erect his empire. Every hundred years, he sends his dwarfs to see if the ravens are still circling around the mountain. If this is the case, the time for the emperor's awakening is not yet, and he again falls back into his enchanted sleep.

After the death of the last Staufer (the Hohenstaufen dynasty), Emperor Frederick II, in the year 1250, the German empire, after a nearly 100-year blossoming, broke down into many small states with partly contradictory interests. The Barbarossa saga mirrors the desire of simple people for a unified state led by a wise and just ruler.

Originally, the emperor's saga was applied to Frederick II, the nephew and successor of Barbarossa. However, by the later middle ages, it was Barbarossa who was seen as the sleeping emperor in the mountain.

At the beginning of the 19th century, during the time of Bismarck, strong efforts were made to recreate a unified German national state. During that time, the Barbarossa legend became a German national story. ◆

OPERATION BARBAROSSA

Hitler's preemptive strike on the Soviet Union was to prevent Europe from being overrun and subjugated by the armies of Josef Stalin. Above, German troops at the Soviet state border marker on X-Day, 22 June 1941. PHOTO: GERMAN FEDERAL ARCHIVES

CHAPTER 5

HITLER STRIKES FIRST WITH OPERATION BARBAROSSA

Translators' Introduction: Hitler explains he had no other choice but to attack the Soviet Union before Germany was attacked by her. Even though Churchill refused all efforts to bring peace in Europe, Hitler signed the Directive No. 21 on Dec. 10, 1940—the order to prepare to invade the Soviet Union. It was a gigantic undertaking: 153 German divisions, nearly 3 million German soldiers, together with Hungarian, Italian, Romanian and Bulgarian forces, crossed a 1600 km border line from Northern Norway to the south shores of the Black Sea in the early morning hours of June 22, 1941. The scene opens on an evening in the late summer of 1942 at Hitler's headquarters in Winniza/*Werwolf*, where Giesler is staying as a guest of the Fuehrer. Giesler has Hitler speaking in the first person as they work on building plans for German cities.

HITLER REVEALS HIS REASONING

"I planned the preventive stroke against Russia with still more care than the west campaign. The threat from the east was too obvious. After the French campaign, I declared to the Reichstag that there was no reason to continue the senseless war against England. The British answer to that peace gesture was a rude denial. England wanted to go on with the war; Churchill was serious with his "Germany must perish!"

"From then on I spent long nights over the maps of East Europe, full of sorrow, pondering and reviewing England's typical conduct toward a conflict-free Europe. Looking for her advantage, England had always interfered in continental affairs—provoking or inflaming disputes via middlemen. She always tried to find a continental saber to fight for her and spare her own strength.

"With France now eliminated, England—sure of the support of Roosevelt's America—would try with all means available to let Russia fight for her.

"I paid dearly for the pact with Stalin in August 1939. It cost me a lot for a pragmatic friendship for the sake of a pretended limitation of the war or, if the conflict expanded, to avoid facing Soviet bayonets at my back. Stalin turned agreed-upon spheres of interest into the brutal occupation of the Baltic states, the separation of Bessarabia and the forcing of Finland to her knees by a war of deceit.

"After the military occupation of the Baltic states, Bessarabia and Bukovina, Stalin's goal was clearly recognizable: to become ruler over northeastern Europe and the Balkans. He wanted free access to the Mediterranean and an all-important starting position against Europe.

"Stalin saw those possibilities at a time when we were tied up in the west. He had the England-United States constellation in view; he had made up his mind and was preparing to attack Germany, the only nation that could block both aims. The threat could be seen; the Soviet deployment began.

"The military deployment of the Soviets on our eastern border would soon be followed by political blackmail. I was convinced of that. It was also obvious to me that the pan-Russian sphere-of-interest thrust was increased toward the west because of the demand of Bolshevism—it had already earlier jumped over its natural eastern border at the Pacific Ocean.[1]

"Soon, Stalin would be found on the side that offered him the greatest advantage: elimination of the only power that could resist the further advance of Bolshevism into European areas—National Socialist Germany.

"I not only saw the threat in the ready positioning of Russian armies at our eastern border, with only a thin veil of a few divisions opposing

Some of the 5 million Soviet prisoners captured by German forces during Operation Barbarossa are shown in this photograph taken near Minsk. PHOTO: GERMAN FEDERAL ARCHIVES

them, but my concern was much more for our dependence on raw material—such as oil from Romania, but also ore, bauxite, molybdenum, manganese, chromium and nickel from Finland—the supply of which could be blocked at any time by the Russians.

"I again negotiated with Russia. It was an honest effort. Molotov, however, arrogantly delivered Stalin's demands: a free hand for Russia in Romania, Bulgaria and Finland and, in addition, free access to the Baltic Sea and the Dardanelles. That meant abandoning Europe.

"My only alternative was the defense by a preventive stroke. Not only Germany was at stake, but the very existence of Europe. Still, the decision for me wasn't an easy one.

"Regardless of all other matters, it meant the postponement of the realization of the social part of the tasks I set for myself and which required a secure time of peace. To those tasks, as you know, belonged the reconstruction of German cities.

"When I ordered the beginning of the preparations, that sinister treason occurred again that we experienced during the campaign against Poland, before the Operation *Weseruebung* (in Norway and Denmark) and the French offensive.[2]

"Nevertheless, great initial success occurred due to the unique strengths and élan of the German soldier, the strategic planning and supreme tactical leadership.

"After the stormy successes, the wear and tear of men and materiel came to light. The vast spaces, for which we had to fight hard, tired out the troops. We had to take a breather (the supply problem forced it also) before we could take up the decisive moves incorporated in my strategic ideas.

"Egoism and the one-track thinking of my generals crossed that strategic planning. In that month of August, so decisive for the Barbarossa operations, I fell ill and was so weakened that I could not gather the necessary insistence and steadfastness to push my plans through against my generals.

"Twice I thought to be close to victory. I was mistaken; and it turned out to be deceptive."

We were sitting on stools at the worktable, drawing details of the Linz City House. Adolf Hitler, however, was soon at the war scene again in his thoughts.

"I talked with you already about my strategy because I knew you, as a talented architect of multi-faceted city projects, could appreciate the importance and the scope of complex planning.

"Above all, a sober, mathematical thinking is needed, not only for various military dimensions, but more so for the immense distances, estimates of timing and transport routes for securing supply. Specifically in the wide-open Russian spaces, one has to think about locations of raw materials and food; also regions of concentrated armament industries. All these things determine the basic idea for strategic planning, and at the same time influence the order of military targets, which again demand the ability for imagination, intuition, invention and audacity.

"One can pretty well figure one's own forces, their battle strength and experience. But judging your adversary? Evaluating the enemy's strength?

PHOTO: GERMAN FEDERAL ARCHIVES

"The vast spaces, for which we had to fight hard, tired out the troops". Here, Wehrmacht soldiers pull a car from the mud during the *rasputitsa* (sea of mud) period in Fall 1941. Ice and snow presented a unique challenge, but the difficulty of moving men and materiel through the thick Russian mud was even worse.

OUTSMARTED BY THE RUSSIANS

"A complete failure of intelligence by our general staff and the military information service, and by the spy-agents and all the way up to the military attaché at the embassy in Moscow—nothing of real information! During the occupation of Poland and the winter offensive in Finland, our military experts were outsmarted by the Russians.

"We did not know anything about the strength of their divisions. We knew what was opposite us, but nothing of what we had to expect in the depth of the Russian spaces.

"During battle, it was revealed that the shells of our PaK [7.5-cm *'Panzerabwehrkanone* 97/38' cannon] only caused a knock on the steel protection of the T34.[3]

"Only our 8.8-cm flak [*Flieger Abwehr Kanone* = anti-aircraft gun] shells were able to pierce the strong armor of the 50- and 100-ton tanks.

"An impenetrable camouflage made the buildup of an incredible military and armament force possible. In the struggle for information, we were, and remained, hopelessly beaten."

I then remembered a remark Hitler made to me in December 1941, when he said: "Giesler, we just got away and escaped destruction by the Bolsheviks—Stalin was nearly ready to pounce upon us."

Now Hitler explained the connection between the Russian campaign planned by him, and his experiences after the invasion:

"Added to the complete underestimation of the enemy, the wrong reports about its reserves and armament strength, its deceits and confusions, was that incomprehensible treason. The preventive stroke was really no surprise at all for the enemy; it was reported on time and exact to the day and the hour. But that's not all: every detail, every offensive plan was given to the enemy by German traitors.

"I expected the treason of the X-Day. The surprise had to be rooted in the strategic development of our offensive. That strategy had been carefully thought out. In order to keep it secret and be sure of the surprise, I kept my plans only to the smallest circle. The orders for the development of the strategic tactical operations had to depend on the given situation of the offensive, the factors of space, time, weather and, above all, on the forces of the adversary.

"Now to the strategic structure: The armies were organized in three army groups: North, Center and South. Main emphasis lay with Army Group Center's thrust toward Moscow. That was an intentional deception; I did not have Moscow in mind at all. The enemy forces should be confronted with our thrust; they should be tied down and not evaded. Then they should be destroyed by massive encirclement."

Adolf Hitler sketched on drawing paper the arrows of the attacking directions of the army groups, between the outlined Baltic and Black seas. In front of the arrows he put three points and circled each one.

"Leningrad, Moscow, Rostov," he said.

The arrow of Army Group Center, he reinforced on both sides by additional arrow lines. Big circles between those five lines indicated the en-

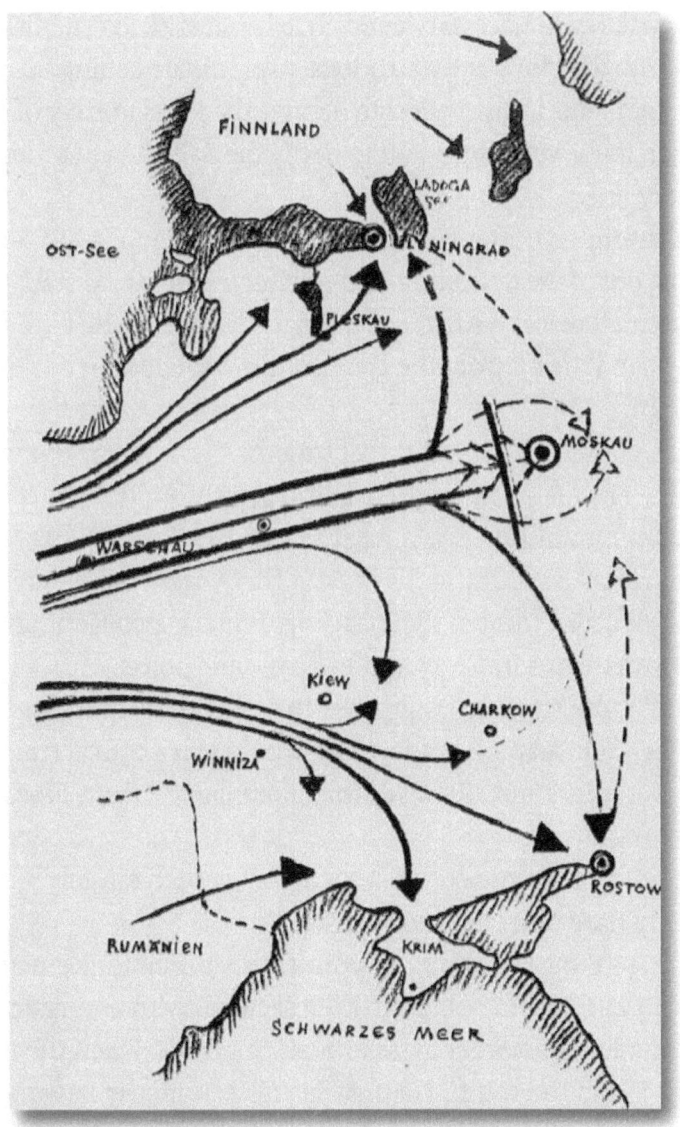

Giesler's recreation of the map Hitler made of his battle plan.
[IMAGE: GIESLER PERSONAL FILES]

circlement of enemies' armies. A fat cross line he drew in front of Army Group Center, marking Moscow.

"The attacking thrust should stop there; the tank forces with their rapid units should turn to Army Group North and South. That primary order was now decisive for the further necessary operations. Moscow was not my goal. It was necessary to encircle Leningrad, to establish the connection with the Finns at Lake Ladoga, to eliminate Leningrad as a center of the armaments industry and to deprive the Russian navy of its base at Kronstadt. It was very important to pacify the Baltic Sea in order to secure the supply line.

"Still more important was the thrust of Army Group South. The spreading out of the tank and rapid-unit forces into the distant space had to be executed twice. We had to obtain the harvest of the fertile Ukraine, the wheat and the oil from the giant sunflower fields, for our troops and the nation.

"The second north-south thrust from Army Group South was aimed toward the raw materials—the coal, iron ore, chromium and manganese, and the important power plants at the Dnieper and Donets region all the way to Rostov and the Black Sea. There, right at the raw material sources, were also located the industrial centers, a concentration of the Russian armaments industry and its economic power.

"At the same time we could gain the takeoff position for the thrust toward the Caucasian oil. And we also would win a critical region to protect the war-important supply of the Romanian oil from Ploesti against surprise attacks.

"The political rewards of such a surprising, successful military operation would have been quite significant."

While speaking, Adolf Hitler pointed his pencil to the marks of his strategic planning and completed the sketches with energetic lines. He quickly shaded the border areas around the Baltic Sea in the north and the Black Sea in the south. He drew circles around the raw material, industrial and armament centers, and once more around the encirclement of the Russian armies.

Then the arrow points of Army Group Center pierced through the heavy marked "stop line" in front of Moscow, and out of the operative areas of all army groups, he drew dotted bow-shaped lines that encircled Moscow completely.

"If strength, time and space made it possible, it should be the finale.

Only a wide, all-encompassing scissors movement would give us the possibility to take Moscow and smash the Russian forces decisively at the same time.

"Strategically and tactically, I considered those flank and encirclement operations as the only possibility to destroy the enemy; to avoid a frontal confrontation with heavy losses. We neither could match the enemy with the number of our divisions nor, as it later turned out, with our tanks and heavy weapons.

"In order to overcome the massive Russian formations and tear up rigid fronts, we should concentrate on mobile units—taking advantage of the fighting strength of our soldiers and the tactical supremacy of our leadership.

"The generals reported to me that the panzer divisions and rapid forces are completely exhausted; the tanks have to be overhauled; they are not fit for battle. They told me how many weeks they will need for it. Thus, they wanted to block my flanking thrusts northward toward Leningrad and to the south into Ukraine and the Donets.

"I was sick and without any willpower—weakened, I could not get anywhere against their 'ego sense' and 'ego will.'

"'We generals can judge the military situation much better.' That's how they were stubbornly thinking.

"Way back, a military personality once gave me the advice that, from an army general upwards, obedience decreases, and any order is subject to a personal critique. I often had the same experience.

"Again and again I noticed that my generals, in their deliberations, completely disregarded political, geopolitical and economic matters. Mostly, they kept to a purely military viewpoint, and that turned out to be traumatic when directed toward Moscow in the Russian campaign.

"As I found out later, my generals insinuated that I reflected a Napoleon-related Moscow shyness. Yet, by no means did I misjudge the military and political importance of taking Moscow; but first, the prerequisites for that were successful attacks toward the north and south, those two strategic pillars. Then, Moscow might be the last stage of the gigantic Russian undertaking.

94 | THE ARTIST WITHIN THE WARLORD

"The time favorable for mobile warfare ran out—the valuable time. It was always too little time and too much space in this war.

"At the end of September, when I was healthy again, I could still push through one of the flank-and-encirclement thrusts toward the south. That operation I had to literally wrest from my generals—yes, I had to enforce it by harsh orders. The result: four Russian armies were destroyed, and 650,000 prisoners taken. Even that success did not convince my generals of the only possible strategy within the vast Russian distances.

"Against my inner conviction, they set up the frontal offensive against Moscow. Moscow was never in my mind, but they would not or could not understand that.

"To carry the great strategy through, it was, however, too late. The offensive toward Moscow met an increasingly stiffened Russian defense. Our divisions, tired and weakened by the month-long hard battles, had the target before their eyes and clashed against fresh Siberian forces continually moving in from the far regions.

"The frontal offensive toward Moscow lost its momentum against the massive Russian defense. Soon afterward, the front froze in snow and icy cold; the winter equipment, ordered in time, never reached the troops.

"Now my generals were for retreat, which meant a Napoleon-like end: the catastrophe." ◆

CHAPTER NOTES:
1 Referring to the Russo-Japanese War of 1904-1905, and specifically the result of Russia's Far East expansionist policy to gain control of Manchuria and Korea, and the warm-water Port Arthur.
2 See Chapter 1 and Chapter 2 of this book.
3 The Soviet medium tank produced from 1940 to 1958, credited by some as the single most effective, efficient and influential design of WWII. It was the mainstay of Soviet armored forces, more heavily armored than previous models, and the most-produced tank of the war.

Strategy: Leningrad, Moscow or Kiev?

By Wilhelm Kriessmann, Ph.D.

By early August 1941, five weeks after the beginning of Barbarossa, opinions among the *Oberkommando der Wehrmacht* (OKW), the *Oberkommando des Heeres* (OKH) and some of the field generals diverged.

The first idea of Hitler and OKW was for Field Marshal Wilhelm Ritter von Leeb, leader of Army Group North, to move northeast and take Leningrad with a strong, decisive thrust that would cut the city and its immediate hinterland from Moscow, join with the Finnish forces

Gen. Heinz Guderian, commander of Germany's *Panzergruppe* 2, is shown with members of a tank crew on the Russian front, Sept. 3, 1941.

PHOTO: GERMAN FEDERAL ARCHIVES

and secure the supply for his army group through the Baltic Sea. The larger part of Army Group Center would support the move south to obtain the treasures of the Ukraine; then conquer Moscow without too great military risks.

Col. Rudolf Schmundt, Hitler's chief adjutant, had relayed this to Col. Gen. Heinz Guderian at their July 29 meeting on the east bank of the Dnieper River, on the occasion of rewarding him with the Oak Leaf of the Knight's Cross. With all his power as Germany's tank expert, convincingly successful in the Polish and French campaigns, Guderian argued for the Moscow thrust.

Guderian's *Panzergruppe* 2 and Col. Gen. Hermann Hoth's *Panzerkorp* 3 were the powerful spearheads of Army Group Center. It was known that Field Marshal Guenther von Kluge, commander-in-chief of the Fourth Army and Guderian's superior, sided with the OKW, advising more caution. Further complicating matters, the relationship between the two was strained.

OKH's chief of staff Col. Gen. Franz Halder and his chief of operations, Col. Adolf Heusinger, were at first uncommitted, but then pleaded with the generals for the Moscow thrust, as also did their chief, Field Marshal Fedor von Bock.

On August 4, at the headquarters of Army Group Center in Novy Borrisow, northeast of Minsk, the decisive meeting took place. Hitler, accompanied by Schmundt, requested reports and opinions from von Bock, Guderian, Hoth and Heusinger.

In von Bock's map room, the Fuehrer met, one on one, first with Heusinger, then von Bock, followed by Guderian and Hoth. Assembling all again after the individual meetings, Adolf Hitler announced his decision: first the thrust north to take Leningrad; then, depending on the military situation, either east to Moscow or south to Kiev and the heart of Ukraine.

This was at the time that Hitler became incapacitated by severe stomach and sleeping problems.

It was on August 18 that Hitler issued Directive No. 34, pressed by the surprising Soviet offensive in the north that was endangering Col.

German mechanized troops rest at Stariza, Russia on Nov. 21, 1941, only just evacuated by the Russians, before continuing the fight for Kiev. The gutted buildings in the background testify to the thoroughness of the Russians "scorched earth" policy.

PHOTO: GERMAN FEDERAL ARCHIVES

Gen. Erich von Manstein's offensive toward Narva—and Manstein's request for help from *Panzerkorps Hoth*. Army Group Center's offensive power moved southeast, to Kiev.

On August 24, three weeks after Hitler's original decision and six days since the directive was issued, Guderian was called by his superior von Bock to attend a meeting at headquarters that Halder also attended. The three discussed how Hitler's "irrefutable decision" could be changed, and after hours-long deliberation, von Bock suggested that Guderian and Halder should visit Hitler at *Wolfsschanze*.

Guderian described the scene in his book *Erinnerungen Eines Soldaten*:

> . . . [A]fter the landing I reported to C&C Army, Field Marshal [Walther] von Brauchitsch. He received me with the words: "I forbid you to discuss with the Fuehrer the question of Moscow. The offensive toward the south is ordered; and it

is only a question of the 'how'. Any argument is useless." I then requested to fly back to my *Panzergruppe*, because any argument with Hitler [was], under the given conditions, of no avail. But Brauchitsch did not like this either and gave me the order to see Hitler and report the situation at my *Panzergruppe*, but without mentioning Moscow.[1]

Guderian continued:

"I then went to Hitler and reported in the presence of a large group of officers—Keitel, Jodl, Schmundt and others, but regretfully without Brauchitsch or Halder and no representative of the OKH—the situation at, and condition of, my *Panzergruppe*. Hitler asked, 'Do you think your troops will, after all your achievements, still be able to endure great efforts?'

"I answered: If the troops are told of a great goal, understandable to each soldier, yes.

"Hitler replied: 'You naturally mean Moscow.'

"I answered: Permit me to present my reasons after you touched on the subject.

"Hitler agreed, and I argued my case. He let me finish and did not interrupt once. Then he talked and explained why he arrived at a different decision. For the first time, I heard the sentence: "My generals do not know anything about war economy."

"Once the final decision was made, I supported the offensive to Ukraine with all my power and asked Hitler to issue an order to keep my *Panzergruppe* together as a solid unit. He agreed to issue that order."[2]

A few days later, Army Group Center moved with decisive force toward Kiev—and was successful.[3] ◆

ENDNOTES:
1 Guderian, Heinz, *Erinnerungen Eines Soldaten* ("Memoirs of a Soldier"), Motorbuch Verlag, Stuttgart, 13th edition, 1994, p. 180.
2 *Ibid.*, p. 182.
3 The *Wehrmacht* took 665,000 Red Army prisoners from the Battle of Kiev, 1941, deemed the greatest defeat of its kind in history.

M-Day: Stalin's Mobilization

VIKTOR SUVOROV

If there is any proof strong enough to correct and revise the traditional "court" historiography of World War II, which names Adolf Hitler's regime in Germany as the sole aggressor, it can be found in Victor Suvorov's excellent book *The Chief Culprit* (*Der Tag M* in its German publication)[1]. It follows Suvorov's first book *Icebreaker*, published in 1990, which became a sensation in Russia, Germany, and also in Israel.

In both books he outlines how Stalin and his General Staff, well in advance of the Molotov-Ribbentrop pact, planned to attack Germany. New detail and documentary evidence have been brought into *Chief Culprit*.

"M-Day"—the mobilization—fell on June 13, 1941, but the preparations went back to early February the same year, and even further back into 1939 and 1940 when, shortly after the end of Germany's campaign in Poland, the Soviet army occupied the eastern part of that country.

Marshal G.K. Zhukov and Marshal A.M. Vasilevsky—both major generals at that time—and staff officers at high army commands were planning, on Stalin's orders and in deep secrecy, the attack on Germany.

Suvorov quotes Vasilevsky: "Since May 1940, the deputy head of the Operations Directorate of the General Staff worked on the operational part of a plan of strategic deployment of Soviet armed forces in the northern, northwestern and western directions."[2] That meant war preparations against Germany.

If Maj. Gen. Vasilevsky worked on such plans at that time for his operational section, from the Baltic Sea to the Pripet marshes in White Russia, one has to assume—and Suvorov indicates it—that similar plans were developed at the other four military districts on the Russian west border. At the Kiev Military District, one of special importance because of its strategic position vis-à-vis the new eastern borders of Germany, those military operations are described in detail.

On "M-Day" (June 13), orders marked "Top Secret, Special Importance"[3] were received at the Kiev military district for the "transfer (of) all deep-rear divisions and corps commands with the corps formations to new camps closer to the state border." It was signed by Marshal Timoshenko and Maj. Gen. Zhukov.[4]

MARSHAL ALEXANDER VASILEVSKY

Immediately, massive troop movements of the First Strategic Echelon, consisting of 170 divisions, began. Fifty-six divisions moved clandestinely all along the five military districts from the Baltic to Odessa, mostly at night, to areas within 20 km of the borderline, in an operation camouflaged as summer maneuvers. The remaining 114 divisions moved into the deeper territories of the western border area, fully equipped and ready to attack.

In the meantime, forces of the Second Strategic Echelon Far-East in the Siberian Baikal and Altai military districts, received similar "Top Secret, Special Importance" orders to move to new camps westward. It was an immense logistical task—thousands of railway cars transported those masses of rifle, tank and artillery corps, and with or behind them their ammunition, food, sanitary and other supplies.

But not only the army moved; the airplanes of the Russian air forces—not an independent branch of the Soviet forces but attached to army units—flew in, landed and parked on fields close to the border, cramped and looking like busy ant hills. Also the navy submarines and mine sweepers, destroyers and torpedo boats left the ports of Kronstadt and Narva, taking positions farther west.

This gigantic deployment was nearly completed when, in the early morning hours of June 22, Hitler executed his preventive masterstroke. The military disaster for the Soviet forces that followed within the next four weeks brought the worst that can happen to a deploying, marching force: encirclement. The *Blitzkrieg* pincer movements of the Army Group North in the Riga-Luga-Staraja areas, the Army Group Middle in Bryansk-Minsk-Smolensk region and the Army Group South at Kiev-Uman smashed the Soviet armies.

More than three-quarters of a million prisoners were taken; 10,000 tanks, artillery pieces, trucks, machine guns and thousands of tons of ammunition were destroyed or taken over. Yet, in spite of this auspicious beginning, the massive size, huge population, raw materials and great industrial strength of the Soviet Union eventually asserted themselves—as Suvorov insists they were destined to do from the start. ✦

—W.K & C.Y.

ENDNOTES:

1 Suvorov, Viktor, *The Chief Culprit: Stalin's Grand Design to Start World War II*, Naval Institute Press, Maryland, 2008.

2 VIZh=*Voenno-istoricheshy Zhournal* ("Military History Journal"), Marshal A.M.Vasilevsky, VIZ7 (1979), p. 43.

3 Only one classification was higher than "Top Secret, Special Importance"—that was "Top Secret, Special File," which meant that only one copy was produced and could not leave the premises of the Kremlin. Thus Top Secret, Special Importance was the highest level of secrecy used beyond the Kremlin. (*Culprit*, p. 208.)

4 *Culprit*, pp. 208-9.

Field Marshal Wilhelm List, who commanded forces throughout the war, walks with Adolf Hitler along a path at *Werwolf*, the headquarters at Winniza, Ukraine.

PHOTO GETTY IMAGES

CHAPTER 6

INSIDE HITLER'S SECRET MILITARY HEADQUARTERS EAST, 1942

Translators' Introduction: This interesting chapter takes place at *Wolfschaanze* (Wolf's Lair) near Rastenburg in East Prussia, Hitler's largest headquarters, and at *Werwolf* near Winniza in Ukraine, his farthest east headquarters. The discussions range from hidden problems that came to light because of the extra-harsh early winter in 1941, conveyed by General Schmundt and Col. Gen. Jodl . . . to Hitler's vision for the future of Europe. Giesler also recounts walks among the local Ukrainian people with the Fuehrer's personal physician Karl Brandt, and Hitler's additional positive comments about them. The chapter ends with more discussion of architecture—the historic building achievements in Italy and Germania.

WOLFSSCHANZE—WINTER 1941/1942

MINISTER DR. FRITZ TODT had asked me to undertake important war construction work at the *Balticum* (Baltic area) within the Army Group North. From December 1941 on, all of my co-workers—architects and engineers, plus the workers of the construction companies with their equipment—were working in that area. To support the supply line for the troops, we built railways and de-icing sheds for the railway engines, along with side tracks and "fast lane" tracks.

I arrived at the Fuehrer headquarters *Wolfsschanze* for a few days of meetings. After the discussions with the officers of the army transport department, I called the adjutant's office about reporting to Hitler. Generals Rudolf Schmundt and Walter Scherf informed me about the situation at the front. Both pointed out how serious the situation had become during the past weeks. With elemental force, the winter attacked the hard-fighting troops—the engines of tanks and transport carriers failed under the biting cold, guns froze, machineguns and other automatic weapons did not work. In icy snowstorms, without winter equipment, lacking accommodations and short of supplies, the German soldier fought doggedly and grimly against the massive onslaught of fresh, winter-proven units of the Red Army's far eastern areas and Siberia.

The frontline staggered. Russian breakthroughs shattered troops and leadership. Gen. Schmundt told me Hitler faced very hard decisions.

Up until now the troops successfully led attacks with confidence. But now, a sacrificing and desperate defense required the hardest resistance from the soldiers. Many commanding generals pleaded for a withdrawal in order to shorten the frontline. The Fuehrer had to make a very hard decision. The army had to hang tough, fight and withdraw only step by step where serious resistance was impossible. The front has to hold and will hold. The Fuehrer did not lose his nerve. His strong attitude influenced the troops. The soldier understood him and recognized his decision was right and the order necessary—he stood fast and fought. The army of the east was saved, because a retreat would have turned into a chaotic flight and destruction.

Today we know that we not only lost the weeks of the unforeseen Balkan campaign,[1] but also some of the strength that would have been available for the north, center and south divisions in the east. Why did the winter equipment not reach the troops in time? I had heard that the *Waffen* SS and the *Luftwaffe* got theirs in time. I asked Gen. Schmundt.

"That is painful, but I do not like to comment—even though I could say a lot about it," he replied. "Although the winter arrived unusually early and hard, not only was winter equipment missing, but also general supplies and ammunition. We did not have front-experienced divisions at our disposal when the Russians threw fresh Siberian troops into the battle."

CHAPTER 6 | 105

PHOTO: GERMAN FEDERAL ARCHIVES

Adolf Hitler and his generals study maps at a *Lagebesprechung* (military situation meeting). To Hitler's left is General Erich von Manstein, whom Hitler highly praised for his victories at the Crimea and Sebastopol, considering him the "right man for the job" of the second attempt to break through east of Leningrad, with the objective of cutting off the Russian supply lines around Oranianburg and relieving the German supply roads to the Baltic Sea area. To Hitler's right is General Kurt Zeitzler (nicknamed "Kugelblitz"—lightning-ball), appointed Chief of the Army General Staff in September 1942 as a replacement for Franz Halder, who had become an impossible irritant to Hitler. At the far right is General Ewald von Kleist of Army Group South, commander of troops whose mission was to capture important oil wells in the Caucasus. Background: General Theodor Busse, who served under Manstein as Chief of Operations, Army Group Don.

I sensed restraint and evasion. Only later I received information about the true happenings. I also had a chance to talk to Gen. Jodl (chief of staff at OKW). He told me: "I admired the Fuehrer when he laid out his strategy for the west campaign, but I was much more impressed during the last weeks by his unbelievable energy and will power, his faith and suggestive strength which held the staggering eastern front and avoided a catastrophe. A leader-personality of outstanding greatness."

When I reported to Hitler, I told him I consider it the utmost satisfaction to serve the war tasks at the Balticum and the Army Group North with all my heart. I am the right man for that task. Already in World War I, I served as a "pioneer" at the front. But that was not said quite right for him. When Dr. Todt informed Hitler about my team activities, he ap-

Above, **Hitler's workroom/office** in *Wolfsschanze*. Could the round table have been used for nightly tea and when Giesler took private meals with Hitler? **Below, the radio control center** in a blockhouse at Hitler's *Wolfsschanze* headquarters.

proved. Hitler said my architects and engineers had to deploy all available manpower at the Balticum for urgently needed railway/ bridge/ road/port construction in order to secure the supply lines and relieve the troops. At the same time, all my co-workers—unless they were drafted by the army—remain as a unit for future peaceful tasks.

Hitler said:

> I expect you to continue to work on the city-building plans, as well as the design details for Munich and Linz. If you need some assistance, your staff of experts from your construction team is at your disposal. Within the OT (Organization Todt)[2], you manage the activities of your team. You step in if difficulties occur, when discussions with higher military are necessary or decisions have to be made.
>
> You are going to stay more often now at my headquarters, which suits me perfectly. The courier airplanes are at your disposal, and you can talk to your department heads anytime. That task certainly means an additional burden for you. But, Giesler, don't take away from me the chance to get involved for a few hours in tasks which I consider so important and which are so close to my heart. Don't take the only remaining joy away from me: peace tasks of the future!

HITLER ENVISIONS EUROPE'S FUTURE

After the evening situation reports, Hitler talked about Europe's future. For me, it was especially interesting to see how convincingly he presented his visionary ideas. To overcome national chauvinism, he thought it was absolutely necessary to unify Europe and thus guarantee its future. The mere threat of an Asian-Bolshevik pummeling, destroying the basic fundamentals of Western culture, forces the union. Hitler said:

"Presently, each nation thinks egoistically for itself and not for a European condominium; that has to be our goal—a Germanic social revolution to overcome Marxism! Logically, that would lead to a league of Germanic states—not too closely knitted, but within a wise boundary—because England, for instance, is not Europe oriented, but worldwide.

We have really experienced that recently.

"Also, the Mediterranean states will remain outside that Germanic League, but still belonging to the New Europe.

"Already, voluntary military units are being formed—hope for that future Germanic League. Let me say it a little differently: the swastika flag flies right now as our national symbol. It will one day be a Germanic symbol and Germany the magnetic power field. That power field will draw in and win over all those who sense the aura of the time. That conviction has to rise— and it will. We belong together regardless of national ties and separation throughout centuries. Nothing stops us from remaining Danes, Dutch, Walloons, Flemings or Norwegians.

"A parallel example: Bismarck set a historical fact by unifying separated states like Prussia, Bavaria and Wuertemberg to the Reich. A new, strong and historical order always arises from struggle and war, or—we always have to be aware of that danger—chaos, splitting up of ethnic entities, degeneration of nations, rigor, loss and decline. So it happened when the Thirty Years War ended with the peace treaty of Münster and Osnabrück—but also at the Seven Years War when the great king's faith did not falter and Prussia's military and cultural-moral leadership was founded. The 'war of liberation' was fought against France's hegemony under Napoleon, causing the old reactionary forces to return. The wars of 1866 and 1870-71 unified the Reich. We have to think about World War I also, when, after a sacrificing struggle, the dictates of Versailles and St. Germain plunged Germany and Austria into chaos.

"We therefore had to be always aware what this war means. Not only Germany's existence and lebensraum is at stake, but we defend the culture of the *Abendland* (Occident) against Bolshevism, which according to Lenin's prophecy will roll over Europe, supported by Asia."

Hitler answered a question—No, he does not think about Moscow. That area will be ignored. What he considers necessary is a protection of Europe's flanks—the Baltic Sea in the north and the Black Sea in the south. In between something like the limes of the Roman empire has to be built, a European east wall with fortifications to protect the new European settlements. He sees the east wall in connection with a "no-man's land" occupied by German-Germanic troop units. It will be a giant connected military training area, which makes all former facilities within the Germanic lebensraum unnecessary. Those areas will then be returned to cultured land and forests.

But before we can accomplish these cultural goals, we must face the battle for our existence.

WERWOLF—SUMMER/FALL 1942

Translators' Commentary: It is now September 1942. In the north, Field Marshal von Manstein is able to stop the Russian counter-offensive at MGA, south of Lake Ladoga, during Giesler's talks with Hitler. The Fuehrer shows his confidence in his architect as a friend and loyal party member, but also values the company of a fellow artist. We learn from Giesler just how much Adolf Hitler needed a creative outlet for his artistic nature—continuing with the re-designing of German cities and buildings in the midst of monitoring battles and the devastation of war.

HITLER NEEDS A CREATIVE OUTLET

Martin Bormann[3] called from Hitler's headquarters Winniza[4] and requested my immediate departure for there. "*Parteigenosse* (party comrade) Giesler, you are urgently needed. Bring all your Linz[5] plans with you and expect to stay a few weeks. Hurry, please."

A little later Field Marshal Wilhelm Keitel[6] called and asked me to depart as soon as possible and take all architectural plans with me. An adjutant informed me which courier airplane to take for the flight out of Berlin. My alarm bells were already ringing from Bormann's call; even more so when Field Marshal Keitel called.

When I reported to Hitler in Winniza, I found him changed. After the serious discord with his generals, he stayed away from routine personal contact with them and stopped attending the joint lunches and dinners. After the *Lagebesprechung*, (*"Lage"*)[7] he withdrew. At first he

DR. KARL BRANDT

Dr. Karl Brandt became the personal physician for Adolf Hitler in August 1933, after impressing the Fuehrer by his treatment of Hitler's adjutant, Wilhelm Bruckner, who had been injured in an automobile accident. Brandt joined the NSDAP in 1932, the SA in '33 and the SS in '34. He and his wife Anni were frequent guests at Berchtesgaden, Hitler's home; they had a residence nearby. Brandt was hanged at Nuremberg June 2, 1948 at the age of 44 for his part in the short-lived Reich euthanasia program. Having defended his actions as humanely motivated, on the scaffold he said: "It is not surprising that the nation which . . . will forever bear the guilt for Hiroshima and Nagasaki . . . wants victims. I am such a victim."

did not discuss the problems with me. Bormann was also silent; he only told me that Hitler wanted to talk to me about the Linz plans whenever military matters permit it. Only talks about city building and architecture can relax him, Bormann said. I found it interesting that Field Marshal Keitel had the same idea: only Giesler with his design plans could bring relief.

During my stay at the Winniza headquarters, most of the time I was Hitler's only guest. We took our meals together and I spent long evenings and nights with him, not only in intense discussion of matters of architectural design. We often talked in detail about city building till early morning. Hitler went to bed only after he received the latest reports from the front and the night air bombing. When, exhausted by the tension of all those different discussions, I left for the bed site in my hut, I noticed that Bormann was still working in his office. Once we met in front of my hut: "Professor, rest now; you certainly realize how important your presence is."

When the others assembled for the midday *Lage* meeting, I very often walked with Dr. Brandt, a friend and Hitler's surgeon and attending physician, outside the restricted area (*Sperrzone*) through Ukrainian sunflower fields in full bloom.

We exchanged greetings with friendly natives.

Brandt said: "They show traces of the Goths. The chief (Hitler) believes that also. The women and girls look so strong and healthy because of their labor as farmers and their simple diet. . . . By the way, did you notice the change of the chief's face? Chin and mouth are hardened, the forehead tighter, more strongly chiseled, specifically above the eyes. Worry and willpower are very apparent. Did he talk to you already about his worries? I am curious what he is going to tell you."

During dinner, I talked about my impressions of the country and its people during my walk with Brandt, and his remark about the Ukrainian people. "Yes," said Hitler, "as far as I can judge, some are wonderful human beings, with valuable roots in their ancestry." He sees it in the faces of the women and girls, and especially the children; they not only look healthy, but they are also so energetic, simple and clean—used to hard work in the fields. No nibbling on sweets—where would they get it anyway? Sunflower seeds, yes. Here and there one believes one finds features of the Goths in their faces—it is certainly more an intuitive recognition that cannot be proved. Then again, the broad faces mirror the wide spaces and their closeness to Mother Earth. Anyhow, Ukraine once belonged to the great empire of the Goth. Adolf Hitler will see that he gets more information.

After the evening *Lage*, we were again dealing with the planning of the Danube bank of Linz. Adolf Hitler talked at first about his idea for the Linz city hall. He decided that the location should be at the Urfahr[8] site, upstream from the Nibelungen Bridge. The city of Linz should be represented by the mayor, not the *Gauleiter* from Oberdonau, as in Hamburg and Bremen[9]. "That's why we plan the city hall—it should become the pride of Linz." Full of fantasy, thinking of all details, he then developed his ideas. They proved that he had a fundamental knowledge of building sites of similar scales—he went far back into the past and pointed to the uniqueness of those buildings. He mentioned the Quiri-

Architectural perfection: Hitler praised the design and construction of the City Hall in Stockholm by Ragmar Oestberg, completed in 1923.

PHOTO: ARILD VÅGEN

nal and the Roman Capitol, the Palace of the Senate, as well as the Palazzo Venetia and the Palace of the Doge in Venice.

That was one side of his explanations. He then referred to the *Kaiserpfalzen*,[10] the buildings of the Staufer[11] in Apulia, the Rempter,[12] the townhouses in Flanders. He talked about the Guerzenich in Cologne and, naturally, also about the medieval city hall of Elias Halle in Augsburg: a city house, not a typical office building for scribes and their files. And then, in a kind of final statement, he mentioned the City Hall in Stockholm, designed by Ragmar Oestberg, as an outstanding achievement, a work created by tradition and knowledge of the proper location, built with masterly perfection. He praised specifically the tower and the "Blue Room." ✦

CHAPTER NOTES:

1 The Russian campaign, planned to begin in May, was delayed when Serbian air force Gen. Simonitsch started a putsch in Belgrade, which brought down the Axis-friendly regime of Prince Paul. German forces then spent five weeks to reach Greece and pacify the Balkan region.

2 The Organization Todt was a civil and military engineering group named for its founder, Fritz Todt, an engineer and senior National Socialist figure. The organization was responsible for a huge range of engineering projects both in pre-World War II Germany, and in Greater Germany (Grossdeutschland) during the war.

3 Martin Bormann was Reischsleiter and chief of Adolf Hitler's office at the headquarters.

4 Located in Ukraine, about 140 miles southwest of Kiev.

5 The capital of Upper Austria during the Third Reich, where Hitler attended school as a boy and strongly identified with all his life. Hitler and Giesler were working on great rebuilding plans for Linz.

6 Wilhelm Keitel was chief of the OKW (*Oberkommando der Wehrmacht*), the Supreme Command of the Armed Forces. Hitler established that office opposite the OKH (*Oberrkommando des Heeres*), the Supreme Command of the Army.

7 Military Situation Meeting. Usually three situation meetings took place—morning, noon and evening—in a large room with maps. They were attended by Keitel, Jodl, staff officers and generals who were called in with reports.

8 Urfahr is a suburb of Linz on the north side of the Danube.

9 Oberdonau is now Oberoesterreich/Upper Austria. Hamburg and Bremen were both free Hansa League cities.

10 Emperor's seats, not palaces, in the Middle Ages. Charles the Great built several in his vast empire, and would visit and/or stay there for awhile.

11 A German family of kings. The last one, Konradin, was decapitated in Naples by the French count of Anjou.

12 Knight's Hall in Marienburg, seat of the German Knights Order in East Prussia; now Malbork in Poland.

TRAITOR TURNS PROSECUTION WITNESS

From 1945 on, former chief of the German General Staff Franz Halder worked closely with the U.S. Army to carefully construct a military record and history of the Third Reich. Halder's diary served as evidence in the prosecution of his fellow officers at the 1948 High Command Trial, the last of the 12 trials for war crimes the U.S. authorities held in Nuremberg after the end of World War II.

[PHOTO: U.S. ARMY, TELFORD TAYLOR PAPERS]

CHAPTER 7

HITLER DISCLOSES HIDDEN TREACHERY AT THE FRONT

Translators' Introduction: In this chapter, Adolf Hitler, still at *Werwolf*/Winniza, confides to Giesler his discoveries of misconduct and disloyalty among the highest level of military command, and possibly within his headquarters. Although difficult to ferret out, he learned that the devastating, surprise attack by the Russians at Wolchow resulted from a total failure to erect the defenses he had ordered. At this time, he fired Chief of Staff Gen. Halder, replacing him with Gen. Zeitzler. Giesler then turns to his design for Hitler's retirement home, and, for a humorous interlude, recounts the visit from the renowned surgeon Professor Dr. Sauerbruch.

HITLER REVEALS HIGH-LEVEL SABOTAGE

When we were again alone after the evening tea, Hitler told me of the shattering situation he is confronted with: "Giesler, I want to talk to you about my worries—in confidence. I live and work with the depressing certainty that I am surrounded by treason. Who can I trust absolutely? How can I make final decisions and issue orders; how can I lead decisively when deceit, wrong reports and obvious betrayal cause mistrust, and uncertainty creeps into an otherwise justified caution? When, right from the beginning, mistrust stays with me."

Speechless, I looked at him. My face obviously expressed alarm.

"Yet, that's it—it starts with wrong reports and ends at sabotage. Clear, formulated orders are not executed, or fail because of stubbornness that leads to total failure. From time to time I can interfere, find the responsible people, who then use all kind of—sometimes dishonest—excuses, like: 'but the situation demanded it. . . . I interpreted it differently. . . . Out at the front everything looks different.'

"If I challenge them when they do not follow orders, or if they inform me incorrectly or incompletely and make excuses, they then click their heels and say, 'I beg for my dismissal!' Just like that!

"'It is up to me to let you know when I let you go; the soldier at the front also cannot say, I don't like it; I want to go home,' is my answer.

"Before the Russian campaign, I was making very careful plans and thinking about the strategic possibilities and how they have to be tactically executed, like when we began the offensive in the west. Naturally, the imponderables were much greater in the east, all the more because our information about the strength and fighting power of the Russians was poor and incomplete. It's useless to ponder about it now. But after the terribly desperate fight last winter—very close to a catastrophe—I put together an offensive thrust with the greatest care and checked every detail.

"Still, everything went wrong—or should I say, there was something fishy! Not only did unauthorized actions occur, but orders were deviated from. At fighting areas so far apart, that might have been necessary if a given situation requested it, but it must then end in success. The general who disregards my order has to have what Frederick the Great called 'Fortune.'"

A little detail revealed his bitterness: "Instead of opening the road for the thrust to the south of the Caucasus as ordered, they climb the Elbrus[1] to hoist a flag!"

Now, I know the "Elbrus conqueror," an enthusiastic mountaineer, Maj. [*Hauptman* Heinz] Groth, from the Sonthofen[2] regiment—a judge in his private life. For a short while I was silent. Then I said, "That mountaineering adventure had a tremendous propaganda effect in the Allgaeu

The "world's highest weather station" on Mount Elbrus (then in the USSR), after members of the 1st *Gebirgsjaeger* Division captured it in August 1942 on their way to Batu and Baku. Hitler dismissed the propaganda coup as not worth the diversion from his plan to capture oil resources. See commentary on next page.

(Groth's home province); they were proud of Maj. Groth and his *Gebirgsjaeger*."

"Crazy climbers at best," said Hitler. "Yet here is an exact, interconnecting timetable. But instead they climb an idiotic glacier mountain. They should have taken Sukhumi, and not the Elbrus. Any further comment I consider useless."

Translators' commentary: Hitler planned the summer offensive of Army Group South to push east and west of the Caucasus Mountains and take the oil centers Batu, at the southeast corner of the Black Sea, and Baku at the southwest corner of the Caspian Sea—or at least, as a first stage, Grozny and Sukhumi in 1942. From Rostow at the Don, the eastern thrust advanced very well, and their spearhead, the 1st *Gebirgsjaeger* Division, reached the Terek River. In his talk with Giesler, Hitler apparently referred to the task of crossing the river or opening the road further toward Nalchik. On August 17, part of the 1st *Gebirgsjaeger*—3rd Company of Regiment 99 Sonthofen under Maj. Groth—instead overpowered the Russian troops occupying the Elbrus hut at the 4,000-meter-high Khotiutau Pass.

Four days later, they climbed to the 5,600-meter peak and raised the Reich's war banner (swastika and Iron Cross on a red/white/black field), creating a propaganda coup. The Soviets tried to bomb the hut, and on September 21 they even tried to take it back with their own mountain troops, but failed in both attempts. The Germans kept possession of the hut until January 1943.

The thrust to the oil fields came to a sudden stop at the east side around Grozny, and broke down around the narrow road and steep mountains around Tuapse, on the Black Sea.

Giesler continues quoting Hitler:

***

"It is not easy for me to say. Unauthorized actions and treason I can sense, but cannot understand lies that are happening—yes, they lie to me. Therefore, I am now forced to have stenographers at our situation room so that every single word regarding messages, reports and orders is recorded.

"I let Halder go [on Sept. 24, 1942]. It just does not work anymore. I have to control myself when I look at his face and read in it hate, and an arrogance not at all justified by only an average intellect. It gets still worse! If I said previously I feel I am surrounded by treason, I did not mean enemy intelligence agents, professional spies or political adversaries. I do not mean those crooks and high traitors whom one can decode, detect and catch—those you have to reckon with all the time. No, this treason roots deeper, is inconceivable, and I have no way to tackle it. Who is the one I cannot trust? Who can do something like that?

"Regardless whether basic questions of strategy are concerned or detailed tactical operations which I ordered—the enemy already has knowledge of it, as I have to find out later! Who shall I suspect? I change my young SS adjutants—so what? Shall I extend my distrust to the participants in the situation room?—an impossible predicament! Or are traitors sitting at the intelligence center, where all the orders are transmitted? Obviously, they are officers, maybe even high-ranking ones!"

"But that's not possible. It cannot...!" I exclaimed.

"Ah, Giesler, listen—a small, simple example—that's why I could detect it fully; a small example only. You are familiar with the situation at the Army Group North? It is your area, where your engineers and working force for the—my God, yes—rebuilding of cities is now involved in war construction work (*Pionierarbeit*). Now, after everything went wrong, I can talk openly about that military disaster. About other events I still have to be silent. Well, at the 18th Army a thrust to the Northeast should have been executed to eliminate the Oranienbaum[3] enclave and connect with the Finns. That thrust was strategically, but, much more, politically, very important.

"Already at the beginning of the 1941 offensive, I targeted that northeast thrust. They did not follow the order; and it did not succeed—because of obstinacy, I believe. No, not because of the 'early winter,' but more about that later!

"Who could I now entrust with the new offensive? [*Generalfeldmarshall* Erich] Von Manstein was the right man for this task. He just captured, with his courageous divisions, Kertsch and Sebastopol. I discussed with him in detail the breakthrough east of Leningrad and told him what is important: the connection with the Finnish front, to cut off the supply line of the Russian army around Leningrad and Oranienbaum, and thus to shorten the frontline and, above all, pacify the Baltic Sea area and relieve our own supply roads.

German soldiers man a position at the Wolchow battlefield, near Leningrad. Thousands of Russian soldiers died in the Wolchow swamps, despite the Soviet launching of a sneak attack along this front. The massive Russian attack prevented the Leningrad operation from taking place as planned. PHOTO: GERMAN FEDERAL ARCHIVES

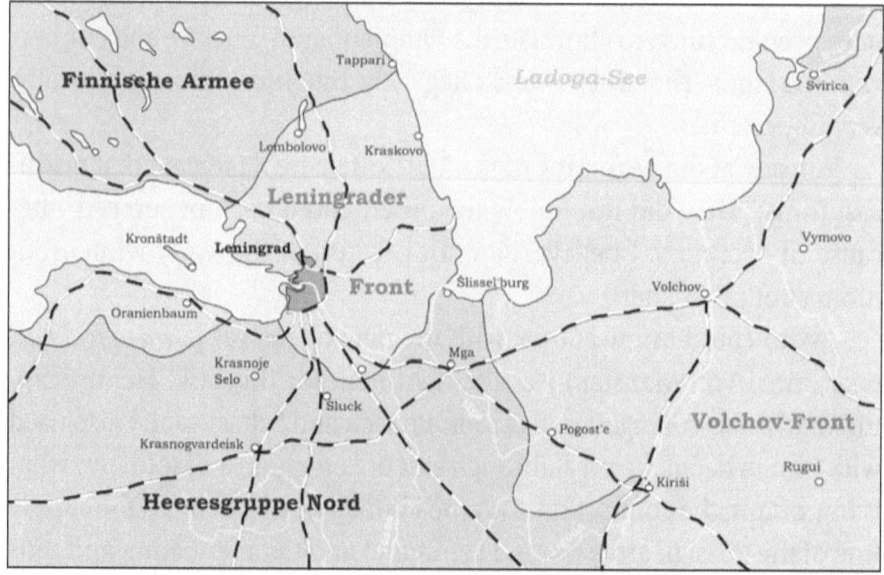

Map showing the situation on the Eastern Front at Leningrad and Wolchow from May 1942 till January 1943.

"Neither the leadership of Army Group, even less the one of the 18th Army, was capable enough for a successful operation. Manstein was the right man. The glory of the Crimea and Sebastopol was identified with his name and his army. From the beginning on, my worry was to secure the right flank, the area from the *Ilmensee* to the north—the Wolchow front.[4]

"I took the necessary steps right away. On the maps of the divisional, regimental and battalion sectors, I marked the minefields with the barricades, supported the defense by adding heavy weapons, stationary tanks and artillery, and transferred the given orders on the enlarged aerial photos and maps. I demanded and received temporary reports and finally the 'all done' confirmation—a big relief. Manstein's attacking army already moved into the area of the offensive. Then, on August 27, the Russian offensive at the Wolchow started.

"Parts of the 18th Army that I thought secured were overrun. The Russians deployed 20 divisions, plus five tank brigades—alarming! Naturally, the Russians had knowledge of the troop movements of Manstein's attack army, but that they beat us to our attack and surprised us with such a massive thrust exactly at the sector I was so worried about—strange! The Russians overran Gaitolowo and advanced close to 'MGA.'[5]

"Well, he therefore had early knowledge of our strategic plan; that means he was able to mass his forces to counterattack before our troop movements even began. How could that Russian attack intention be hidden from us?

"And now, Giesler, pay attention: How did the Russian divisions cross the minefields; how did they force their way through the barricades, through the positions secured by tanks and artillery? Right away, that puzzled me. I was forced to order Manstein to, at once, move the army, planned for the Leningrad operation, to the Wolchow front—prepared to defend as well as attack, thus avoiding a catastrophe. Since then, several battles have been fought there. The situation is not stabilized yet.

"All our forces supposed to operate at the Leningrad front are now engaged at the Wolchow. There is no longer any chance to carry out that so strategically important operation. If there was treason involved or not, we have to leave that open. But now to the facts that I was able to discover: How were the Russian divisions able to move through the barricaded fortifications, the widespread minefield? How did they overrun the tanks and defensive weapons? As unbelievable as it may sound, there were none there—they existed only in reports of the 18th Army and the Army Group! I investigated and received hypocritical excuses only.

"I had no other choice but to order all officers directly involved in the Wolchow front, as they were available, to report to headquarters—regiment, battalion, and company leaders. I interviewed them thoroughly, chatted with them, laid out the maps with the marked minefields, barricaded fortifications and so on. All the officers questioned had the same answer—the minefields, barricaded fortifications and tanks were on paper only. My instructions and orders were not carried out. The reports of having carried out my orders—lies.

"Giesler, not just an isolated example ... enough for today!"

Next morning I talked to Gen. Schmundt, chief adjutant of the armed forces (*Wehrmacht*). He confirmed those facts and explained to me the situation at the Wolchow, showing maps of the general staff. Gen. Zeitzler became new chief of the general staff, a vivacious soldier. The adjutants characterized him aptly as *Kugelblitz*—"lightning ball." The frank character of the new chief of the general staff contrasted with the reserved, chilly attitude of Gen. Halder.

HITLER'S INTENDED RETIREMENT HOME

One late afternoon Hitler again allowed himself an hour of relaxation. On the map table, we were drawing together on the Linz city rebuilding plan. I wanted to clarify some details concerning his retirement home at the rock-plateau above the Danube. He thought my idea to develop his house from the cubic form of an Upper Austrian farmhouse, the "Vierkanter,"[6] pleasing. Add to it the four protruding bays, which then might give him a view toward Linz and the surrounding country, and especially down toward the Danube and the new Danube-bank development. Its solid, robust design incorporates some of the powerful, but lucid features of Frederick II's priceless Castel del Monte [a Swabian castle in Puglia, southern Italy]. "By the way, Giesler, remember the painting of the Weimar artist—was his name Gugg? Castel del Monte, jewel of Apulia, which I ordered—find out how advanced he is with his art."

Adolf Hitler saw it at the last art exhibit in Munich and liked it very much—praised it. We discussed further details of his house: "As far as my rooms are concerned, the ground plan is set in its final form. The great hall with the terrace, its sides framed by the bays, the proper room for an 'Artus Runde' (King Arthur's Round Table); I like having it that way. You, as my architect, will be a member." I tried to get some more of his design ideas, like utility rooms, garden and the roofed pergola to the tea garden. Hitler said, "No, that's Ms. Braun's business. All those questions, you discuss first with her; she will be the lady of the house. When I designate my successor and retire, I will marry Ms. Braun."

Soon afterward, we were interrupted when an adjutant announced the arrival of Professor Dr. Sauerbruch, the surgeon. Hitler gave me a hand signal and asked me to stay—I witnessed the talk. First a friendly greeting, then:

"I thank you very much, dear Professor, that you answered my request. As a world-famous and internationally acknowledged physician and surgeon, you are at the same time also the best representative and ambassador of the nation. The task you've agreed to take on is therefore of special importance. What I can do for your support, will be done.

"My pilot and my aircraft are at your disposal. Naturally, your assisting physicians, the anesthetist and nurses will accompany you. Everything will be done to assist your effort. The ambassador in Ankara has been instructed accordingly. If you want to make your doctors and nurses happy, land on your return flight in Athens—the Acropolis should be of interest to all disciples of *Aeskulap*.

"For your intuitive finding as an operating surgeon looking for the source of the sickness, I wish you a lucky hand and full success."

Hitler bade him goodbye and again turned his attention to our work. He explained quickly: A high-ranking Turkish person is involved, of importance because of our rather delicate political situation.

Ernst Ferdinand Sauerbruch (July 3, 1875-July 2, 1951) was one of the 20th century's most outstanding surgeons and chair of surgery at Berlin's Charity Hospital from 1927 to 1949. Professor Dr. Sauerbruch overtly supported National Socialism in his public statements and in his position as head of the medical section of the Reich Research Council. He was appointed state councilor and received the Knight's Cross of the War Merit Cross. But Sauerbruch in private expressed his criticism of National Socialists. The ambiguous stance of Sauerbruch is probably typical of the role physicians played during the National Socialist era. He was also a teller of (very) tall tales, as in the madcap story he told about Adolf Hitler going bonkers about his dog, as related by Hermann Giesler. (See page 127.) The above painting is by his friend Max Lieberman, created in 1932.

A FANTASTIC STORYTELLER

Translators' Commentary: Giesler sees a side of Dr. Sauerbruch that strikes him as pretentious. He finishes the chapter with what he personally witnessed at *Werwolf*, setting the record straight, as it were, from what Sauerbruch wrote in his memoirs *Das war mein Leben* ("That Was My Life") about this very visit.

As background, *Geheimrat* Professor Dr. Ferdinand Sauerbruch was born in 1875 and had a distinguished academic career in medicine. Between 1903 and 1905, he developed a revolutionary device for heart and lung surgery now called the hyperbaric chamber. As a master surgeon, he operated on hearts, lungs, brains and bones. He treated both Lenin in Zurich and Reichs President Paul von Hindenburg in Berlin. In 1937, he received the German National Prize for Art and Science even though he was not a fan of National Socialism. In 1942, he became surgeon general of the army. His friendship with the Jewish painter Max Liebermann and people in the Stauffenberg circle, and his increasing criticism of the regime, was tolerated because of his worldwide reputation.

However, by 1949, marred by dementia, he was dismissed and died two years later in the same year he published his book *Das war mein Leben*. Armed with this information, the reader can judge this interesting and amusing, but possibly controversial, section for himself.

* * *

At the time of the situation room reports in the evening, I was invited to a cocktail party. Prof. Sauerbruch, surrounded by the top military medical brass, was the center of the party. The mood among Aesculapius' disciples was a rather enhanced one, as "Josef Filser"[7] would have phrased it. Well, they were also hosted by Julius Schaub,[8] with a cunning look. Sauerbruch was bragging—I really cannot call it otherwise—about his forthcoming Turkish mission, his tired mouth highly alcoholized: "... and how well the Fuehrer treated me—amazing personality—his airplane I get, and everything that I consider necessary—he told me so—he knows quite well how useful I am."

He shed tears—no, it was the *Steinhaeger*[9] that dripped out of his eyes. He wiped it off and then said: "Who is this one here? I have seen him once before!" He pointed at me. Sure, he had seen me before, just late that afternoon. Still, I was surprised at his ability for "intuitive recognizing." He was in such a good mood he would have removed our appendix without charge! I was thinking about my evening mission and withdrew.

Exactly 10 years later at the war crimes prison in Landsberg, fall 1952, I read Sauerbruch's book *Das war mein Leben*, his memoirs—first in a magazine, then a book (an edition of 170,000 copies). The *Herr Geheimrat* ("secret counselor") presented descriptions of his profound surgical art and serious scientific knowledge, garnished with gossipy untruths. He describes that visit at the Fuehrer headquarters in Winniza, what he had to go through when meeting Hitler. Well, I was present with close attention and interest at these meetings and talks, because the name "Sauerbruch" was well known.

According to Sauerbruch, the headquarters were "30 meters below ground level." He got drunk that evening when the headquarters also existed for him as wooden houses, huts and barracks! A general "hissed" at him. He does not really know who he was, but it only could have been the very courteous, amiable Gen. Schmundt, chief adjutant of the *Wehrmacht*. "Will you undo your belt? Nobody is allowed to visit the Fuehrer with a weapon."

But *Herr Geheimrat*, that directive was not issued until after the assassination attempt, July 20, 1944.

"Sixteen generals" could not have an audience with Hitler because *Herr Geheimrat* was late. The situation meeting time was long past— Hitler and I were drawing and planning well over an hour when the *Geheimrat* was announced. When the *Geheimrat* entered the large, lavishly furnished room, a giant dog "shot" at him, barking at his chest with bared teeth and its snout on his neck—that would have been the German shepherd bitch, Blondi, lying quietly on her blanket, her muzzle between her paws, from time to time wiggling her ears. And all of Hitler's rooms were furnished very simply. But in the meantime, the dog expert Sauerbruch called Blondi back to order—yes, the dog "smiled friendly" at him, he writes, "when Hitler entered." I saw it differently: the adjutant let Sauerbruch in.

"The scene now following was the most terrible one I ever experienced," the *Herr Geheimrat* writes. But I stood in the same room and saw the courteous, friendly greeting.

"In his eyes sparkled fury; he clenched both his fists, plunged toward me [Hitler, naturally, not Blondi] and yelled: 'What have you done to my dog?!'" They had nothing together, the *Herr Geheimrat* and the dog. "Hitler raised a wild, furious yell. 'I want the dog shot!'" Then with a "jarring, shrill discant" which must have echoed through the whole subterranean vaults (of the wood house), "I give you that bitch!" and "I'll have you arrested!" And so it continues, by the *Geheimrat*'s description. The *Herr Geheimrat* notes: "I was somehow flabbergasted."

Well, I, too, reading that stuff.

When walking around the center yard of the Landsberg prison, I asked the internist and scientist Dr. Beiglboeck, a very civilized and humorous Viennese: What do you think of Sauerbruch? "A super *Aufschneider*,"[10] he remarked ambiguously, smiling slightly.

Then I talked to the top brass of the military physicians, *Generaloberstarzt* Professor Dr. [Siegfried] Handloser. Naturally, he read Sauerbruch's memoirs. He answered with a question: "Why do you ask me about Sauerbruch's Winniza story?"

"Well, I was present most of the time, from the beginning until close to the drunken end, first with the chief and his dog in the vault '30 meters underground,' and then at the cocktail party, or symposium as you medical men call it!"

"Ah, that was you. All the years here in Landsberg, I always asked myself, how do I know you?"

"Well, dear Dr. Handloser, Sauerbruch was superior to you then regarding the 'intuitive recognizing' because he already had to face that question after only a few hours."

"Well, then we might be again 'off the dog,'"[11] Dr. Handloser remarked. "I believe the medical and surgical chapters are Sauerbruch's;

128 | THE ARTIST WITHIN THE WARLORD

Above, Hitler with his dog Blondi, who was always well-behaved. Why Dr. Ferdinand Sauerbruch (left) would write what he did in his memoir, that the dog "shot at him, bared her teeth and barked at his chest," would be a mystery except that, as Giesler explains, it was the style of the time after the war to make up wild stories about Adolf Hitler. *Generaloberst* Prof. Dr. Siegfried Handloser (right), thought Dr. Sauerbruch a great surgeon and the slander and lies were added by someone else.

everything else was written by his interviewer, and he writes as the fashion of the present time demands."

"I see that a little differently," I said. "It might well be that one of those dirty scribblers was at it, but he could never have mentioned all these details—fantasies—without *Herr Geheimrat* Sauerbruch's authorization. I believe that a physician is bound by truth and committed to Paracelsus."[12]

Dr. Handloser, an ascetic man with a sound attitude and tolerance, finally said, "Disregard the nonsense that was certainly added by another man—Sauerbruch was a great physician and a fantastic fellow."

Well, I question neither his surgical abilities nor his fantasizing efforts to color his book according to the fashion of the time. The "Sauerbruch audience in Winniza" is for all matters symptomatic. ✦

CHAPTER NOTES:

1 Mount Elbrus is the highest mountain in the Caucasus (and for that matter in all of Europe), at 18,506 feet (5,642 meters). It is in the Republic of Kabardino-Balkaria, Russia.

2 Hometown of the mountaineer regiment.

3 Twenty-four miles southwest of Leningrad/St. Petersburg. Today named Lomonosov, at the east end of the Baltic Sea/Gulf of Finland.

4 Referring to the Wolchow-Kessel Region, and the Wolchow River.

5 "MGA" denotes a road-railway junction about 10 km SSW of Gaitolowo. It was the target of the Russian thrust.

6 *Vierkanter* means four corners: a rectangular shape with a court in the center.

7 An invented Bavarian character by the Bavarian author Ludwig Thoma, known for his down-to-earth language.

8 One of Hitler's oldest adjutants, from the 1923 putsch in Munich.

9 German clear schnapps.

10 An *Aufschneider* is one who cuts, as a surgeon, but also a teller of fairy tales.

11 *Beim Hund* means at the end of a problem, or at a loss for a solution.

12 Philippus Aureolus Theophrastus Bombastus von Hohenheim, German-Swiss physician of the Middle Ages, whose successful but unorthodox practice caused him to be persecuted as a heretic by the medical authorities of his day.

TRUSTED OFFICER BETRAYS HIS OATH

Col. Claus von Stauffenberg stands erect at far left and Field Marshal Keitel at right, as General Karl Bodenschatz shakes hands with Adolf Hitler at his camouflaged military headquarters east of Rastenburg on 15 July 1944. Five days later, Bodenschatz would be seriously wounded by Stauffenberg's cowardly bomb.

PHOTO: GERMAN FEDERAL ARCHIVES

CHAPTER 8

VALKYRIE: THE FINAL PLOT AGAINST ADOLF HITLER

Translators' Introduction: The background of the Valkyrie plot can be understood as the conflict between the worldview of the old military-industrial aristocracy versus that of the new National Socialists. These men from old, aristocratic families with long military traditions felt resentment toward Hitler's strategic and tactical directives and often disagreed with his decisions, considering them interference with general staff's established knowledge and wisdom. Their conspiring had built up over time until a "now or never" feeling took over, especially in Stauffenberg. Giesler's account begins in Munich on that fateful July 20th day.

GIESLER LEARNS OF THE BOMBING

On the late afternoon of July 20, 1944 my brother called me. "Close your office; organize all your co-workers who have military training and form a guard unit—if necessary, supply them with weapons. Send the rest home and stay by your telephone.

"After you give the necessary orders, drive immediately to my office and by no means allow yourself to be stopped on your way, even by military police. Do you have a weapon? No? It may be better I send a car and driver to pick you up. Your place now should be at my office."

"What happened?"

"Assassination of the Fuehrer, and the military is alarmed; Valkyrie has been unloosed in Berlin; the situation is still unclear."

My brother, as an experienced company commander, secured his post and the immediate surrounding area. We then waited tensely for further news from Fuehrer headquarters via the telegraph, from telephones, from the liaison office of the *Wehrkreis* (military district), for messages from the party office, from the SS and the Gau[1]. It was with great relief when finally, in the late evening, we heard the Fuehrer's voice. In Munich and the whole *Wehrkreis VII*, everything was quiet; it remained that way, as far as we could judge, during the night.

* * *

Translators' Commentary: A week later, architect and Minister of Armaments Albert Speer, under time pressure, picked up Giesler on his way to Stuttgart so they could discuss war construction, the labor force and steel quotas.

* * *

We then talked about July 20. . . . Speer had been at Fuehrer headquarters and gave me his impressions of the fuller extent of the conspiracy. Worried, he said: "Even now, after the assassination, the Fuehrer is still very much involved with the military and political consequences. He needs some distance from the assassination (attempt) and all the disappointments. I believe that it's time that you arrive at headquarters, Giesler, as you are the only one who can distract him, even for a few hours a day. Present him with city building plans—Linz and the Danube Bank construction; that will still be of interest and lead him out of permanent worrying."

After a few days, the call came from Fuehrer headquarters. Bormann was short: "Please come as soon as possible; the Fuehrer is expecting you. Please bring along all the plans that might interest him; naturally everything that refers to Linz."

Full of excitement to see Hitler and talk to him, I arrived at Hitler Headquarters *Wolfsschanze*. But what he told me confidentially during the following week, and what I found out, as ordered by him, from others; what I was reading in documents and protocols, and what I saw around me—shattered me deeply. All that I learned I would have thought

CHAPTER 8 | 133

PHOTO: GERMAN FEDERAL ARCHIVES

The scene in the barrack where the bomb went off. Hitler had been standing at the middle of the table facing the three open windows, leaning on the table with his head on his hands. There were 23 other people in the room. The survivors described the explosion as a powerful blow of air, accompanied by loud noise and flames. Almost everyone was thrown on the floor by the impact, but no one was thrown through a window. Suddenly someone cried: "Where is the Fuehrer?" —it was Keitel. After several seconds he found Hitler and helped him leave the premises. Below, a map of the room. Circled figure is Hitler. "X" marks the spot of the bomb.

WIKIPEDIA

impossible; it felt as unreal as spooks in the night.

Now that controls had been introduced, I entered *Sperrkreis* (restricted zone) I to report to Hitler; I met him in front of his bunker, talking to his adjutant. Actually, Hitler made a few steps toward me: "I expected you, and I'm glad to see you." He shook my hand, guarding his right arm which was bent and held in a sling, and his right leg also, obviously hurting. The side of his face that was toward the explosion was slightly swollen; he had cotton in his ears. But I was surprised by his posture—I thought it would be worse.

At teatime, to which he invited me, he mentioned the assassination only briefly and spoke little about his injuries. Linge (his servant) showed me Hitler's coat and the torn trousers, which were split lengthwise like the ones worn by medieval mercenary soldiers. "They did check you, Giesler—understand that. It is an order for the time being, caused by the assassination. In the future, it will not be done with you."

I didn't agree. After all that happened here, I thought the control was naturally necessary—it could have been that someone put something into my briefcase. "No," Hitler said, "you check for yourself before you cross the checkpoints."

Apparently he gave the orders, because any checking in the future didn't happen—as in late autumn, as well as January/February 1945 in the command bunker at the Reich Chancellery. I always, however, checked my own briefcase and blueprints.

On the first evening we talked about city construction in Linz and Munich. For me, it was an unexpected and rare conversation during days of turbulent military and political events. At the beginning, Hitler looked deflated. But in the course of our discussion he became visibly more energetic and open-minded.

THE KALTENBRUNNER REPORTS

The next morning Bormann asked me to see him, giving me this advice: "Please don't put any questions to the Fuehrer about July 20 and all that was connected with it, unless he himself talks about it. Try, however, to distract him—talk with him primarily about Linz. That's what

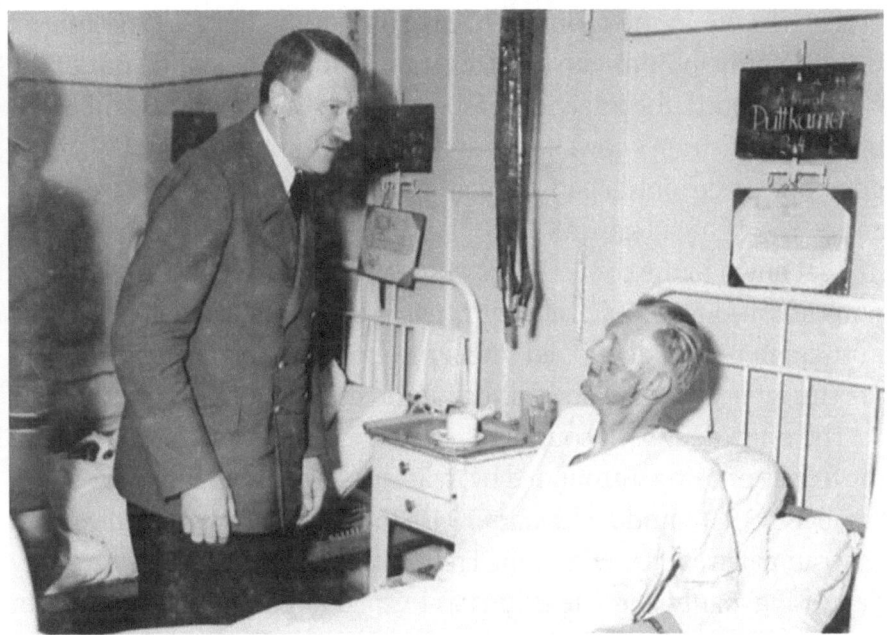

Several high-level officers were injured by the bomb and four were killed. Afterward, the sympathetic leader visited the injured at the hospital. Above he is shown with Rear Adm. Karl-Jesco von Puttkamer. Also injured in the blast were Gen. Walter Scherff, Capt. Heinz Assman, Lt. Col. Heinrich Borgmann, Gen. Karl Bodenschatz and Gen. Adolf Heusinger. Killed were stenographer Heinrich Berger, Gen. Rudolf Schmundt, Col. Heinz Brandt and Gen. Guenther Korten.   PHOTO: GERMAN FEDERAL ARCHIVES

interests him most. On the other hand, I think it proper that you be informed correctly about all the happenings of July 20. I will see to it that you will be informed about every detail of the deep web."

After a short pause:

"One happening is under absolute secrecy—the Fuehrer will decide if you are to have knowledge about it. But I urgently ask, don't approach Hitler on that matter."

However, I could see all the supporting documents and interview protocols delivered by Kaltenbrunner to Bormann's office. By getting an overview of the total network of the clique of traitors and the larger circle of people involved, I would be more likely to refrain from asking Hitler about the affair during our discussions.

Only later was it clear to me what Bormann really meant by that.

From then on, in the morning hours and during the *Lage*² meetings, I was primarily in Bormann's office. At those times, he pulled out of the vault the reports, the interview protocols, and lists of persons and investigations, which are known today as the Kaltenbrunner Reports. But those documents were only a part—even though a very important one—of the entire web of high treason.

I sat down in the corner of his office and began reading the sober reports of conspiracy, which already began pre-war and gradually increased in strength until it developed into a perfect form—betraying, above all, the struggling frontline and killing hundreds of thousands of soldiers.

The often dissonant-sounding remarks of Hitler since 1939: "I have the feeling of being surrounded by treason"—his former hints, as on November 6, 1939; middle January 1940; then, during *Weseruebung* (Norway campaign) at the end of the French campaign; adding in the partly depressing, partly angry reactions as I experienced them at Winniza in 1942 and *Wolfsschanze* in 1943—now, by these reports and protocols, his suspicion was confirmed. But far more than that: happenings up to now unexplainable became transparent and finally made sense, worse than ever imagined.

I began with the reading of the (prepared) appeals to the armed forces and the German people. [Carl Friedrich] Goerdeler³ to the armed forces: "something additional threatens to deprive you of the success of your victories which you gained from a leadership of educated and experienced men: Hitler's 'strategic genius,' which he claimed in an irrational delusion, and was disgustingly idolized by his lackeys."

Another appeal, still better: "The Fuehrer is dead. An immoral clique of battle-ignorant party leaders, misusing the present situation, is trying to take over the government for selfish reasons, stabbing the fighting troops in their back..."

With that, [Field Marshal] von Witzleben wanted to address the German people and the Armed Forces, to introduce himself as the new Supreme Commander. I knew him—then still fresh from the glory of crossed marshal batons⁴. At the People's Court they took pictures when he denied having any knowledge of the assassination and the military conspiracy, which was immediately refuted. When questioned: Well, what were your thoughts then, what was going to happen if the assassination would have succeeded?—he answered: "I am a military, I don't know anything about political and civilian matters." In the second part of the sentence he sounded absolutely convincing.

The next documents were photocopies: kind of an operational plan of the putsch-government and a list of the ministers selected for the *Reichskanzler* (Federal Chancellor) Goerdeler. On both documents 'Speer' was listed as minister—with a question mark, however. Surprised, I jumped up and went to Bormann, "What does that mean?—that's not possible." Bormann looked up, "Comrade Giesler, on that matter everything is possible."

Slowly he stood up, went to the vault, took out a voluminous file, opened it and showed me the top sheet—there was the name 'Speer.' Only that. "For your personal information," he said, and returned the file to the vault. "Keep silent about all that," he said, sitting down at his desk. That was enough for that day; I could not continue reading.

GIESLER REFLECTS ON THE ROLE OF SPEER

My thoughts went back to a talk with [Karl] Hanke, *Gauleiter* of Silesia. A war construction site in lower Silesia caused me to meet him several times in March 1944. In my judgment, he was a man full of character, with wise, attentive eyes and a well-shaped head. Hanke proved himself during the political battles in Berlin, and later as a soldier at the front. His clear formulations corresponded with his long activities as an undersecretary of state at Dr. Goebbels's office.

One evening in Salzbrunn, Hanke asked me to advise him after the war with his plans for city rebuilding and solutions for traffic problems in Breslau, the capitol of Silesia. "Well," I said to him, "aren't you closely associated with Speer? If I agree to fulfill your request, apart from being overloaded with my own work, it would be an affront against him which I don't want to happen." Up till then, Speer could not even overlook the fact that I got the Munich assignment, and then in addition Linz. My job as an architect included, with the exception of Weimar, most of the Southwestern region of Germany.

"But, you also advise Mayor Freyberg in Leipzig."

"Yes," I answered, "but only because of the Fuehrer's order when problems at the fair (Leipzig's annual International Trade Fair) arose in connection with the planned extension of the railway system."

That was one more reason for him to talk to the Fuehrer. For various reasons, he wanted me and not Speer as an advisor for Breslau. He had a very clear opinion of Speer's goals, knowing what's going on in his office. That worried him and did not sit well—the Fuehrer should know about it. His particular mistrust extended to two of Speer's closest co-workers. Hanke mentioned the names—I knew both of them, one highly ranked in the SA, the other in the SS.

"Do you know that Speer is after succeeding Hitler?"

Yes, I had heard about it, but I considered it gossip—as an incorrect and overbearing opinion of Speer's personality by his staff. Here, wish might be the father of the thought.

"No," contradicted Hanke, "there is more to it."

He doesn't want to burden me with that stuff, but the Fuehrer should know about it. He, however, cannot get an appointment; Bormann is completely shielding Hitler, isolates him from everything—that worries him also. I could . . ."

"The protection by Bormann is Hitler's order," I interrupted him. "And Hitler considers me only as his architect and would strongly object if I would dare to get mixed up in matters that are none of my business. Please understand that."

"You're right—I have to try by myself to talk to the Fuehrer."

Remembering that talk with Hanke, his critique of Speer and Speer's two co-workers, made me pensive. But how was Speer's attitude after the July 20th assassination to be explained, when he expressed to me his deep worry about Hitler, and when he asked me to take the Linz plans with me to the Fuehrer headquarters? Other small events before the assassination, unimportant as they were then, seemed to me now rather strange.

At the end of June 1944, for instance, Speer called the leaders of the defense industry, the armament industry and the directors of the building industry to Linz and urged their utmost effort to increase the production

Albert Speer, Hitler's Berlin architect and later armaments minister, had the full confidence of the Fuehrer and even his friendship, but at the same time Speer's personality harbored something of the ambitious and calculating within it. Giesler experienced it painfully on numerous occasions in the area of their common city renovation tasks. Giesler recounts an incident in which Hitler seems to be letting Giesler know that Speer, in spite of his many talents, is not being considered to succeed him as Fuehrer.   GERMAN FEDERAL ARCHIVES

of the armament industry. That "Linzer convention" ended with Hitler's speech at the Platterhof at the Obersalzberg.

Speer and I were Hitler's guests that evening at the Berghof. After dinner, Speer said with urgency, "Giesler, by all means, find a moment to tell Hitler about the Linz convention and let him know that I ended it with the performance of Bruckner's 4th Symphony at the aula of the St. Florian Abbey." Speer knew how much Hitler liked that symphony. Late that evening, he suggested, "My Fuehrer, I propose that Giesler should tell some funny anecdotes."

With Speer, everything was practical and calculated—even as a 'friend' I considered him a stranger and full of riddles. Now his name appeared, though with a question mark, on the list of ministers of the traitors.

In the evening, Hitler talked to me about his successor. Was it a coincidence or was it a hint by Bormann, caused by my reaction in the morning? Hitler said, "After this terrible war, the only one who is privileged to appear in front of the nation is he who, as a soldier, risked his life, and justified it with his bravery and willingness to sacrifice. Naturally, he has to show the quality of a leader and charisma; he has to be wise and think logically—above all, however, he has to have character. Only a brave soldier of that war has the right to lead the nation."

Then he was silent for a long time. Next morning, I was sitting again in the corner of Bormann's office and reading more messages, reports, documents. No further mention of Speer.

THE PEOPLE'S COURT

The reports and interrogations got more and more complicated. One peculiar incident of the interrogation of Theodor Struenck[5], for instance, impressed me quite a bit. He called Adm. Canaris shameless because, at Struenck's interrogation, Canaris requested that he put everything on Oster and Dohnanyi.[6]

During the evening hours, primarily around the time the *Lage* took place, the first film clips of the trial at the People's Court were shown. I did not want to miss anything and looked at the film for a while. Some of the accused I knew personally; of the others, I had formed impressions from reading the protocols, which the films now completed. Hoepner, von Witzleben, Stieff—how much they differed from the young officers like Klausing and Bernardis. These admitted their deeds with military composure and yet still wanted to distance themselves. Well, if the younger ones would only have known what a miserable attitude dominated the plotter's heads.

I saw the counter-position of Major Von Leonrod with his confessor-priest, Father Wehrle,[7] and listened to their terrifying discussion—I felt my way to the door and avoided further films.

On one evening, for one reason or another, Hitler talked about the 20th of July. I told him I had seen some films of the trials at the People's Court and I was shattered. Hitler remarked:

"I don't want to see anything of that; it is enough that I have to read the reports. The assassination revealed very clearly to me that not only high treason—but also the ugly *Landesverrat*[8] lost its disguise. For a long time I had already suspected treason; in Winniza I felt it directly—often I thought I felt physically furtive glances. But much more, far beyond what has been reported, I have now learned. After a sober consideration, I think it's proper to be silent—for the sake of the fighting troops and the unity of the nation.

"That reactionary clique plotted since 1938, if not earlier, for my fall by revolt or assassination. But it was not in accordance with their character to confront me openly with a weapon. How they must have hated me, and National Socialism, when they betrayed without scruple, and so miserably, even the fighting troops. The whole scope of that shameful plot one can now see—it is so revolting. Rattenhuber and Hoegl will tell you some of it; however, keep it confidential. I've bound everyone who knows about it to silence; that also includes you."

GIESLER REMEMBERS MARTIN BORMANN

Translators' Introduction: Giesler wrote the following description of Martin Bormann in the middle of the chapter. In order not to interrupt the flow of the Valkyrie narrative, we moved it to the end.

I didn't only read reports; I also watched what was going on at Martin Bormann's desk, and his method of work. I gained new insight into the character of that powerful man, feared by many and even hated as the "party's gray eminence." During that period he appeared to me more transparent and more understandable than in previous years. I will describe him as I saw him.

Here he was sitting, this so-bedeviled man, with his shirtsleeves rolled up during the summer heat. With lively alertness and immense industriousness, he worked through piles of files, dictated and phoned without a break. He had the endurance of a fighting bull. I think Adolf Hitler saw him correctly when he told me once: "Bormann is like his signature, and that is like the *Hoehe Goell*." (A mountain peak near the

Berghof, Hitler's home.)

I was often present at that time when Bormann reported [to Hitler]; he did so in a matter-of-fact and concentrated way, with all the pros and cons, mostly about very important matters. Sometimes, when persons and happenings were involved that I was familiar with, I could see how clearly and correctly it had been reported. Then Adolf Hitler decided it. That information given to the Fuehrer covered all areas of the State, the Party and the whole civil sector, and lasted sometimes hours.

I was drawing while this went on, but still listened carefully. An adjutant would appear, reporting the *Lage*. Or an interruption because of an established appointment—then Hitler would say: "Giesler, we'll continue later." Or to Bormann: "See that Giesler gets some refreshments."

A little later, I was again sitting in my corner, refreshments there, reading the reports or silently watching Bormann at work. He often dictated to two or three secretaries at a time. But—rather strange and surprising— at the same time that Bormann dictated to give the gist of the matter, he memorized Hitler's decisions word for word, following the sentences exactly as they were spoken by Hitler, while in between he shaped the letters and orders that he derived from them. Telephone calls came in; disturbing messages were handed to him; after which he continued dictating where he had stopped before.

Again a call came. Bormann looked at me: "The *Lage* is over; the Fuehrer expects you," and turned again to his work.

Who could endure that, day in and day out, always deep into the night, and for years? Indeed, Bormann was like the *Hoehe Goell*, and, like that *Goell*, he sometimes cast a shadow in bright light. Naturally he cast shadows. Sometimes, I had real quarrels with him, or he with me. Twice, Hitler intervened: "Giesler, please go along with Bormann." Once at the Berghof, in spring 1944, he said to me: "Giesler, if you want to drive away from here early, mad because of Bormann . . . but you are Mrs. Bormann's guest, and you are also my guest—no, you cannot do that to us! By the way, let it be said to you, in that case Bormann acted absolutely correctly. He naturally should have given you some explanation, which I herewith do now. . . . Well, see! Giesler, I need Bormann and his working strength.

BORMANN IN THE BUNKER

Martin Bormann, adjutant SS-*Standartenfuehrer* Wilhelm Zander, and his secretary, Else Krueger, were with Hitler in the Fuehrer's shelter during the Battle of Berlin. The *Fuehrerbunker* was located under the Reich Chancellery in the center of Berlin. On April 28, Bormann wired the following message to German Admiral Karl Doenitz: "Situation very serious. Those ordered to rescue the Fuehrer are keeping silent. Disloyalty seems to gain the upper hand everywhere. Reich Chancellery a heap of rubble."

PHOTO: GERMAN FEDERAL ARCHIVES

He relieves me; he is steady, unshakable and an achiever—I can depend on him!"

In retrospect, I always found out on my own that Bormann was correct to get tough on me, or that he acted on Hitler's order.

Bormann noticed everything; it reflected his former job as an estate administrator. I accompanied him once on an inspection trip at the small farm that supplied the Obersalzberg. He checked out everything, down to the *champignon* [mushroom] cellar—nothing missed his eyes. Then we climbed into the forest above the Berghof.

There he showed me his animal world in its free, natural surroundings. An owl was there, a squirrel—what else was jumping around there, I cannot remember. He allowed beehives to be brought in to the *Hoehe Goell* when the trees were blooming. He got enthusiastic about that magnificent mountain. Dr. Todt had personally searched for that high track and marked it through the sheer rocks—it is the most beautiful and daring road I know of, by far. "I hold Dr. Todt in high esteem and still think about him often," Bormann said.

On the way back, turning off the road, he looked around and asked how I liked it. I remarked one has a wonderful view from here, all around—it's beautiful up here. "Yes, a good location," Bormann said.

"Connection with the street, which in winter is cleared from snow; a well is close by.... You are going to be settled here after the war, so you are present for the Fuehrer at any time." Striding on, he whistled *"Alle mi presente al vostra, signori!"*—an old *Landsknecht* song. [Translated: "Oh, you men prepare yourselves for muster, one and all," from *Wir Zogen in das Feld* ("We Marched Away to War").]

During the difficult days in August 1944, when the disloyalty and treason were apparent, Bormann said to me, with a very serious meaning: "I have one task and one goal; and that is to serve the Fuehrer as a National Socialist. My only ambition is to do that as well as I am able. The Fuehrer gives me the authority that I need to do it. I activate it, but solely for this, my task. Certainly you have no doubts that I am totally obligated to the Fuehrer. I don't want anything else but to take some of the heavy burden off his shoulders; and that is not easy!"

I believed him. ✦

CHAPTER NOTES:
1 A Gau is a party district. It usually covered the same territory as the state administration, but the *Gauleiter* was the NSDAP head of the Gau, while the *Reichstatthalter* was the chief administrator for the State.

2 Short for "Lagebesprechung," a military situation meeting, held twice a day with all the Fuehrer's close advisors, and field commanders called in as needed.

3 Carl Friedrich Goerdeler was mayor of Liepzig from 1930 until his resignation in 1937. He then became director of the overseas sales department at the firm of Robert Bosch GmbH and used the cover of his job to travel abroad promoting an anti-Nazi position. He was the leading instigator in several planned putschs against Hitler and was to be the new federal chancellor upon the success of the Valkyrie plot.

4 Under Hitler, colonel generals received the new rank of Fieldmarshal, in a ceremony in which they were given ornate gold and ivory batons.

5 An insurance executive who also worked in Canaris's *Abwehr*; clandestinely active with the heads of the conspiracy.

6 Hans Oster was a general and deputy of Adm. Canaris at the *Abwehr*. Hans von Dohnanyi was a civil servant, a high-ranked lawyer recruited by Oster for the *Abwehr*.

7 Leonrod, a member of Bavaria's old nobility, was designated in the Valkyrie plans as liaison officer in military district VII (Munich). He said in his defense that he consulted his "father confessor" Chaplain Hermann Wehrle, who did not take him into the confessional, but advised him to stay away from treasonable enterprises. Thus Wehrle was implicated and both were executed.

8 *Landesverrat* is a kind of treason of passing domestic or military secrets to a foreign power.

Previous Assassination Attempts

Many of the participants in Valkyrie were involved in earlier assassination attempts, in November 1939 and March 1943. There was even a plot in 1938 led by Lt Colonel **Hans von Oster** meant to prevent a feared military invasion of Czechoslovakia that never took place. Their secret contacts with the British Foreign Office at that time led a shocked Undersecretary Vansittart to comment: "But that is treachery!" After the war, publication of an account of those contacts was forbidden in England.

In 1939, Georg Elser planted a bomb near the lectern at the Nov. 8, 1923 Putsch Anniversary dinner in Munich, but Hitler left early, escaping the explosion that left several dead and injured.

In 1942 and 1943, resistance member Helmuth von Moltke, a grandson of the famous general, persisted in trying to arrange meetings in Stockholm with the British Political Warfare Executive. It was blocked by Churchill. In this regard, it should be remembered that beginning in 1939 the Hitler government was itself sponsoring secret peace feelers, and even detailed proposals, to high British government officials. All were rejected.

March 1943 saw two attempts to kill Hitler masterminded by Gen. Henning von Tresckow, offspring of an old East Elbe nobility. The first was a bomb placed on Hitler's plane that failed to detonate. It had been put in a box that supposedly contained two bottles of rare cognac meant to be delivered to another traitor, Gen. Stieff, at headquarters. A week later Tresckow got Col. Freiherr von Gersdorff to act as a suicide bomber at an exhibition Hitler would be attending. With two 10-minute fuse bombs in his coat pockets, he was to get near to Hitler before they went off. But Hitler stayed only eight minutes, leaving Gersdorff to run to the lavatory to defuse his bombs.

Hitler repeatedly escaped harm, making it seem that fate was on his side. ♦

Erich Fellgiebel had an unblemished military career when he attained the rank of major general in 1938, at the age of 52, and was appointed chief of the army's signal establishment and chief of communications liaison to the *Wehrmacht*'s Supreme Command. In August 1940, he was promoted to general of the communications troops (chief of communications). In this sensitive post, he was trusted with every military secret of the Reich, including the rocketry work at Peenemuende. Fellgiebel's main job in Operation Valkyrie was to cut headquarters off from all telecommunications, which he was not entirely successful in doing. When Hitler survived, Fellgiebel had to override the communications black-out that he had set up.

CHAPTER 9

VALKYRIE: THE STORY

Translators' Introduction: After a period of time reading the "Kaltenbrunner Reports" in Martin Bormann's office, Hermann Giesler was personally briefed by Hitler's own SS briefers, *Brigadefuehrer* Hans Rattenhuber and SD Capt. Peter Hoegl. The account they give to Giesler is surprising only in the revelation of the "double phone system" that was discovered at Headquarters, with a secret parallel or bridge switching that allowed a third party to listen in. But this was a bombshell. The Chief of Communications at Headquarters, and one of the conspirators, was Gen. Erich Fellgiebel. This phone system is what turned high treason (plotting against the regime) into the even worse *Landesverrat* (passing state secrets to a foreign power). Now we let Hermann Giesler tell what he calls in his book "The Story":

GIESLER DETAILS THE 1944 ATTACK ON HITLER

*"For Brutus is an honorable man;
So are they all, all honorable men."*

The chief of the security detachment, SS *Brigadefuehrer* [Generalmajor Hans] Rattenhuber and *Kriminaldirektor* [Peter] Hoegl, SS captain at the SD [*Sicherheitsdienst* (Security Service)], visited with me. Rattenhuber said Hitler sent them to inform me about matters connected with July 20th and the investigation after the assassination.

What they tell me is strictly confidential.

Hoegl meant that it might be better if we go outside. We walked up and down along the way between Bormann's wood hut and the casino barrack.

The two men were very different: Rattenhuber in uniform, tall and strong; Hoegl in civilian clothes, small, sturdy, serious and with attentive eyes.

Rattenhuber narrates: "First the assassination attempt—well, Stauffenberg waited for the explosion, standing by the car within the *Sperrkreis* (security zone) II.

"When the explosive detonated, Stauffenberg drove immediately to the airfield with his adjutant. On the way, they threw a packet of explosives off the forest road into the bushes—strangely enough, they didn't add it into the briefcase. The explosive and the igniter came from the English, and they surely knew of the planned assassination—the gentlemen had contact with each other for quite awhile. Stauffenberg was taken by surprise when the time for the map room meeting (*Lage*) was moved forward and he did not find the time to stuff additional explosives into the briefcase—otherwise everybody would have had it!"

Rattenhuber meant they were disrupted during their preparations. "I am sure of that. They went all out without any concern—Stauffenberg blew his co-plotter Col. [Heinz] Brandt[1] into the air.

"Lt. [Werner von] Haeften took Stauffenberg out of the meeting with a faked call—it was carefully planned. Stauffenberg laid the briefcase, with the igniter facing him, on top of the maps on the meeting table, then stood up, leaning on his briefcase and pressing down the igniter. A light bow toward the Fuehrer, excusing himself, indicating a telephone call, and then he disappears.

"The meeting continues. A village is named as a battle location—exactly where the briefcase sits. Gen. Schmundt puts the briefcase on the floor; then it is pushed to the table base."

"That's known to me," I said.

"Well, now it gets interesting. Both are now out of *Sperrkreis* toward their car. Beside the car stands Fellgiebel—you know him?—the general

Hitler's Personal Security: Johann Rattenhuber, center, relaxes with Hitler's personal driver, Erich Kempka, left, and Bruno Gesche, chief of Hitler's escort commando, right, at Klessheim Castle near Salzburg in March 1944. From 1935 on, Rattenhuber was head of Hitler's security detachment and achieved the high rank of lieutenant general in the Waffen SS. He was in Soviet captivity from 1945 until 1951.

and chief of communications. They all look with suspense toward the meeting barrack."

"How do you know about it?" I interrupted.

"Lt. Col. [Ludolf] Sander stood at their side—he was present. Now it happens, and Stauffenberg with Haeften drives to the airport. They were convinced that they blew the Fuehrer and everyone at the *Lage* to kingdom come. One had to have the impression they were all dead.

"You can imagine what was now going on here: security escort detachment, physicians, medics, officers, adjutants, Organization Todt workers from bunker construction sites, all confused. Seeing that, Fellgiebel enters *Sperrkreis I* and observes all the emergency activities.

"When he then noticed that Hitler was alive and only slightly injured, helped by Field Marshal Keitel to exit the destroyed meeting barrack, he steps toward the Fuehrer and congratulates him for his escape. He—God knows—said, 'That happens when you set up headquarters so close behind the front line.' He stood to attention—*Hosen in denselben* (a military expression meaning trousers in his high boots)—pistol on his belt," Rattenhuber said.

Hoegl continued: "The investigations revealed that, within the clique, it was specifically Fellgiebel who pleaded that the so-called 'initial ignition' for the revolt could only be triggered by Hitler's assassination—successful, naturally. Once that no longer functioned, Fellgiebel must have known that his participation in the whole affair could not be hidden, without doubt he was done for. Why did he not draw his pistol and shoot? Nobody could have hindered him, because none of us could have that figured out. But for a real deed these people were cowards, and ready only for treachery."

"Yes," I interrupted, "all that is already known to me from reading the interrogation reports. The Fuehrer, however, gave me hints that there was much more beside the Fellgiebel affair and communication system, not only knowledge of and participation in the assassination and the Valkyrie putsch. He told me it was too disgusting for him to talk about it. You should tell me."

"We'll do it, just wait. Well, still a little dazed from the explosion, the Fuehrer asked, 'What is Fellgiebel doing here?' On this, he based his first suspicion. But, initially, it is pretty hard to believe that such a contemptible infamy is at all possible—for us they were 'sacred cows'."

"Not for me anymore," Rattenhuber responded, "since Seydlitz[2] with his committee works for the Russians against the German front."

"Well, well," Hoegl said. "Anyway, at first, suspicion flew around in all directions until it was definite that a military clique had planned the assassination attempt Stauffenberg carried out. As part of this clique, Fellgiebel had the task of paralyzing the communication system. He was successful with the major wire lines, but for one reason or another, perhaps out of ignorance, some lines were not disconnected. That's how Dr.

Inside the Communications Center: The communication center at the Wolf's Lair was a marvel of advanced technology for its day, equipped with the latest systems developed by German companies Siemens, Ascania and Lorenz. From the center, Hitler and his closest advisers could call the remotest staff officer from Norway to Libya. The chancellery in Berlin, the party office in Munich and Mussolini in Rome could be reached within minutes. Though the personnel went through a thorough screening process, its chief, Gen. Erich Fellgiebel, was a key member of the conspiracy to kill Hitler.   PHOTO: GERMAN FEDERAL ARCHIVES

Goebbels and Maj. [Otto] Remer could telephone the Fuehrer, and the Berlin putsch collapsed.

"It is strange, however, that Fellgiebel never tried to warn the clique in the Bendlerstrasse that, as far as killing Hitler was concerned, the plot failed. They tried to continue the putsch, which ended in 'thin air'."

[For a more detailed account of these events, see "A Day at the Bendlerblock" following this article.]

"Yeah," said Rattenhuber, "maybe Fellgiebel tried to camouflage himself by staying in the background, like the 'Herr' General ["Fritz"] Thiele, his deputy and successor, did during the following days. All in all, the plot from 'above' was doomed to fail because they didn't count the decent officers and soldiers, who did not take part, kept their oath and stood by their oath-bearer (commandant). They did not have even one company at their disposal, and not one of the entire clique had the courage to draw his pistol against the Fuehrer. At first, we only knew that Fellgiebel belonged to the inner circle of the conspirators and that he insisted at the clique's meetings on getting rid of the Fuehrer as a requirement for success with the 'Valkyrie putsch.' We arrested him.

"But then something very strange happened: A sergeant with the communication unit at the Fuehrer headquarters reported an unusual double switchboard: parallel or bridge switching. Messages, reports, operative directives and strategic details by 'officers-only telephone' could be listened in on by a third party by turning on that switch.

"This sergeant was an expert and knew the communication stuff. He became attentive, but strongly suspicious only after Fellgiebel was arrested. It emerged that by some kind of coupling, a direct connection from the Fuehrer headquarters to Switzerland was established; through a switchboard in or around Berlin, messages and reports could be tapped."

"Those treacherous reports went to Switzerland via wire," Hoegl added, "and not wireless—that's absolutely certain now. We believe that the Swiss secret service stood at the other end of the wire—some of them must have had connections with Soviet spy groups—and they radioed-in codes to the enemy. That went on for years.

"We knew all the time of Soviet wireless centers in 'neutral' Switzerland which were fed by various spy groups—they were exactly located by directing sound waves. They could only operate there with the knowledge and tolerance of a certain group of responsible members of the Swiss secret service who, knowingly or not, were in the service of the Soviets. [Walter] Schellenberg[3] already negotiated and tried to disrupt that spy business in Switzerland."

"And what did you do then?" I asked.

"At first, nothing," Rattenhuber said. "We did not wish to upset the

The military disagreements **Ludwig Beck** (left) had with Hitler caused Beck to resign his position as chief of the general staff in August 1938—replaced by Gen. Franz Halder. Designated to be head of state in the new government, Beck failed in his suicide attempt following the arrest of the group. Werner von Haeften (right) became Stauffenberg's adjutant in 1943, and traveled with him to *Wolfsschanze* on July 20th. He helped Stauffenberg ready the bomb and returned with him to Berlin to complete the putsch and take over the reins of government.

whole thing right away. The Fuehrer said that Fellgiebel was not alone— he might have known about it. Hitler gave orders for secrecy and constant control of the switchboard; that paid off quite a bit, and a lot of things happened afterward.

"Well, now we will start with case No. 2. Fellgiebel was arrested at the time only for his participation in the plot and knowledge of the assassination attempt. We still didn't have any information about how the communication system worked to constantly betray the fighting front, even though we had suspected it for a long time. On the suggestion of Field Marshal Keitel, Gen. Thiele, Fellgiebel's deputy, succeeded him. As the new chief entrusted with communications, he was sworn in with the oath of allegiance and reported to the Fuehrer.

"In the meantime, the report of the sergeant from the communication unit came in. Secretly, the observation begins, and it did not take long before it was certain: the Herr General 'played the flute' with that macabre chapel choir.[4] He knows of the secret switchboard—the technicians call it parallel switching.

"Because one (Fellgiebel) is drawing in the other (Thiele), his membership in the conspirator clique is now obvious. And now it comes apart further at Communications: Fellgiebel's chief of staff, a Col. Hahn, and the chief of the communication department for Fromm's Reserve Army, a Col. Hassel—they are all being arrested. With Thiele we did it, Hoegl and I, with all the politeness and respect to which a general is entitled."

Something awkward happened then to the general. Rattenhuber mentioned it, but it does not belong in my story.

"Now, professor, you wonder why that is so revolting to the Fuehrer and why he did not want to talk to you about it. That treason against the fighting front took more out of him than the assassination. Recently, he told us that for some time he expected to be shot by one of that reactionary gang, but he never could believe that an officer would commit such a devious act, betraying the fighting soldiers who daily put their lives at risk for Germany."

"How could they play their game for so long?" I asked. "Why didn't someone get wise to their deceit? Since 1939, the Chief hinted about treason in talks with me. After the capitulation of France, he told me that he now knows for sure that treason was rooted at a high military level, some details of which he already knew about in Winniza. I still remember his exact words: 'Should I extend my distrust to the members of the *Lage* or are the traitors located at the seams?' Certainly he was at that time already considering the communication center."

Rattenhuber answered, "That's exactly what depresses us so much, because we felt we were responsible for not only the Fuehrer's security.

"But even so, limits were set for us. Up to July 20, everybody could approach the Fuehrer with a weapon, well, even with bulky explosives like Stauffenberg did with his briefcase—one only needed to be known or carrying a pass for the *Sperrkreis I*. Just the thought that an officer, even a general, could commit treason or assassinate the Fuehrer was, until now—how do you call it—a sacrilege. For all of us, that's the big shock."

"What's going to happen now?"

"For the time being, a big silence. One cannot imagine what would happen if the front and the homeland knew about it. Only the Fuehrer will decide who will have knowledge of that treason-mess."

THE WORST OF THE TREASON

A lot of moving took place at communications now. Before the assassination attempt, Fellgiebel started to replace officers—the ones he did not trust, good soldiers who kept their oath and would not have participated in the infamy the clique wanted to start, exactly like many at the Bendlerstrasse and its communications who stopped it in time. Otherwise, the Valkyrie confusion would have extended further.

Naturally, caution was now demanded. Guderian proposed a new communication chief; he reported today to the Fuehrer. Towards evening, after the talk with Rattenhuber and Hoegl, I met Col. Gen. [Heinz] Guderian at the teahouse as I did several times already during the week, and to my surprise, Gen. [Albert] Praun.

Guderian—I liked him very much for his lively manner and soldier-like aura—was obviously under great tension. We carried on with a short, polite talk; I sensed that his thoughts were with faraway military problems. I had a longer discussion afterward with Gen. Praun, who was the brother of my co-worker, Dr. Theo Praun. I thought a lot of Theo; he was the head of the law department at my office "General Building Counselor, Munich"; then a leader within the OT group Russia North and Balticum, a job which Dr. Todt entrusted to me at the end of 1942.

In January 1944, Dr. Praun, together with the front leader Baerkessel, was murdered by partisans when they visited an OT unit in the 16th Army region. The murder has been "gloriously" reported by the Russian radio. At the funeral service of my co-workers, I met Gen. Praun. At that time, he was the commander of a division, and before that he became, because of his technical expertise, Guderian's communication officer during the French campaign.

Now, on Guderian's suggestion, the Fuehrer installed him as the new chief of communications. During our conversation I asked Gen. Praun about his impressions. He answered hesitantly and acted rather withdrawn. Cautiously, I addressed my questions to find out how much the Fuehrer had informed him about the treason affair. Gen. Praun said the talk was a short one; the Fuehrer pointed very briefly to the serious disruption at communications and asked him to put it back in order again.

I had the impression that the first veil had already fallen over the macabre treason affair. Gen. Praun tried hard to trace the rumors about the treason whenever they trickled through. I know he talked with *Kriminaldirektor* Hoegl, who referred him to Kaltenbrunner's investigating group. He might have asked around some more, but any additional information about Fellgiebel, Thiele, Hahn and Hassel has been withheld.

Strange—but for me very understandable—was the behavior of Hoegl, who referred Praun to Kaltenbrunner, who gave him the reasonable advice to have Fellgiebel questioned by staff officers, and finally of "Gestapo Mueller" [this was a way of referring to Gestapo Chief Heinrich Mueller], who refused Praun any information on Fellgiebel, Thiele, Hahn and Hassel.

I was not surprised that the raid-like checking of the parallel connection showed no results; it was removed long before.

But the treason was there; it was permanent and of an unbelievable scope. When German soldiers overran Russian battle stations, they found there their own operation and attacking plans. Most of the responsible and carefully planned strategic and tactical German operations, advancing with fighting and sacrificing spirit, were beaten back by the enemy's counteractions made possible by that treason. The all-important moment for a successful surprise attack was never gained.

Judged by this major treason affair at headquarters, the Red Chapel plot appears trivial, even though Adm. Canaris from the German *Abwehr* testified at the state war court (*Reichskriegsgericht*)—at that time still a confidant—that the treason of the Red Chapel cost at least a quarter million victims.

But what did that alarming, yet wretched treason mean compared to

CHAPTER 9 | 157

Reiter Regiment 17: A rare photo from the German national archives shows Claus von Stauffenberg mounted. At least five of the anti-Hitler plotters were from the same cavalry regiment—Reiter Regiment 17—in Bamberg.

the incomprehensible plot at a high military level and right at headquarters, only in part revealed by the assassination attempt? It fluctuates between high treason and *Landesverrat*. Hate, craving for admiration, lack of character and a stick-in-the-mud reactionary attitude were the reasons for an unbelievable conspiring with the enemy, an enemy whose goal it was to destroy Germany. Naturally, the traitors interpreted their action as necessary and in the interest of a higher humanity. They didn't offer themselves as a sacrificing gift, however, but instead the German soldier who paid for it with his life.

Therefore, it could not be a revolution from the top; there was no necessity for it, there was nothing there, no substance, no program that could claim to be taken seriously, no sparkling thought or serious plans of how to proceed if the putsch succeeded. There was just no personality there. Civil war and hate would have followed a successful assassination and putsch—for generations. Nothing would have changed the relentless enemy.

Terrible things happened; much might simmer away; a lot can be buried. A lot, however, one will not forget—the treason, above all. One can try to belittle it as unimportant, to cover it up, or even to glorify it—it won't help, because treason cries throughout the centuries. ✦

CHAPTER NOTES:
1 Not to be confused with Dr. Karl Brandt. One of Col. Brandt's legs was blown off in the explosion.

2 Walther von Seydlitz was one of the German Stalingrad generals to turn against his country while in Soviet captivity.

3 Schellenberg was an SS officer in the SD who, as a master spy, was able to travel freely. Schellenberg moved up in the SS ranks under Heinrich Himmler and eventually replaced *Abwehr* Chief Adm. Wilhelm Canaris as head of the new, combined Secret Service in 1944. He was arrested by the British in Denmark in June 1945, while attempting to surrender to the Allies.

4 By "macabre chapel," Giesler is referring to the Red Chapel [*Rote Kapelle*], the German cryptonym for a European-wide Soviet espionage network that transmitted information via radio directly to the Soviets. It was headed by a Polish Communist Jew, Léopold Trepper, and was first discovered in Brussels in 1941. In Germany, the leaders were Harro Schulze-Boysen, a desk officer at the Reich ministry of aviation, Dr. Arvid Hanack of the ministry of economics, and Rudolf von Scheiliha, head of the foreign office information department. All three of these men had access to sensitive and/or secret information. *Abwehr* Chief Canaris and others estimated that the Rote Kapelle in Germany cost the lives of 200,000 German men. By the end of 1942, the leaders had been apprehended and the network shut down, or so it was thought.

A Day at the Bendlerblock

THE EVENTS OF JULY 20, 1944 IN DRAMATIC DETAIL

By WILHELM KRIESSMANN, PH.D.

As a supplement to Hermann Giesler's story of the day's events, Wilhelm Kriessmann—who was serving as a soldier of the *Wehrmacht* at the time—has written his own dramatic account of how the conspiracy unfolded and collapsed within the walls of the Bendlerblock, which became the makeshift headquarters of the hopeful new governing elite of the Reich. The Bendlerblock was a complex of buildings taking up most of a city block that housed the main military offices in Berlin. It was so named because it was located on Bendlerstrasse (Bendler Street) in central Berlin. Bendlerstrasse and Bendlerblock were used interchangeably to identify the military headquarters. Today it serves as a secondary office of the German Federal Ministry of Defense. In 1955, the street name was changed to Stauffenbergstrasse, as part of the glorification of the July 20th assassin as a hero of the nation.

Trusted generals of the Third Reich waited nervously in their offices at the Bendlerblock—Berlin headquarters of the OKW Home Command and General Army Office (AHA)—for the call from Col. Claus von Stauffenberg that the bomb had this time exploded and killed Adolf Hitler.
Notable among them were: Col. Gen. Ludwig Beck (retired since 1938); Col. Gen. Friedrich Fromm, chief of the Home Army Command; Gen. Friedrich Olbricht, Chief of the AHA and his chief of staff Col. Albrecht Mertz von Quirnheim; Gen. Fritz Thiele, deputy chief of communications (under Gen. Erich Fellgiebel); Col. Gen. Erich Hoepner, retired but now in uniform again; and Hans Bernt Gisevius, ex-Gestapo man just in from Switzerland.

Shortly after 1 p.m. the message came in from *Wolfsschanze*, and it was Fellgiebel's voice: "Something fearful has happened; the Fuehrer's alive."
Gen. Thiele and Gen. Olbricht listened on the phone. Fellgiebel, chief of com-

At top, a photo taken outside of the Bendlerblock on July 20, 1944, shows two German officers in front of a line of armed guards. **Below left:** Gen. Friedrich "Fritz" Thiele, deputy chief of communications under Fellgiebel, had the task at Bendlerblock of severing communications between loyal officers and field units. He wasn't implicated immediately; he took over as chief of communications until arrested on Aug. 11. **Below right:** Col. Gen. Friedrich Fromm, who controlled the Replacement Army, wasn't a principal in the conspiracy, but looked the other way until he found out Hitler hadn't been killed.

munications at headquarters, did not tell them that, shortly before, hoping to avoid serious complications for himself, he had congratulated Hitler on his escape. The two didn't know what really happened—if the bomb didn't explode or Stauffenberg failed to place the briefcase that contained it. They didn't convey the message to anyone else either, but instead decided to wait and went to lunch, or—as Thiele was said to do—walked uneasily through the nearby Tiergarten Park.

By 3 p.m. they were back at Bendlerstrasse, still very cautious, unsure what to do. Rumors of a failed bomb attempt were floating. Communication between different army offices and headquarters went on, causing further confusion—the telephone line from *Wolfsschanze* remained open (an error by Fellgiebel), so Field Marshal Wilhelm Keitel and Lt. Gen. Wilhelm Burgdorf were able to call various *Wehrkreise* and individual commanding officers to counteract the Valkyrie order.

Stauffenberg landed at Berlin-Rangsdorf airport shortly after 3 o'clock and called Bendlerstreet with the message: "Hitler is dead." When the colonel arrived after 4 p.m., Gen. Olbricht was still hesitant to act. Without his authority, his chief of staff Col. Mertz von Quirnheim initiated the first written and verbal orders of Valkyrie. "He railroaded me," Olbricht said later to Gisevius.

Stauffenberg and Olbricht together entered the office of Home Army Chief Fromm and informed him of Hitler's death, then requested that the Army take over as the governing authority of Germany. Fromm expressed strong doubts. Olbricht, now convinced that Stauffenberg was telling the truth that Hitler had been killed, suggested that Fromm might call Field Marshal Keitel at *Wolfsschanze* to find out. Upon doing so, Keitel assured him that Hitler was alive.

A highly dramatic exchange of words, blunt confrontations and even physical encounters with drawn revolvers followed.

Fromm: "Keitel told me Hitler is alive!"

Stauffenberg: "Keitel is a liar—he has lied often in the past. I saw Hitler carried out dead."

Olbricht: "We issued Valkyrie."

At that Fromm exploded. He raised his fist, accused the three of high treason and put them under arrest. Stauffenberg turned it around and tried to put Fromm under arrest—a comic situation except for the seriousness of it. Stauffenberg shouted, "I activated the bomb—Hitler is dead." Fromm countered: "You shoot yourself, the assassination failed." Stauffenberg moved toward Fromm; Fromm jumped up and threatened Stauffenberg. Now von Kleist and von Haeften, Stauffenberg's aides, rushed in with drawn pistols, and the turbulence settled at once.

No longer in authority, Gen. Fromm was given another chance to change his mind—he did not. He and his adjutant, Capt. Bartram, were locked in his office with their telephone blocked and Col. Gen. Hoepner took over. Now the new commander of the Home Army, Hoepner had been stripped of his army command a few years ago and had arrived at the Bendlerblock in civilian clothes, carrying his uniform in a suitcase.

In the meantime, the teleprinters had started to dispatch the Valkyrie code and follow-up orders to all the 16 *Wehrkreise*. It was a slow process as the order sheets had to first be coded, and then decoded at the other end; some *Wehrkreis* offices didn't receive it until the whole affair was over.

Gen. Paul von Hase, the Berlin city commander, was now supposed to move the various military units in and around Berlin—to occupy or cordon off all the places, offices and ministries, according to the Valkyrie plan.

Between 4:00 and 5:00 p.m., the Bendlerblock saw many new arrivals. It began to look like a gathering of the old *Reichswehr*, with the Prussian/Bavarian/Silesian nobility: Ludwig Beck, retired colonel general and former chief of staff, now designated commander of the revolt government, dressed in civilian clothes; the counts von Schulenburg, York von Wartenburg, von Bismark-Schoenhausen, von Schwerin-Schwanenfeld, von Hammerstein, and Berthold von Stauffenberg (brother of Claus); Klaus Bonhoeffer and Dr. Otto John. Shortly afterward, Berlin's Chief of Police Wolf-Heinrich Count von Helldorf arrived with Hans Gisevius.

Only Carl Goerdeler, the future chancellor, and Field Marshal Erwin von Witzleben, the new chief of the *Wehrmacht*, were missing. Goerdeler's whereabouts was unknown; he had gone into hiding several days before. Beck asked about Witzleben and was told by Gisevius that he was on his way to Zossen (OKH *Oberkommando Heer*/Army Supreme Command) to take over command of the *Wehrmacht*.

The commander of *Wehrkreis III*-Berlin, Gen. Joachim von Kortzfleisch, was called to Bendlerstrasse and told by Olbricht that Hitler was dead, the army was taking over and the troops in Berlin should be dispatched according to Valkyrie plans. Kortzfleisch refused and shouted, "The Fuehrer is not dead—Fuehrer is not dead!" When he tried to leave the offices, he was detained at gunpoint. Gen. von Thuengen took over for Kortzfleisch, going to his headquarters at Hohenzollerndamm, where he was not involved in any further action.

Olbricht gave chief of police Helldorf the order to alert his police forces and await further instructions; after a short while Helldorf left for the police headquarters and Olbricht returned to his office. Increasingly impatient, Gisevius asked Beck to call Lt. Gen. Wagner, the deputy chief of staff in Zossen, and order him to proceed according to the Valkyrie plans.

But at Zossen, Lt. Gen. Wagner informed Witzleben that Hitler was alive. When Witzleben arrived at the Bendlerblock around 8:00 p.m. he was furious about the course of events. "This is a fine mess," he said, and vehemently argued with both Stauffenberg and Beck, banging his fist on the table. He left for Zossen in a rage; the conspiracy was without its military commander—the commander never had any troops. Witzleben was not seen again; he realized the putsch was over.

The talking, arguing and telephoning continued. Beck quietly overlooked the operation, not saying a word. Stauffenberg feverishly telephoned the *Wehrkreise* to get Valkyrie activated. Gisevius urged "action now" and argued for forming assault parties of officers to go into the field, pending the arrival of troops. Soon after, he left for Helldorf's police headquarters to answer Helldorf's urgent request to know the situation at Bendlerblock.

In the middle of all the turbulence, an unbelievable scene occurred: The silver-black uniformed *Oberfuehrer SS* Pifrader from the RSHA (*Reichs Sicherheits Hauptamt-SS*) walked in and requested that Colonel Stauffenberg accompany him for an interview at the RSHA office. He was immediately apprehended by the conspirators and put under guard.

REMER'S DECISIVE MOVE

The Guard Battalion *Grossdeutschland*, commanded by Maj. Otto Ernst Remer (right) was an elite troop of battle-hardened soldiers and highly decorated front officers. It was divided into four companies of about 1,000 to 1,200 men. Remer dispatched three companies to cordon off the center of the city, according to Gen. Hase's order. He kept one company in reserve at the *Lustgarten* area. As a good soldier, Remer obeyed the order but when Gen. Hase gave him a lieutenant colonel as a liaison, he became suspicious.

By 6 p.m. the platoons were all in their positioned places. Remer checked them out and returned to Hase's headquarters at Unter den Linden. When he overheard a muffled talk between Hase and his chief of staff Lt. Col. Schoene to arrest Goebbels, he knew there was something fishy going on. He called his officers to a meeting.

Josef Goebbels was *gauleiter* for Berlin and minister for propaganda and cultural affairs, but also Reichs defense commissioner for the Gau-Berlin. Lt. Hagen, one of Maj. Remer's officers who worked for a time at Goebbels' ministry, suggested he visit Goebbels at his residence immediately. Remer was suspicious that perhaps Goebbels was involved in a party conspiracy against Hitler, and Goebbels was not sure about Remer. After a dramatic verbal exchange between the two in Goebbels' apartment, Remer was handed the telephone and heard the Fuehrer at the other end of a direct line to *Wolfsschanze*, never blocked by Fellgiebel.

"Do you recognize my voice, major?" asked Hitler, and Remer acknowledged that he did, having spoken privately with Hitler not long ago. Hitler gave him the order to snuff out the plot with all his might and energy. He made Remer the *de facto* commandant of Berlin until the newly appointed commander of the Home Army, *Reichsfuehrer SS* Himmler, arrived. At Goebbels' invitation, Remer set up a new command post in the downstairs room of the house. It was 6:30 p.m.

ALEA IACTA EST

By that time, the teleprinter and telephones at Bendlerblock had ordered the *Wehrmacht* units located in and around Berlin to their specified areas. When most of the marching military units reached the areas cordoned-off by Remer, his officers contacted the commanders of the arriving units and they were put under Remer's command. For a short while a serious problem occurred—Remer's platoons were confronted with an armored group from Krampnitz, a suburb of Berlin. Their tanks were on standby not far away from Goebbels' residence. It took some talking, telephoning and some pushing by Remer's subalterns before they learned that the unit would only obey orders from Col. Gen. Guderian, and Guderian was on Hitler's side. Clear road all the way.

Remer sealed off the whole district around the Bendlerblock and set guards at all street corners and building entrances; he issued strict instructions to accept orders only from his command post. Lt. Schlee, one of Remer's platoon leaders who guarded the front and main entrance of the Bendlerblock, was shuttling between Remer and Olbricht, receiving different orders. He was detained at one point by Col. Mertz von Quirnheim, but when Quirnheim left the room, he walked out without being checked or held up. He immediately reported to Remer the situation there, including discovering Gen. Kortzfleish locked in an upper story room, and that none of the orders of Fromm's Home Army had been dispatched. (The men in the communications center, starting to catch on, deliberately delayed sending the messages, or in some cases didn't dispatch them at all.) This report convinced Remer that the center of the conspiracy was located in the building on Bendlerstrasse.

Col. Gen. Fromm and his adjutant Capt. Bartram were still locked up at Fromm's office without a telephone connection, but with a functioning radio, which told them that the assassination failed. A small, little known exit in their office made it possible for Bartram to slip out several times and deliver a counteraction order from Fromm to the staff officers of the AHA on a different floor of the building. Fromm was also allowed by Olbricht to move to his apartment in another part of the building.

Herbert, von Heyden, Pridun and Harnack—officers of AHA not in the conspiracy—were ordered to Olbricht's office for guard duty. They instead requested answers about the tumultuous goings-on in his offices and the Bendlerblock entrance. Olbricht's answer was halting and evasive. The four officers refused cooperation and let Olbricht know their soldier's oath to Hitler was binding.

They left the office without any hindrance.

All of a sudden, shots were fired. A dozen officers entered with weapons—Herbert was shooting, Pridun was shot by Stauffenberg, who in turn took a hit in his arm. Bullets were flying; blood was on the floor—an unbelievable tumult.

During all this tangled confusion, Lt. Col. Herbert was able to get Fromm out of his apartment and back to his office, where Beck, Stauffenberg, Hoeppner, Olbricht, Mertz von Quirnheim and Haeften were held at gunpoint by the AHA officers. Fromm then said to them, "Well, gentlemen, I am now going to do to you what you did to me this afternoon." They were disarmed and a court-martial was set up. Gen. Beck asked to keep his revolver; he was granted permission, with Fromm telling him to "hurry." He raised his gun and shot himself through the temple, but the wound was not fatal. He staggered and, helped by Stauffenberg, tried again, collapsed, but remained alive.

Fromm ordered Capt. Bartram to form a firing squad and gave the five men time to write their last words and wishes. Olbricht immediately began writing, while Hoepner asked Fromm for a man-to-man talk. After a half hour, Fromm urged them to finish.

In the meantime, the order was given by Major Remer to the lieutenants Schlee, Arnds and Schady to enter the Bendlerblock and arrest the leaders of the conspiracy. When they approached the building, a scuffle began with a group of officers guarding the entrance. Fists were swinging, bodies pushing, but no shots exchanged. The officers who tried to block them were locked up in the porter's lounge. When Schlee entered the hall, shouts and shots echoed through the floor and ceilings.

Informed that Schlee's Guard Battalion soldiers were entering the building, Fromm quickly announced, "In the name of the Fuehrer . . . (naming the accused) . . . are condemned to death." Stauffenberg then spoke, trying to take responsibility for the whole thing, saying the others were only following his orders, to which Fromm said nothing. The condemned men, except for Hoepner, who was taken away to a military prison after his private meeting with Fromm, were marched out of the office. Fromm now ordered a staff officer to give Gen. Beck the mercy shot and left the building for Goebbel's residence.

In the courtyard of the Bendlerblock, shortly after midnight, under the glare of some automobile headlights, Valkyrie found its bloody end. ✦

BIBLIOGRAPHY:
Gisevius, Hans Bernd, *To the Bitter End*, Houghton Mifflin Co., Boston, 1947.
Goerlitz, Walter, *History of the German General Staff 1657-1945*, Barnes & Noble Inc., 1995.
Hoffmann, Peter, *The History of the German Resistance 1933-1945*, McGill-Queen's University Press, Montreal & Kingston, Ont., 3rd Ed., 1996.
Remer, Otto Ernst, "My Role in Berlin on July 20, 1944," *The Journal for Historical Review*, Vol. 8, No. 1, 1988.
Warlimont, General Walter, *Inside Hitler's Headquarters, 1939-1945*, Presidio Press, Novato, Cal., Bernard & Graeve Verlag, 1962.

Claus von Stauffenberg—"Count of Stauffenberg" (left) and Albrecht Mertz von Quirnheim, both from elite, long-established military families and close in age, became friends in 1925. The two, along with Friedrich Olbricht, Quirnheim's superior general, planned Operation Valkyrie to be implemented after Hitler was killed. The three died by the same firing squad on the night of the attempted coup. GERMAN FEDERAL ARCHIVES

CHAPTER 10

VALKYRIE: THE LAST CIRCLE

Translators' Introduction: The final reaches of the multiple conspiracies and related treasons and betrayals are probed. An expanding group of plotters spoke an idealistic, sometimes religious language but revealed an egoistic fixation on personal beliefs over national goals. From Stieff to Stauffenberg, to the men in the *Abwehr*—Canaris, Oster, Dohnanyi—to the Churchmen such as Bonhoeffer, all the way to Stuelpnagel, Hofacker, Von Kluge and Speidel on the Western front, these are men who failed to honor their oaths. Both Hitler and Giesler express not only anger and arguments against these men and their methods, but the sharp pain and deep sadness they felt at the inestimable damage done to the war effort.

GIESLER RECALLS PAST BEHAVIORS OF THE TRAITORS

The hard and sober Kaltenbrunner reports about the interrogations and confessions of the conspirators continued to come in; I had a backlog of reading. For quite a while in my off hours I was busy with design sketches—partly as supporting material for new discussions, partly due to the ideas and suggestions Adolf Hitler brought to our nightly talks. Moreover, I needed time in order to absorb and gain some distance from what SS investigators Johann Rattenhuber and Peter Hoegl had told me.

One morning as I visited Bormann again, he handed me the reports about the interrogation of Maj. Gen. [Helmuth] Stieff. One could get the impression that instead of working for the tasks they were supposed to

Helmuth Stieff was born in West Prussia (now Poland) and from 1927 served on the *Reichswehr* General Staff, joining the *Wehrmacht* General Staff in 1938. From the September 1939 invasion onward, he was greatly disturbed by the strategy of the war in Poland. This must have been known because Hitler disliked the diminutive Stieff and called him a "poisonous little dwarf."

PHOTO: GERMAN FEDERAL ARCHIVES

perform, the plotters spent most of their time brooding about setups and ways to kill their supreme commander—by means of the least danger for themselves. They must stay alive.

According to Stieff, Stauffenberg, at least for a while, thought to let his adjutant, Lt. [Werner von] Haeften, attempt to shoot the Fuehrer; that would be possible at the *Fuehrer-Lage* or at a weapons demonstration. Then, however, they thought that might not be secure enough.[1]

After that much hesitation, Stieff himself—so he said—wanted to take over the assassination on the occasion of a weapons demonstration at the Klessheim Castle near Salzburg, built by Fischer von Erlach.[2] I had participated in redesigning it into a guesthouse of the Reich.

After the heavy weapons demonstration, the Fuehrer was to be shown the new assault uniform for the attack units: backpack, assault rifle and hand grenades. Three sergeants and non-commissioned officers, highly decorated with the Gold Ranger Bar (*Nahkampf-spange*),[3] were selected.

Maj. Gen. Stieff intended to have the packs loaded with English explosives and a time igniter—to be sure to keep himself at a proper distance from the explosion. But because of a delay and a predetermined appointment, the Fuehrer canceled the presentation of the new assault equipment after the weapons demonstration, and we returned to the Berghof.

During the demonstration, a smallish general kept my attention: nervously busy, he stood out among the rest of the military staff. "Who is that little one here?" I had asked the SS adjutant. "That is Maj. Gen. Stieff." I recalled that particular moment as I continued to read the Rattenhuber report: "... true horror among the population, especially amidst soldiers and low ranked leaders, caused by the fact that the traitors planned to lay the bomb into the knapsacks of three battle-proven soldiers who would demonstrate the new uniforms for the Fuehrer. ..."

I looked at Bormann and said, "If what Stieff admitted is correct, then he is really a special jewel of this conspiracy clique! Do you judge Stauffenberg, who carries out the assassination without consideration for his co-conspirator Brandt, whom he blows into the air, as the better one? For me, the overall picture is very clear: when Stauffenberg landed at Berlin-

The Dining Hall at the Berghof where Stauffenberg was discovered by an orderly on July 11th alone, carrying his briefcase and standing behind Hitler's chair at the center of the long table, facing the large window. He excused himself by saying he was admiring the mountain view.

Rangsdorf and reported the—what he thought successful—assassination to those waiting at Bendlerstrasse, didn't he say then: 'Gen. Stauffenberg speaking here!' Look at that, he had promoted himself to a general."

"By the way, do you remember the report of the ordnance officer about the strange behavior of Stauffenberg at the Berghof on July 11? The meeting held in the large living room at the Berghof was not yet over," Bormann said. "Stauffenberg was no longer needed and asked for permission to be absent—it happened not so long ago.

"We were both chatting at the back of the hall toward the small living room when the orderly appeared and reported: 'I just looked over the dining room to make sure that everything was ready for lunch, and there in the middle, behind the Fuehrer's chair, stands the colonel with the one arm. I told him: "The room is private, may I ask you. . . ?"' He interrupted me: 'Pardon, I only wanted to have a look at it.'

"Yes," I said to Bormann, "I remember that the colonel with the one

CHAPTER 10 | 171

Schloss Klessheim in Salzburg, Austria was used to host guests and conferences, such as the weapons demonstration on July 7, 1944, attended by both Hitler and Giesler, and organized by Stieff, who placed bombs in the new uniforms to be shown to the Fuehrer. By leaving early due to time constraints, Hitler foiled the plotters once again.

PHOTO: GERMAN FEDERAL ARCHIVES

arm also said to the orderly: 'Very neat here, beautiful, especially with the bay window'—before the orderly asked him to leave the dining room."

Bormann said, "I then questioned the orderly further—I found out he (Stauffenberg) had a briefcase with him. What do you think was in it?"

"Turnip salad and pudding—in order to contribute something for lunch?" was my joking remark.

Bormann grimaced and said: "Today we know that nobody would have noticed the briefcase under the broad, long table with the low-hanging tablecloth. At that time, you were the honored guest, sitting across from the Fuehrer. Sometime you might thank that corporal!"

I replied, "Those repeated assassination tries which ended in vain seem to be fateful. I think about the plot at the Buergerbraeu[4]—and with a bomb on the airplane[5] they have tried it once before. Now I'm reading about the infamy at Klessheim, and the memory of the affair at the Berghof. Then the 20th July—miraculously the Fuehrer survives with only

General Hans von Oster (left), along with Tresckow and Spiedel, was one of the earliest and most active members of the anti-Hitler army group. As early as 1934 his attitude had soured, and by 1938 he had developed a fanatical hatred of Nazism. Oster was directly involved in four assassination attempts, and countless overtures to the British under cover of his high-level *Abwehr* position. His most important recruit was **Gen. Friedrich Olbricht** (right), deputy head of the General Army Office headquartered at the Bendlerblock in central Berlin, who controlled an independent system of communications to reserve units all over Germany.

light injuries. Are there still some more attempts I don't know about?"

"That attempt with the slight injury is only one side of the coin," Bormann said. "The other one sits much deeper, believe me! To your question: Yes, there were more assassination attempts which only now we are aware of. Talk about it with both of them[6]—I don't have time."

For a while I continued reading the interrogation protocols of Adm. Canaris and his protégé Maj. Gen. Hans von Oster—very opaque, strangely blurred. Dark and depressing as those reports were, an amusing moment occurred: the copy of a letter to Oster from his son Achim, at an army corps in Upper Silesia. Its content stayed strongly engraved in my mind. It read like: "Conditions are very pleasant here. The commanding general is a horseman and *grand signeur* of the ancient regime—a real general, not one of those 'people' soldiers."

I would like to have had a look at that general.

Admiral Wilhelm Canaris, *Abwehr* intelligence chief (left), was responsible for rooting out domestic spy rings—yet he kept up regular contact with Germany's enemies. Under his leadership, Hans von Dohnanyi (middle) and Dietrich Bonhoeffer (right) smuggled Jews, money and messages out of Germany.

TREASON IN THE ABWEHR AND ARMY GROUP CENTER

Translators' Commentary: Maj. Gen. Hans von Oster was an early opponent of what he feared would be inopportune military solutions for the Czechoslovak and Polish questions. He was a religious man (as were Stieff and Stauffenberg) who was forced to resign from the army in 1932 because of an indiscretion involving the wife of another officer. After a job in connection with the Prussian Police, he was able to transfer to the *Abwehr*, the state intelligence agency, the following year, where he met Hans Berne Gisevius and Arthur Nebe, working in the Gestapo, and became a confidant of Wilhelm Canaris, the chief of the spy agency.

By 1935, Oster was allowed to re-enlist in the army, but never on the General Staff. When Canaris reorganized the *Abwehr* in 1938, he made Oster head of the Central Division (*Zentralamt*), in charge of personnel and finances. As such, Oster was able to build up a dense network of contacts to Western countries. He was in the thick of secret efforts to prevent a Czech invasion in 1938; through his office, he arranged for emissaries to Great Britain to urge the British to stand firm over the Czech/Sudeten crisis—clear treason.

Hitler's diplomatic triumph with Chamberlain in Munich left the conspirators disheartened. Some lost interest, at least temporarily, but Oster did not give up. He took upon himself the central planning of all future plot plans.

To understand the contempt that Hermann Giesler expresses for Hans Oster, the following incident should suffice: Oster informed the Dutch military attaché, his friend Bert Sas in Berlin, more than 20 times of the exact date of the many-times-weather-delayed invasion of the Netherlands. Sas passed the information to his government, but was not believed! Oster himself said he calculated that his treason could cost the lives of 40,000 German soldiers, but concluded that it was necessary to prevent even more deaths during a protracted war should Germany achieve an early victory.

Oster worked closely with Henning von Tresckow, chief of Army Group Center, and with General Friedrich Olbricht, head of the General Army Office at the Bendlerblock in Berlin. It was Oster's *Abwehr* group that supplied the English-made bombs that Tresckow used in the assassination attempts of 1943. One of this group was Hans von Dohnanyi, Dietrich Bonhoeffer's part-Hungarian brother-in-law.

But trouble came in April 1943, when the Gestapo entered the *Abwehr* to arrest Dohnanyi for violations of foreign exchange regulations (illegal money transfers, to be exact), including cash transactions with Jauch & Huebener, Germany's largest insurance company. (Today it is the American firm Aon. Walter Jauch was related by marriage to Hans Oster.)

Present at the time, Oster was caught trying to hide incriminating notes. That was the end of his *Abwehr* intrigues; he was dismissed and closely watched by the Gestapo from then on. Dohnanyi was eventually sent to the Sachsenhausen detention camp for political prisoners, where he was put to death on April 8, 1945 as a July 20 conspirator. Oster was arrested on July 21, 1944, the day after the assassination; on April 4, 1945, the diaries of Wilhelm Canaris were discovered. That sealed the fate of both men.

Thus on April 9, Oster and Canaris, along with Bonhoeffer and four other men, were hanged at Flossenbuerg as traitors to their country.

Wilhelm Canaris had been playing a double game for a long time. Enough evidence had finally come to light that Hitler had already dismissed him from the *Abwehr* in February 1944, replacing him with Walter Schellenberg and merging much of the *Abwehr* with the *Sicherheitsdienst* (SD), the SS Security Office headed by Ernst Kaltenbrunner. Canaris was put under house arrest, preventing him from taking part in the July 20 plot.

An interesting detail: Under Canaris (and Oster and Dohnanyi), hundreds of Jews were given token *Abwehr* training and issued papers to leave Germany. One of those is said to have been the Lubavitcher Rebbe in Warsaw, Rabbi Yosef Schneersohn.[7] If true, we can thank Canaris for the strong presence of the Lubavitch tribe in the United States. Giesler writes:

* * *

Years later as a "war criminal" at Landsberg WCP (war criminal prison), I would hear at our round walks in the jail yard the rather dreamy opinions held by Oster: By betraying the German operation plans, causing the death of countless German soldiers—no, that was by no means treason—Oster just wanted to avoid an extension of the war goals to the north and west. He only wanted to counteract the attack on Denmark and Norway, Belgium and Holland— all neutral states. The governments of those states had only been warned by Oster so they could protest in time, before God and the world, about Hitler's intention to attack. That might stop Hitler and force him to a peaceful settlement of all conflicts. (These were) unlikely explanations and justifications for high treason and *Landesverrat*.[8]

Another of these prophets—who thought they could define treason as a cavalier offense and considered it proper to sacrifice German soldiers and endanger the nation's existence for the higher cause of humanity— was the diplomat and former undersecretary at the Foreign Office, [Ernst] von Weizsaecker. I am sure he expressed that opinion in order to justify his own behavior. I met him at the Landsberg WCP with open contempt.

To the ones who were influenced by that prattle, I said, "A peaceful settlement of all conflicts had just been successfully prevented by those new propagandists, because Adolf Hitler did not want war, and the war in the East was forced upon him by the East as well as by the West." I said to them, "Combined with a reasonable land reform,[9] Adolf Hitler would have preferred to build, perform social work and do an outstanding job of renewing cities. Many of those imbeciles really believed the Autobahn was nothing else but a road-megalomania!"

All that mental confusion I met with a quotation which was attributed to Napoleon, but was really by Josef Goerres from the *Rheinische Merkur* newspaper, 1814: "No people are more gullible than the Germans. . . . [A]mong them they strangled each other and believed, by doing it, they have done their duty. No other nation on this earth is dumber. No sillier lie can be dreamed up—yet Germans believe it. A slogan handed to them will cause persecution of their own people more severe than against their real enemies."

The weeks I spent at the Fuehrer Headquarters *Wolfsschanze* in August 1944 were the most turbulent ones I ever experienced in my life. What I saw troubled me deeply; I felt the downfall, I thought the Reich would now collapse. The fronts were shaking; threat closed in from all sides. Add to that the depression of being more and more aware of the scope of the treason done.

The assassination attempt of July 20 was like a stone thrown into calm water, causing first a bubbling stir, then, by the interrogations and confessions, forming circle after circle until finally Goerdeler's grandiose, mad obsession of confessing, traitor now of the traitors.[10] But now—when in the center the bubbles are still rising and bursting— a last circle is formed before the water's viscosity holds to its own. But just that circle, for many not visible anymore, caused Adolf Hitler a big shock: the front itself.

For years he asked himself: Why all those failures? The enemy knew about our military operations at the same time as our commanding officers received them!

Already in 1942 in Winniza, he told me something wrong is going on, he suspects treason at the highest level. After the catastrophe of Stalingrad, communist emigrants worked openly together with part of the

Wilhelm Leuschner is shown appearing at the People's Court. He had agreed to be vice chancellor under Goerdeler in the "new regime." A Social Democrat minister of the Interior in the state of Hesse prior to 1933, he was a union supporter who had always opposed the NSDAP. After 1933 and a year of confinement, he built up a resistance network. He was arrested on August 16, 1944 and executed on September 29.

officers captured by the Russians.[11] The collapse of Army Group Center from the Russian attack of July 1944 caused the loss of 25 German divisions and hit Adolf Hitler hard. He suspected treason here also, as he did at the failure of the Citadel offensive[12] the previous year.

The investigations following the assassination revealed and then confirmed Adolf Hitler's suspicion of high treason. General Henning von Tresckow, general staff officer of Army Group Center, shot himself; general staff officer Maj. [Joachim] Kuhn deserted to the Russians. The statement of [Wilhelm] Leuschner, former Hessian secretary of the interior and future vice chancellor under Goerdeler, clarified the situation further. Leuschner's statement didn't get much attention at first at *Wolfsschanze*, but he made his statement after his conviction and, faced with death, there is hardly any doubt that he spoke the truth.

By that statement the scope of the treason causing the destruction of Army Group Center became clearer. At the same time, Ludwig Beck, the former chief of the General Staff, glimmered in an enigmatic light. Knowing that the assassination failed and the revolt fell apart, he took his life on that evening of July 20, at the Bendlerstrasse.

TREASON IN THE WEST

Translator's Commentary: Giesler says little about how Valkyrie played out on the Western front. To fill in: Conspirator Lt. Col. Caesar von Hofacker, officer on the staff of Gen. Karl-Heinrich von Stuelpnagel, military chief of France, received the call from Stauffenberg at 4 o'clock in the afternoon telling him Hitler was dead. Based on that, Stuelpnagel issued the order to arrest members of the SS command post in Paris according to the "Valkyrie" plan. Field Marshal Guenther von Kluge's chief of staff, Gen. Hans Speidel, got the call from Stuelpnagel's chief of staff, Gen. Blumentritt, but decided to wait for Kluge to return from the front. The arrest of around 120 members took place before a heavy-armored navy attachment was alarmed, and threatened to march on Paris in an armed intervention unless the SS prisoners were released. By then, radio and telephone were revealing that Hitler was alive.

Kluge returned to headquarters at 6 p.m. and summoned Stuelpnagel and generals Sperrle, Blumentritt and Speidel to report to him. During the following two hours they shared a tense, but civil dinner until a call from Gen. Stieff at OKH gave the definite word that Hitler was alive and any action on Stauffenberg's Valkyrie *ist Wahnsinn* (is madness).

After Stuelpnagel returned to Paris, von Kluge relieved him of his command, replaced him with Blumentritt, who he ordered to "tidy up and get back to normal." But this was not possible; it became another inglorious end of suicide and suicide attempts for the conspirators.

Back to Giesler:

* * *

To complete the score of treason and infidelity, sometime during the 15th and 18th of August, Hitler learned of a conspiracy attempt between the German military leadership in the West and the Allies.

The breach of loyalty and suicide attempt by Gen. von Stuelpnagel, military commander of France, was alarming. Kluge was relieved of his service and called back to headquarters for report. On the way to the air-

HANS SPEIDEL: THE MAN WHO LOST D-DAY?

General Hans Speidel (left), "Valkyrie" conspirator and chief of staff of Army Group B under Erwin Rommel, and then under Guenther von Kluge (center), was in one of the most commanding spots at the Normandy invasion front. He continued to tell OKW to hold back divisions because the landing location was not certain. Spanish superspy for Germany Alcazar de Velasco said after the war: "It's because of him (Speidel) we lost the war." Speidel survived to become a four-star general in charge of NATO Land Forces, Middle Europe! Gen. Stuelpnagel (right), as military chief of France, was responsible in "Valkyrie" to arrest the SS command post in Paris. He was later fired by Kluge for doing so.

field, he took poison. A contradiction in itself was, on one side, the at-that-time known efforts of the field marshal to enter into negotiations with the Allies for an armistice without the Fuehrer's knowledge—even though he must have known that would cause the collapse of all fronts—and, on the other side, the fact that shortly before his death he sent the Fuehrer a letter assuring him of his loyalty.

At one of those evenings at the Wolf's Lair, Adolf Hitler talked to me about those treasonous affairs and said:

"Those were the worst days of my life! How easy and simple it would be for me to terminate my life. What is my life? Added to all those disappointments—only struggle and worry and grinding responsibility.

"Fate and providence assigned those tasks and burdens to me—and doesn't the last assassination attempt just demand more steadfastness than ever, to continue the struggle with trust and confidence? And if that struggle is to make sense, we must succeed in exterminating the bearers of that treason—because all the effort, all the bravery are in vain against treason within your own people.

"How malicious and wretched is that treason!

"I could sense it through all the years, but struggled with myself to believe that German officers, generals, could be connected with it. Beyond any imagination is treason during a war, treason against the nation and treason against the fighting soldiers.

"I believed I could win them over since the existence of Germany was at risk ... even Europe! I stood up to overcome Marxism and introduce instead a socialism of a unified nation [*Volksgemeinschaft*]. I did win the workingman over, but I misjudged the reactionaries—they were here, in the *Reichswehr*, within industry, the powerful economic and money circles. They were here, too, as failed politicians and diplomats.

"I misjudged their vain ambition, their need for admiration and their intellectual shortcomings—all that I misjudged! I forgot to get rid of those fossils of a long past era. In a time of urgency, reconstruction, reformation, war requirements and burdening pressure, I forgot that I am a revolutionary.

"That someone from that reactionary group might at some time shoot at me—I thought about that and had to live with it. But I never believed it possible that a General Staff officer was able to commit such a characterless crime—even though, due to my experiences since 1938, I ought to have expected all that. They didn't have the courage to openly resist me or shoot me.

"We have to create a new aristocracy, a value and rank order based on character, courage and steadiness. One sentence of Nietzsche's I identify with: What today can prove if one be of value or not?—that he is steadfast."

The evening closed with discussions about city rebuilding and reconstruction. Was it denial and relaxation? Was it confidence? I don't know. That night, Adolf Hitler was dealing with traffic structures of cities. ✦

CHAPTER 10 | 181

CHAPTER NOTES:
1 *Vierteljahreshefte fuer Zeitgeschichte*, 2.Jahrgang 1954, 3.Heft Juli, Ausgewaehlte Briefe des Gen Maj Helmuth Stieff, Seite 295.
2 An Austrian Baroque architect.
3 A special decoration for soldiers involved in close battle.
4 Refers to Buergerbrauekeller in Munich where the reunion of the 1923 Putsch is held every year on Nov. 8. In 1939 a bomb exploded behind the speaker's desk, killing six and injuring many. Hitler said an inner voice urged him, "Get out, get out"; after some hesitation, he followed the urge.
5 The March 1943 assassination attempt by Gen. von Tresckow, who had a bomb placed on Hitler's plane. The bomb failed to go off.
6 Rattenhuber and Hoegl.
7 Altein, R, Zaklikofsky, E, Jacobson, I: "Out of the Inferno: The Efforts That Led to the Rescue of Rabbi Yosef Yitzchak Schneersohn of Lubavitch from War Torn Europe in 1939-40", page 160. Merkos L'Inyonei Chinuch, 2002.
8 *Landesverrat* is considered worse than high treason. It is "country treason"—the passing of state secrets by a citizen to a foreign power through written message, verbal report or otherwise.
9 *Raumordnung*, expansion to the East, according to the party ideology of "Volk ohne Raum", people without space.
10 Goerdeler freely cooperated with the Gestapo in naming names, which made him the object of considerable hatred from the other prisoners, who saw him as a "spineless rat." Manvell, Roger & Frankel, Heinrich, *The Men Who Tried to Kill Hitler*, Skyhouse: New York 2008, pages 178-179.
11 Ullbricht, Markus Wolf, Pieck, von Einsiedel and consortium (all Communist émigrés from Germany) were meeting with POW General Walther von Seydlitz and his Stalingrad clique, working on actions, radio propaganda, and Front voice messages. Seydlitz formed the Committee for a Free Germany.
12 "Operation Citadel" was the military code name for one of the largest military operations in WWII, a pincer offensive to cut off the Soviets from the bulge between Orel and Kursk in July 1943. It was postponed several times, then at first successful, but strong Russian counterattacks caused eventual collapse of the operation, with great losses on both sides.

The People's Court

"They asked for the death sentence and it cannot be anything else. It is just. I erred and did wrong. It was not right to arrogantly interfere as a little human being with God's doing."

Those were the last lines written by Gen. Helmuth Stieff to his wife immediately after being sentenced to death by the People's Court on the afternoon of Aug. 8, 1944—going to the gallows the same day.[1] As Chief of Organization at Army High Command (OKH), Stieff was in a prime position to help the conspiracy—he had regular access to Hitler; he hid the bombs in his office at the OKH

Facing page: Gen Helmuth Stieff faces the People's Court after confessing his role in the July 20th assassination plot. Despite his unusually short stature, as seen in the photo above when welcoming the Fuehrer to a weapons demonstration at Klessheim Palace on July 7th (during which he planned to kill Hitler with a bomb explosion), and Hitler's personal dislike of him, Stieff's exceptional organizational skills enabled him to rise to the level of Chief of Organization at OKH.

headquarters in Mauerwald, East Prussia, not far from *Wolfsschanze*. Stieff's first contact was with Army Group Center Chief Henning von Tresckow; together they met with Generals Friedrich Olbricht and Ludwig Beck in Berlin in August 1943. They approached Gen. Guderian and Gen. Kluge, but neither one would commit. In October, Stauffenberg asked Stieff outright to kill Hitler and Stieff refused. But Stieff put the bombs into the uniforms to be displayed to Hitler at Klessheim Castle. Stieff was in charge of the event at Klessheim; after this failure it was decided that Stauffenberg was the only one who could complete the job.

Gen. Stieff was on the plane with Stauffenberg and his aide Lt. Haeften on their flight to Wolf's Lair July 20. He was arrested that night at the OKH headquarters, interrogated by SS investigator Hans Rattenhuber, and held from then on. ✦

ENDNOTE:
1 *Vierteljahreshefte fuer Zeitgeschichte*, 2.Jahrgang 1954, 3.Heft Juli, Ausgewaehlte Briefe des Gen Maj Helmuth Stieff, Seite 295.

OLD LINE PRUSSIAN

Henning von Tresckow exemplified Giesler's description of the plotters as men guided by "humanitarian" motives, who failed to understand the nature of Bolshevism in the East or the long-held intentions of the Anglo-American-Jewish alliance in the West to destroy Germany once and for all. Born in 1901 to a noble Prussian family with 300 years of military tradition, Tresckow had risen to the rank of Colonel, first serving under FM Fedor von Bock (his wife's cousin) from 1941-43, then under FM Guenther von Kluge as chief operations officer of Army Group Center, and lastly as chief of staff of the 2nd Army in Russia. Described by the Gestapo as a "prime mover" and the "evil spirit" behind the Jan. 20 plot, he had been active in planning incidents to kill Hitler from 1935 onward. When he learned the Valkyrie plot had failed, Tresckow committed suicide on the Eastern Front, leaving word with his friend Schlabrendorff that the attempt was worthwhile to show the world there were still righteous men in Germany.

CHAPTER 11

METHODS & MORALS OF THE TRAITORS

Translators' Introduction: Hitler has time to reflect on the scope and nature of the treason during an illness in September 1944. After he recovers, he gives a thoughtful and accurate summary to Giesler of the character of the "plotters" and their (in)ability to make the necessary decisions.

HITLER CRITIQUES THE PLOT'S LACK OF SUBSTANCE

"Valkyrie" was the code name for the military response to emergency situations in the Reich—troops in their barracks and boot camps, on leave and in training classrooms. Among other things, they should prevent revolts of prisoners of war and foreign workers. "Valkyrie" also meant emergency military actions against enemy landings on the shores and via airborne operations—in short, all actions necessary to protect the Reich. By their nature, the armed forces were in command.

The investigations of the July 20 assassination attempt were now finished in principle. Isolated at his sleeping cell during an illness in September 1944, Hitler had time to reflect. He told me:

"Valkyrie was planned for the protection of the Reich—the plotters used Valkyrie as a deceiving tool for a cunning *coup d'état*. But they could not turn their powerful positions and the potential they had to their advantage, in that they had neither the ability nor the strength to make decisions. The assassination—the 'ignition' as they called it—failed. The conspirators did not have a Brutus.

"An aristocrat—a colonel, with the knowledge and approval of the generals' clique—tried to take me from this world by deceit. I have to admit that the hypocrisy, cowardice and maliciousness—the breach of oath, treason and *Landesverrat*—hurt me more than the explosion of the hellish machine with English explosives that that aristocrat had put under the worktable.

"From a safe distance he watched the explosion—the co-conspirator and general of communications Gen. Erich Fellgiebel at his side; then he flew back to Berlin full of energy to trigger Valkyrie."

It must have been a shock for that general to see that his victim was only lightly injured—yet he was still shameless enough to congratulate him. He considered it too dangerous to warn his fellow conspirators in Berlin. Well, they were ready to command soldiers, to give them orders that could cost them their lives, but they themselves were not ready for that. They would have thought themselves too important.

Not one had the courage to face him openly with a weapon. Instead of entering history by a manly deed, they tried to fell their supreme commander by treachery. Only self-sacrifice would have given them a chance to distinguish their act from that of a cowardly criminal.

How did they justify breaking their oath? Who would give them the right to assassination and revolt at a time of highest pressure and distress, at a time when fierce battles are fought on all fronts? They tried to justify their deed by pretending they were acting in the interest of higher human goals. They saw Churchill and Roosevelt, even Stalin, as their guarantors. They said that for the sake of humanity's higher objectives the blood sacrifice of German soldiers and their comrades is justified.

After the assassination bid, Hitler insisted on being fully informed, and without glossing, of all the results of the interrogations: the statements and testimony of the conspirators. He asked for exact information of the circle of persons involved, and their reasoning; he was also interested in the operational plan for the revolt after Valkyrie.

He soon found there was nothing planned.

"The first proclamations of the bearers of an illusionary power were lies—with lies they confronted the nation and the armed forces. After what they thought was a successful assassination, they didn't have the courage to confess to it.

"Mr. Fellgiebel could not turn off all telephone lines. I was able to talk to Dr. Goebbels and the major[1] of the Berlin Guard Battalion *Gross Deutschland*—who then cleared up the confusion. The putsch collapsed; the conspirators had not one company on their side."

Who would give them the authority for the assassination attempt and the coup? With one voice, the front expressed its anger; the frontline soldier could not understand how officers were able to do such a deed. The front could see the consequences and results; its judgment was also quite clear: it would burden us; only the enemy would benefit.

The reaction of a troubled community was the unanimous rejection of the assassination attempt and coup. Worry and mistrust arose. Neither the nation nor the armed forces gave the conspirators the authority for the assassination or the attempted coup—above all, not for rebellion and contemptible treason.

From the investigation and testimony one could learn that the conspirators didn't think very far ahead—an egocentric attitude led to a euphoric opinion of the political situation, as in: First we get rid of the dictator, then, via Valkyrie, his party—the Allies will then help us. And once again those vague phrases of higher human ideals for which one had to sacrifice—that's what their conscience demanded.

Also his writings gave them a reason for their deeds. Better than many of his party comrades who were reading *Mein Kampf*, they rummaged through the book and found sentences they thought they could interpret to support their shabby thinking. Since he "drags the nation" into destruction, he justifies in *Mein Kampf* their right to stop him through resistance, rebellion and the coup. It is, therefore, not only their right but also their obligation to get rid of him, the tyrant—that's how they read *Mein Kampf*.

He is ready to face the people's criticism at any time. Not "he" dragged the nation into distress, but the openly declared will of Churchill, Roosevelt and their big ally, the international Jews—to destroy us. The reactionaries and the plotters' clique encouraged that intention, and theirs was the best way to push the nation, via the putsch and assassination, beyond the present trouble, into the abyss. No—he denies those men the right of high treason, rebellion and the right to assassinate. Where indeed could they ever have shown the power to build a new state regime made necessary by the last war and the new century?

Again and again he asks himself: Where really are their ideas? What can they offer the nation? Just their names and an honor only they believed in? Both are tattered by their deeds.

One can lift a revolution to a big wave, releasing enthusiasm, national strength and willingness to sacrifice. One cannot keep that wave permanently; one cannot conserve it. But the start of a revolution also depends on the person who carries it and his authority—on the thoughts and ideas, if they are understood, if they have roots and find confirmation in the spirit of the time and the sense of the nation.

His way to the leadership of the nation is proof of his harmony with the national spirit.

The bearers of the assassination attempt imagined a past they themselves did not understand. For him, it had been inconceivable up to now that a German officer—above all a general—could commit treason. Treason in wartime—damaging the German people, burdening the fighting German soldier—impossible.

For a commander, the most important quality is his character, his attitude. Intelligence does not stand higher. The character and the strength of his will alone are decisive when he has to withstand severe blows of fate. Courage, bravery and willingness to sacrifice are the prerequisites of a leader. He always requests that from his soldiers. So he shall and must be a role model—even more, he must be able to give strength and convince.

When he had to accept the capitulation of [Field Marshal Friedrich] Paulus and the behavior of his generals, Hitler had said:

CHAPTER 11 | 189

Walther von Seydlitz-Kurzbach (left), commander of 51st Corps, with Friedrich Paulus, commander of 6th Army, as POWs in the Soviet Union, 1942. During the battle of Stalingrad, Seydlitz urged Paulus to disobey Hitler's order to stay and resist. Seydlitz wanted to break out. Paulus obeyed Hitler and issued a rousing order to stand and fight, following which Hitler promoted him to field marshal. Paulus then became ill and withdrew to his quarters; his staff finalized the surrender. In captivity, Seydlitz organized the "Committee for a Free Germany" which encouraged German soldiers to surrender. Paulus resisted joining the Committee until 1945, after which he cooperated with the Russians, wrote military textbooks and lectured. PHOTO: GERMAN FEDERAL ARCHIVES

Now they will take their way down into the lowlands of wretchedness, the oath being only a fiction. A steady character is not their strength, intellectual self-esteem more so. They may try to work with the Russians and will lose face at the same time. It won't take long, and we are going to hear them on the Russian propaganda radio. Step by step, they will show a lack of character and, in the end, slander their military tradition. They may forget they carry a name of a dutiful obligation.

There were some co-workers here, generals too, who could not believe that something like that was possible. Hitler had said, "Yes it is, sooner or later, and all the way up to field marshal." That he had promoted Paulus to that rank was something he never would forgive himself.

"So one leads an army, the army fights and dies, and he who was entrusted to lead that army and the soldiers—does he die heroically with his soldiers? The meaning of that battle, the heroism and sacrifice of many ten thousands of brave soldiers, officers and generals will lose its value and will be trampled down by the one who should have been their example. He will take the road to Moscow; we will live to see him at the radio station."

Hitler said that, and he had it right, but that it would lead to such a disgusting mess as the so-called "National Committee for a Free Germany" by that Seydlitz-Kurzbach—I myself could never have imagined.

Well, Seydlitz might feel like Yorck at Tauroggen.[2] Seydlitz and his creatures did not grasp that it was Bolsheviks they signed up with; they didn't get it because with their thinking they were still entrenched in the 19th century. They hadn't learned anything at all. They hadn't recognized that this is a war of life or death, not restricted to soldiers, folk or the nation. They could not imagine that we are involved in a fateful struggle, in a revolutionary fight for the existence of Europe—in a battle for a new idea of life (*Lebensbasis*), against destruction and the powers who want to destroy us.

If we still had such schizophrenic twits who thought: We do that with the Russians—we drop our weapons honorably, we hand over our épée[3], which Marshal Stalin honorably hands back to us again—yes, in such a world they still lived. Then we sign a peace agreement with them—that's how those idiots thought, and the ones oriented toward the west thought similarly.

Is it surprising that optimism dwindles? That our allies and the neutrals might lose their confidence? And are we surprised about the demand for unconditional surrender?

What shall the front think, the soldier, when asked by those shameful tracts of cowardice to surrender, to sabotage, to commit treason and to refuse to obey orders—pamphlets signed by former commanders? We have to overcome that moral crisis.

They wanted to end the war and submit the nation to the unconditional surrender; they would have surrendered the soldiers of the eastern front to the Russians—they did not care.

Hitler would have been relieved of worries, sorrows, pressing responsibility and sleepless nights if the infamy of Stauffenberg had succeeded. But what would have been the consequence? Chaos and destruction at the fronts. Hate and civil war and despair.

They wouldn't have understood—it is not about him, but Germany. Churchill declared it frankly and cynically: It is about Germany's destruction. Where can you find in this a legitimate political foundation for a conspiracy that makes history?

Of a rare kind, they found each other: reactionaries, liberals, Marxists, representatives of the church—the *Bekennende Kirche*—the anti-regime "Confessing Church," specifically—they even prayed for Germany to lose the war. And let's not forget the diplomats. And the *herren* generals. Hitler cannot expect to be understood by his generals, but he can request that they obey his orders.

They just could not see that we lived in a changing era and had to endure a fateful war. Instead of fighting for the nation as their oath required, they committed destruction, sabotage and subversion.

"From the first war year on, I suspected treason; often I felt it physically. I am sure that treason started much earlier. Now, after the assassination bid, proof of the permanent treason is clear. Still, not all traitors are recognized. What damage they caused." ✦

CHAPTER NOTES:
1 Referring to Maj. Otto Ernst Remer, later awarded the rank of major general.
2 Hans David Ludwig Yorck was a Prussian general during the Napoleonic war. In Tauroggen in East Prussia, he sided with the Russians against King Friedrich Wilhelm's order.
3 An épée is a blunted fencing sword developed in the 19th century for practice and competition.

JODL: THE "COLONEL GENERAL"

Hermann Giesler: "Whenever I had a chance, I enjoyed talking to the colonel general because of his realism and his precise description of military affairs." As Adolf Hitler's Chief of Operations at OKW (High Command of the Armed Forces), Col. Gen. Alfred Jodl (above with map) was responsible, generally speaking, for conveying Hitler's instructions to the three services (*Heer*, *Kriegsmarine*, *Luftwaffe*). He served under Chief of the OKW FM Wilhelm Keitel, who in turn served the Supreme Commander and Commander-in-Chief of the Armed Forces, Adolf Hitler.

PHOTO: GERMAN FEDERAL ARCHIVES

CHAPTER 12

JODL LOOKS BACK ON STALINGRAD; HITLER FACES UNCONDITIONAL SURRENDER

Translators' Introduction: Hermann Giesler engages Colonel General Alfred Jodl, Chief of Operations of the OKW, in conversation about the fateful battles at Demjansk and Stalingrad. Some of the difficult strategic considerations behind Hitler's orders to resist to the end are explained, putting to rest many false assumptions and making clear that capitulation at that time was unthinkable. The effect of the Unconditional Surrender demand of the Allies, and Hitler's secret hope for Col. Hans Rudel to succeed him as Fuehrer, are also revealed by Giesler.

JODL TALKS ABOUT STALINGRAD

In the fall of 1943, I talked with Col. Gen. Jodl, chief of Operations of *Oberkommando der Wehrmacht* [OKW], about *Demjansk*[1] and the catastrophe of Stalingrad. In the winter of 1941-42, a Russian army encircled a German army corps at the Waldai Heights around Demjansk. The six encircled divisions, about 100,000 men, could only be supplied and remain fit for action by continuous daily air support. They repulsed all Russian attacks, and at their wide, extended "hedgehog" front they kept five Russian armies tied down.[2] The divisions in the "cauldron" [signifying the encircled forces] of Demjansk prevented a decisive breakthrough of the Soviets at the Army Group North.

At that time, I was around Pleskau and Staraja Russia and took a special interest in these operations. My friend Schulte-Frohlinde flew a Ju 52, carrying munitions and supplies into the cauldron and wounded soldiers out.

My Organization Todt units, together with sappers, were building bridges, roadways, military positions and field railway tracks toward the cauldron as necessary preparations for the attack from the outside and the planned breakout from the inside.

The main battle line on the land bridge west of the Demjansk cauldron was in the meantime stabilized and fortified. Four German divisions attacked from the Staraja Russa area in order to relieve the encircled army corps. Through mud, swamps and across the Lowat River, the troops fought that battle in an unprecedented manner.

"An amazing achievement of men and leadership," Col. Gen. Jodl said. "Unique also in the history of war is the fact that a whole army corps, encircled, withstood for a long time an all-around attack of far superior forces. And unique also, and a first, that for months an army corps was supplied with all its needs for military operation solely by transport airplanes."

I said, "Beyond its description in the war histories, Demjansk and Stalingrad will stand as a saga—even with all the bitterness—as a soldier's *Nibelungen* epos."

The colonel general replied: "I know where you want that talk to lead me, but it's not the time for it yet. [Here are] only a few military points. The Stalingrad disaster began with the collapse of the north flank, and also a part of the south flank, of the 6th Army. Those forces could not withstand the attacking thrusts of the Russian elite armies.[3] Encirclement of the 6th Army at Stalingrad was not the only intention of the Russians. Their strategic goal was larger; their thrust was directed toward Rostow."

I asked, "Don't Demjansk and Stalingrad show a certain analogy?"

Jodl answered, "Certainly they have a lot in common." However he [Jodl] sees the fortress [*festung*] Stalingrad as a double-faced Janus head—"on the one hand it did not only concern the position on the Volga and the encircled 6th Army, but also the fate of the Army Group

A German Junkers Ju 52 3/m approaching Stalingrad with much-needed supplies in late 1942. Jodl said that, "Operative considerations, and not thoughts about prestige, kept the 6th Army in Stalingrad."

South with more than 1 million solders and all the area they controlled. On the other hand, you should consider that for six months the 6th Army tied up seven Russian armies at Stalingrad. The rapid release of those enemy forces would certainly have meant a disaster for Army Group A, but it also would have greatly endangered Army Group Don and part of Army Group B. Large parts of the Romanian, Italian and Hungarian armies were already run over by the Russians.[3]

The breakthroughs had to be dammed, and defense fronts along the Don built. The fight of the 6th Army preconditioned the stabilization of the south flank of the east front, where giant gaps were obvious. The situation was extremely threatening.

"Something else is connected with Stalingrad—the Volga, the most important waterway for transporting the Baku oil and the American war deliveries from the Persian Gulf. Looking at the military situation of the south flank—the Volga front is for the time being of secondary importance. But Stalingrad, by its special strategic dimension, is much larger than Demjansk, even if you include Cholm and the Wolchow breakthrough. From both of those gigantic operations one can clearly conclude that the Russians recognized our strategic plans.

"Still some more indications: It surely makes a difference if 100,000 or 250,000 are supplied and made battle-ready by air. The distance and the depth of the enemy's encirclement played a role; its flak and fighters caused serious problems for the flights of our slow Ju 52 transports. To what an extent and for how long the supply could be secured was a decisive, but unanswerable, question.

NEED FOR A CORRIDOR

"Because of operative reasons, a relief from the west along the Don could not be considered," Jodl continued. "Therefore all hope of such a relief was based on Army Group Hoth (Group B) opening a corridor from the southwest. That would have meant freedom of the decision for our combined effort by forces from inside and outside the encirclement.

"It would have been irresponsible to break the Stalingrad encirclement from inside with weakened troops, leaving behind the wounded, without the support of heavy weapons. Operative considerations, and not thoughts about prestige, kept the 6th Army in Stalingrad. The insufficient and weather-dependent supply by the *Luftwaffe* could not keep the army in a fighting capability. To have enough food, fuel and ammunition for the heavy weapons, and also for the breakout of the 6th Army with support from outside, a corridor was absolutely necessary.

"An isolated breakout, without heavy weapons, from an unprotected icy-snowy steppe, and through a deeply staggered ring of the Russian armies, would have been an act of despair and led to total destruction. It would have meant the end of the 6th Army, and freed the enemy forces tied down there before the army groups at the south flank were secured.

"Around Jan. 9 or 10, the Russians actually offered the possibility for the 6th Army to surrender. However, the purpose and goal of that offer was transparent: they wanted to free their tied-down army in order to move it, together with the other armies, against the not-yet secured defense front of the army groups. With regard to the conditions of the surrender, we were well aware what to expect. We were, however, still hoping to organize a sufficient supply line and a breakout through a corridor.

"The detachment of a large fighting force from the enemy, specifically in winter, carries all kinds of risks—it loses its fortified places/positions, and the coverage and protection by heavy weapons. Within the battle area, a detaching move by a division from North to South was carried out. It ended in total destruction—without any cover, the rapidly attacking Russians tore it apart and ran over it. That breakout of one division should be an example of the risk for the breakout of the whole 6th Army."

Was that the action, as we learned it later, that Gen. Seydlitz ordered by his own decision? Very strange. At Demjansk, he was in charge of the attack divisions breaking the cauldron from outside.

"I have to go to work," the colonel general said with a serious face. The discussion about Demjansk-Stalingrad was never carried to an end. Yet the colonel general said the essential about the unavoidable development of that fateful battle.

JODL AT NUREMBERG

Whenever I had a chance, I enjoyed talking to the colonel general because of his realism and his precise description of military affairs.

That heroic fight, and the sacrifice of the Stalingrad soldiers, was to be followed up by triumphant noises from the Allies. Out of their arrogance and blind hate came the harsh and rigid demand of the "unconditional surrender."

Regarding that, in November 1944 I heard some critical observations by the colonel general: "No soldier with responsibility could undergo such a capitulation—it is dishonorable. Knowing all those conditions and the intentions of the enemy, only enraged resistance remains. That has nothing to do with fanaticism; despotism you can counter only with decisiveness, even in hopeless situations."

Many years later, when I read the Nuremberg protocols, I realized what military considerations were behind his words.

When questioned why Hitler did not capitulate in 1944-45, Jodl answered:

> Then, to advise to surrender I did not. That was totally out of the question; no soldier would have done that; it would not have been of any value. . . . Not even after the failure of the Battle of the Bulge . . . the Fuehrer was as well aware of the overall situation as we were and he probably saw it clearer much sooner than we did . . . also nothing needed to be said to him in that matter anyway.
>
> Apart from the fact that the question of a capitulation or giving up the resistance is above all a matter for the supreme commander, there were, in the winter of 1944, many reasons against it. One major point—we had no doubt that it could only be an *unconditional* surrender; at that time the enemy did not leave us in doubt about it. And if we still would have had any doubt about what we had to expect, it was completely eliminated when we got hold of the English 'Eclipse.' The English members of the commission will know what that is. It was the exact order of what the occupying power was going to do in Germany after the capitulation. The capitulation required the standstill on the fronts at the spot where they were, and their capture by the adversaries who stood across the line. The same thing that happened the winter of 1941 at Wjasma had to happen.
>
> Millions of prisoners had to camp in the middle of the winter in open fields. Death would have reaped an immense harvest, and above all, those nearly three and one-half million still standing at the eastern front would have fallen completely into the hands of the eastern adversary. It was our desire to bring as many people as possible to the west. One could do that only if the two fronts moved closer to each other. Anyway, those were the mainly military considerations we deliberated toward the end of the war. I believe that more will be said about that in later years than I can or will tell today.

CHAPTER 12 | 199

Hans Rudel sits in his plane, a Stuka dive bomber armed with "tank destroyer" 37 mm gun cannons under the wings, while a technician cranks up the engine.

PHOTO: GERMAN FEDERAL ARCHIVES

HITLER SEEKS A SUCCESSOR

It was late at night when Adolf Hitler read the last reports. One received his special attention. Again and again he recognizes, he said to me, that modern weapons give brave men the chance to excel. If they risk their life, those weapons will lead them to supreme success. But he [Hitler] has to watch out that the infantryman—the *Panzergrenadier*, who often has to endure much harder battles, does not come out short when his high achievement is evaluated.

Hitler said to me:

"For quite some time I've been aware that only a soldier of great status will be entitled to lead the nation once I retire after the end of the war. That's why I tried to get acquainted with anyone whose soldierly achievement and manly deeds were extraordinary. By having the chance to present the awards for brave soldiers personally, I gained an immediate impression of many. Regardless of his military rank or which part of the armed forces he belonged to, I was open and attentive to him. I talked to everybody in order to find the value of his personality—always searching for the outstanding soldier who could one day lead the nation.

"To his calm audacity and courage, personal charisma has to be added. Thoughtful and logical thinking, combined with an interest in modern technologies and cultural openness, were absolutely necessary. I looked for the soldier with imagination and leadership qualities. That naturally spoke for an officer of inborn authority. He had to be convinced this struggle is not only for Germany but for the whole of Europe. Steady he must be, and of strong character."

Adolf Hitler stood up, made a few steps and said, "I found him—the Stuka pilot Rudel!" I was not surprised, for he had been known to the nation for his courage, his fighting spirit and his success for some time. He was an officer of high reputation and an example of its soldiers.

Adolf Hitler continued:

"I wanted to take him in as my assistant. He should participate in all my sorrows and hopes—not only of military affairs. Rudel's humanistic education is a favorable qualification for further tasks.

"As a confidant, he would assist me. I wanted to introduce him to all the areas of responsibility and make him familiar with my ideas. I would then have had the opportunity to know him still better, to be sure that he will grow into the leadership of the Reich.

"I had to see in him more steadiness than I should expect—that he showed an iron will and knew how to use it. He said to me, 'I belong on the front line! As long as there is fighting, my place is there.' Up to now, I haven't succeeded. I really can't tell him I want to take him in as my successor.

"He has a great ability to evade my wish. Straightforwardly, he told me, 'I can accept that honor only when you allow me to return again to the front.' He felt that I understand him, yes, that I admire him and that I will not tie him down with an order. I hope he will stay alive!"

CHAPTER 12 | 201

"WE WILL WIN THE WAR"

One evening I witnessed an event that impressed me very much. He put a bunch of reports on the working table, reading as usual standing up, and then walked resolutely up and down the room. He said, "We will win the war!" And he repeated it. After a time I heard him again, "We will win the war, I am very certain of that." It was self-talking, not addressed to me.[4]

He rang for an adjutant, took the bunch of reports again into his hand, and turned toward me: "Giesler, I expect you after the *Lage*."

I had the feeling Adolf Hitler stood under a great strain. Just before, during dinner, I noticed his absent-minded pondering. I thought he was still feeling the tension of the previous military discussions, still thinking about decisions. I'm sure those reports were responsible now for that "We will win the war."

For quite awhile I noticed a change in his nature, the slight trembling of his left hand, played down by some joking words. His restlessness is all the way to nervousness; he is overworked. On the previous night, he gave me a hint:

"It is very hard for me to find sleep. Sleeping pills, certainly—but they make me only more tired, they do not give me sleep. Only after a long time awake, mostly around five or six o'clock, I fall asleep. Even in darkness or quietness—I've become accustomed to the humming of the air conditioning—I cannot fall asleep.

"I have the maps of front lines before of my eyes, from the armies to the divisions to the regiments. Anxiously, my thoughts are touching the front lines, something can happen here, something must happen there.

"I simply cannot switch off after the night *Lage* and give in to the demand for rest. I wait for incoming reports either from the front, from bombing attacks or of a world political event. At the nightly tea, talking about matters that interest me, I think I might be able to relax. Yes, sometimes it depends what the day had demanded from me. At the relaxing discussions, I am very picky: city construction, architecture and technology are my favorites—well, you know it!"

GERMAN NEWSPAPER DESCRIBES HEROIC EFFORT AT STALINGRAD

The NSDAP newspaper *Völkischer Beobachter*, on Feb. 4, 1943 ran the headline: "The Battle of the 6th Army around Stalingrad is ended. They died, that Germany lives." In the center, a famous relief sculpture by Arno Breker captioned "Our oath: retaliation!" The left column, headed "True to their Oath," is the official *Wehrmacht* report from Feb. 3, which begins: "The battle for Stalingrad is over. True to their oath and to their life's last stroke, the 6th Army under the exemplary leadership of Field Marshal Paulus succumbed to superior forces and unfavorable conditions. Their destiny is shared by a Flak Division of the German *Luftwaffe*, two Romanian divisions and one Croatian regiment. . . ." The right column, "Heroes of the 6th Army," was written by Alfred Rosenberg, party ideologist and *Reichsminister* for the East Territories, likening the current struggle to the great heroic sagas of old. He wrote: "The battle far away, at the banks of the Volga River, will enter history as the greatest symbol of all time . . . a heroism of a whole army which . . . coming centuries will tell as a struggle fought for the existence of a nation."

Worries and doubts overwhelmed me, also, after Stalingrad—the fateful collapse of Army Group Center, the failed defense of the invasion, and also the assassination attempt of July 20. But whenever I talked to Adolf Hitler, worries and doubts were eliminated by the immense fascination and radiation of his personality. His authority, the enormous power as the chief of state combined with his supreme command over the Armed Forces—all that was increased by his simple modesty. His matter-of-fact attitude impressed me, when, in the middle of hard war campaigns, he was thinking about reconstructing cities, as: "We are going to build that this way"—and it sounded like, "Too bad we cannot start tomorrow because adverse matters do not allow it."

That is what made my worries and doubts disappear, because he was so convinced and believed, "We will win the war." I was not able to resist his conviction and willpower. Again, it seems to me important to repeat: When we discussed plans for city reconstruction, Adolf Hitler combined unexpected ideas with matter-of-fact considerations before he made any decision. Everything was well thought out—in my own realm I could judge it—by his pragmatic evaluation of any problem. It was clear deliberation, well argued and finally, the assuring word, "That's the way we are going to build." Was it different in military matters? I cannot imagine that his high intelligence, his ever-awake senses did not see and consider military situations by the same clear observation and judgment.

And I am convinced that the sober-thinking Col. Gen. Jodl did not have to tell him in late fall 1944 that the military catastrophe was approaching from day to day and cannot be stopped.

Hitler saw the situation clearly, better and sharper than anybody else, because he was able to comprehend the whole scope, from raw materials to weapons, from the fighting strength of the soldiers to the strategic planning. I am also convinced that if it would have concerned only him, he would not have hesitated one day longer. What prevented him? Relentless stubbornness? No, much more—the "unconditional surrender."

That cold formula of destruction he could only counter with his unconditional resistance. That "unconditional surrender" was not targeted and limited to the removal of Hitler and the National Socialists, nor the "system," nor the *Wehrmacht* and its officers—but the German nation. Germany, its substance and living space, were the target.

Even if the leadership of the nation would have been formed by the men of the resistance, or even by those "men of God," annihilation on a much bigger scale than the continuance of the war could have taken place. Unconditional surrender—with that merciless formula the enemy powers not only prolonged the war but recklessly sacrificed German soldiers, civilians, women and children. They also sacrificed their own soldiers.

An additional idea also dominated Adolf Hitler—he felt far superior to Churchill and Roosevelt. To him, both of them were rudimental appearances from the past era of the 19th century. Stalin, however, he considered as a revolutionary who took Lenin's Communism to its final peak. Now he became the European threat—still "good old Uncle Joe," but for how long could that self-deceit of the Western Powers last? That alliance had to break down. That it did not happen yet does not speak against Hitler.

But all that means nothing against those defiant, forceful words: "We will win the war, I am certain about that!" Inconceivable for all who did not know Hitler and thought of him as a nihilist—he was a deeply believing man! His road led him through a changing era, and he was convinced that it was his task to walk that road, predestined by Providence.

Even more than his penetrating intelligence, his faith determined his thinking, his trust in Germany, himself and his mission, but also his belief in Providence. That belief, enforced again and again on his long way from zero to the Fuehrer of the nation, gave him the strength to be an example of steadfastness and optimism for his staff.

Adolf Hitler was well aware of the superior strength and recklessness of his adversaries, and the dangerous war situation. Any sign of weakness he must have seen as a deadly failure for all. That unbelievable strength to resist this weakness was not based on rational sources, but he gained it by his belief in Providence. How many nights did sleep evade him until he could find rest? ✦

CHAPTER NOTES:

1 This refers to the encirclement of German troops by the Red Army around the city of Demyansk (German: Demjansk), southeast of Leningrad. Called the Demyansk Pocket or *Kessel von Demjansk*, it existed mainly from early February until April 21, 1942.

2 This makes the Russian to German advantage in manpower at least 3 to 1.

3 Paul Carell explains in his book *Operation Barbarossa*, Schiffer Publishing Ltd., 1991, 495 pp.: "Catastrophe was already looming by noon on the 19th [November]. Whole divisions from the Romanian front, above all the 13th, 14th and 9th infantry divisions, broke and fled to the rear in panic. The Soviets pushed after them toward the west to the Chir and then to the south and southwest. It became clear that they [Soviets] wanted to break into the German Sixth Army's rear. . . ." Further explanation is found in *Stuka Pilot, Hans-Ulrich Rudel* by Guenther Just (1990), page 25: "A promising relief attempt got to within 30 km. of the pocket, but the main force had to be pulled back to avert the threat to the entire southern front caused by the Italians' failure near Bogoduchov."

4 A possible insight into Hitler's belief and hope that he could still "win the war" is his admiration for Frederick the Great, whom he personified as an example of will power and endurance. On the brink of disaster again and again during a seven-year war, Frederick held on, refusing to sign a cowardly peace treaty after the lost battles of Kunersdorf in 1757 and Hochkirch in 1758, thus saving his Prussian kingdom. At the chancellery in Berlin and in Hitler's *Wolfsschanze* and Berlin bunkers, Adolf von Menzel's painting of Frederick the Great was the only decoration adorning Hitler's simple room.

The most highly decorated German soldier in World War II, Hans Ulrich Rudel. Of him, Gen. Field Marshal Ferdinand Schoerner said, "Rudel alone replaces a whole division." Above, Rudel, on duty, wears the award Adolf Hitler personally designed for him. Hitler believed that Rudel had what it took to succeed him as Fuehrer of the Third Reich. Inset, an official photograph of Rudel.

HANS ULRICH RUDEL:
The Man Who Might Have Been Fuehrer

By Carolyn Yeager

"You are the greatest and most courageous soldier the German people have ever had." So Adolf Hitler told Hans Ulrich Rudel on Jan. 1, 1945 at the bunker headquarters in Berlin on the occasion of promoting Rudel to the rank of colonel and awarding him the highest German WWII decoration: the Knight's Cross with Golden Oak Leaves, Swords and Diamonds.[1]

This was quite a statement considering all the great and courageous soldiers who have fought so valiantly for the Fatherland, yet considering the almost unbelievable accomplishments of this modest man who loved piloting and sports, it was not a rash statement.

Rudel's extraordinary career began after he overcame a childish timidity by plunging himself into sports participation after hearing mocking words from his older sister. Once he had conquered his fear, "no tree was too high, no ski slope too steep, no brook too wide, and no boy's prank too risky"[2] for this son of a Lutheran priest who weighed less than six pounds when he was born July 2, 1916 in Konradswaldau in German Silesia—which since WWII is the section of Poland bordering the Czech Republic.

He developed the conviction that "one can do anything if one wants to." As a soldier, he famously maintained this belief with his personal motto: "Only he who gives up on himself is lost."

Between the Hitler Youth and school sporting meets, "Uli" became a decathlete for whom an Olympic future was predicted. From childhood he had wanted to become a pilot, but after he matriculated from secondary school his father could not afford the expensive training, as his oldest sister was already studying medicine.[3]

When he learned of the formation of a new *Luftwaffe*, he determined,

"I will become a pilot!" He passed the difficult entrance examination and began infantry training in Dec. 1936, but his path to becoming the world's greatest pilot was plagued with disappointment. First, he was a slow learner. After volunteering for dive-bomber school, he couldn't seem to get the hang of Stuka flying. And he was an odd duck, eschewing mess life with the other cadets [he didn't drink or smoke] to spend all his spare moments at sports or hiking in the magnificent hills surrounding Graz, in Styria.

Much to his dismay, he was transferred to reconnaissance flying school and during the Polish campaign the only shots he took were with a camera. He was also present, but not allowed to fly, during the western campaign. Then in September 1940, he was sent back to Graz to a Stuka Replacement *Gruppe* and on a practice mission he suddenly sensed what had so far eluded him and, even more, he had the clear knowing "now I have got it, now I can make the machine do everything I want it to."[4]

THE WARRIOR EMERGES

From then on, no one could touch him for skill and precision bombing; he was master of his machine. After Easter 1941, he was posted, with high hopes, to *I. Gruppe of Stukageschwader 2 Immelmann* on the Greek peninsula, but the CO there refused to allow him to fly operational missions, based on old reports from his adjutant. It wasn't until his group was transferred to the air base at Raczki on the Eastern Front that Rudel was finally given the chance to show what he was capable of.

On Sept. 23, 1941, his first extraordinary action took place. He sank the Soviet battleship *Marat* at the harbor of Kronstadt. By making a steep, up to 90-degree dive, he released the 2,000-kg bomb at about 300 meters, apparently striking right into the ship's magazine, and skyrocketed straight back up into the air, barely avoiding tremendous anti-aircraft shell fire and the explosion itself. He heard his gunner say, "*Herr Oberleutnant*, the ship is blowing up!" Congratulations immediately began pouring in from all sides over his radio.

He followed by sinking a cruiser, a destroyer and numerous landing

Nov. 25, 1943: Rudel (center) receives the Swords for his Knight's Cross with Oak Leaves from the hand of Adolf Hitler. On his right is Dieter Hrabak; on his left his gunner Erwin Hentschel. Hitler believed a man like Rudel might be groomed to become fuehrer after his own retirement. Hitler insisted that the man who was to replace him would have to be one universally respected by the German people.

boats around Kronstadt and the Lake Ladoga area. By the end of the war, Rudel had logged an unmatched 2,530 missions. In his first 90 days of flying against the enemy, he made his 500th flight and received the German Cross in Gold. In January 1942, General der Flieger von Richthofen presented Rudel with the Knight's Cross in the name of the Fuehrer, the citation listing his successes against ships, direct hits on important bridges, supply routes, artillery positions and tanks.

During 1942, Rudel's *Gruppe* flew difficult missions over the Caucasus, directed to their targets by radio. They sealed up a Russian armored train in a mountain tunnel, destroyed harbor installations, airfields, and vessels on the Black Sea. At the end of 1942, they flew missions in support of the heroic defense by the surrounded 6th Army at Stalingrad/Volgograd.

In 1943, following his 1,001st mission, Rudel went to a special unit at Rechlin/Mecklenburg that was testing the new anti-tank Ju 87 armed with two 3.7-cm cannon carried beneath the wings. Flying such an unwieldy but fearsome "cannon bird," Rudel went on to destroy more than 519 Russian tanks by the end of the war.

In April 1943, Rudel was promoted to *Hauptmann* and received the Oak Leaves to the Knight's Cross from Adolf Hitler in the Reich Chancellery, along with 12 others receiving decorations. At this time, Hitler must have already been observing him closely.

PERILOUS FORTUNE

A noted characteristic of Hans Rudel was his unwillingness to stay out of action, even when ill or injured. His healthy lifestyle—which included his continuing regimen of sports and mountain climbing in his spare time—and his positive mental attitude made for a constitution that mended rapidly. He "escaped" from several hospitals before being formally discharged and returned to his group, finishing his recovery while flying again.

Rudel was not immune, however, to the dangers he and his comrades faced daily. His plane was shot down by ground fire or crash-landed over 30 times, but he always managed to return safely. He even landed behind the Russian lines six times to rescue pilot comrades.

On the last such occasion, in March 1944, he landed near the destroyed Dnjester bridge to pick up the two-man crew of a crash-landed Ju 87. As it turned out, the field was so muddy he could not take off again and they were forced to escape by swimming across the ice-cold river. Rudel was the only one of the group to survive, even though he swam back into the river in an effort to assist his floundering gunner, who, however, he could not save. The other two pilots didn't run, as Rudel did, when they were approached by Russians, who took their pistols. He was shot in the shoulder as he zigzagged away, and ran/jogged nearly 30 miles, barefoot, over hard, rocky ground, chased by pursuers with dogs, until he reached the German line.

Following this ordeal, his feet were so damaged he couldn't wear regulation shoes or boots for several weeks while he continued flying missions and, in fact, appeared at the Berghof on March 29 as the 10th German soldier to be awarded the Knight's Cross with Oak Leaves, Swords and Diamonds, the highest existing decoration at that time, from Adolf Hitler, wearing his fur-lined flying boots.

Rudel was recognized by everyone as a phenomenon—a soldier who stepped beyond the limits of fortitude and sacrifice, and took risks nobody else dared. But he could not escape the perils forever. In November 1944, he was badly wounded in the thigh but, after an operation and with his left leg in a plaster cast, he continued flying. It was January 1, 1945, on the occasion of Rudel becoming the first and only German to be awarded the Knight's Cross with Golden Oak Leaves, Swords and Diamonds, that Hitler tried to get his hoped-for heir to stop flying.

According to Guenter Just:

> He received the decoration at Fuehrer Headquarters West at Taunus in the presence of the commanders of all branches of the armed forces, as well as Gen. Field Marshal Keitel, Col. Gen. Jodl and several eastern front generals. At the same time he was promoted to *Oberst*. Rudel's joy turned to dejection when Hitler said to him: "You have done enough flying. You and your experience must remain alive as an example for German youth."
>
> The high-ranking officers held their breath as Rudel answered, "My Fuehrer, I cannot accept this decoration and promotion if I am no longer permitted to fly with my *Geschwader*."
>
> Hitler suddenly smiled. "Very well then, fly. But be careful, the German people need you." Afterward, Rudel spent an hour and a half in conversation with the supreme commander and was astonished by Hitler's knowledge in the field of armaments technology. Subsequently he flew back to his squadron in Hungary.[5]

Within two weeks, the ban on Rudel's operational flying was reinstated, but he ignored the order from Fuehrer Headquarters, crediting his tank kills to the *Geschwader* so that the High Command wouldn't notice he was still flying. During missions over the Frankfurt/Oder-Kustrin area, Rudel and his group rescued an army unit that was surrounded by Soviet armored forces. Their reward was seeing the relieved troops wave and throw their helmets in the air for joy.

But Adolf Hitler's concern was warranted. On Feb. 8, 1945, at the Oder Front east of Berlin, a Russian anti-aircraft shell hit his cockpit, smashing into the lower part of his right leg, nearly severing it. Rudel used all his will power to force-land the plane, after which his gunner, Dr. Ernst Gadermann, saved his life by applying a tourniquet above the knee to stop the bleeding. When Rudel regained consciousness in the SS hospital near Seelow, he learned the crushing news that his leg had been amputated right below the knee. Hitler's reaction to the news: "He was lucky to get off so easy."

But even this would not hold Rudel back. His physician told him, "You are finished with flying." But before six weeks was up, Rudel left the hospital with an only partially healed stump and began commanding his squadron again. Wearing a temporary prosthesis and using a counterweight at his steering rudders, he flew again in April and killed his last 14 tanks.

On April 19, a day before Adolf Hitler's 56th birthday, he was called to the bunker headquarters in Berlin for a report before he left with his group to the airfield Maerisch-Schoenau in Bohemia. The Russians had crossed the Oder River and amassed their forces east of the Seelow heights for the final assault on Berlin. According to his own account, Rudel suggests to the Fuehrer that victory in the east is possible if "we can succeed in getting an armistice" with the west. He writes:

> A rather tired smile flits across his face as he replies: "It is easy for you to talk. Ever since 1943 I have tried incessantly to conclude a peace, but the Allies won't; from the outset they have demanded unconditional surrender.[6]

The entire staff lined up to say goodbye and wish him well when he left the bunker long after midnight.

Rudel's Battle Squadron 2 continued to support Field Marshal

Ferdinand Schoener's ground forces in the east until the final day of the war, when they decided to try to seek safety in the western occupation zones. On the capitulation day, May 8, he and a few comrades purposely landed their Stukas and FW 190's at their home field in Kitzingen in such a way as to shear off the landing gear and even break a wing. He expected to get medical attention for his leg from the American occupation forces, but instead was "relieved," as all the crews, of watch, fountain pen and decorations, and held for interrogation, eventually sent to camps

April 1945: Rudel returns to his squadron without his leg, but undaunted.

in England, then France, without medical attention. With difficulty, he finally obtained a transfer to a German military hospital in Bavaria where German doctors provided excellent care for his amputation wound. By mid-April 1946 he was released and had a top-grade prosthesis built in Kufstein, Tirol.

AFTER THE WAR

With no prospects in Germany for ex-National Socialists, in 1948 he and friends Bauer and Niermann managed, with the help of "Odessa,"[7] to get to Cordoba, Argentina and became consultants to the aviation industry there.

The regime of Gen. Juan Peron welcomed not only Rudel, but also Prof. Kurt Tank, the Focke-Wulf aircraft designer, and several German test pilots and *Luftwaffe* officers. At an aircraft plant in Cordoba, they worked on the first Argentine jet plane, the IAe Pulqui 2. Rudel continued to

Rudel (left) is shown with Evita and Juan Peron in Argentina after the war.

keep his body very fit. He climbed the 22,824-foot Aconcagua in the Argentine Andes; following that he scaled the 22,703-foot Llullay-Yacu peak three times, being the first man to do so even once. He raced wearing his prosthesis on the ski slopes of Bariloche, and completed his book, *Trotzdem* ("Nevertheless" or "In Spite of Everything"), which was translated into many languages and sold more than a million copies. His sports trophies continued to mount into the hundreds.

Early in 1950, after the fall of the Peron government, Rudel returned to Germany and immediately became involved in politics, becoming a leader in the German Reich Party. Hitler would have been pleased. His concern was for the future of the former German soldiers. He justified

Rudel is shown attending a meeting of the DRP (*Deutsche Reichspartei*) in the Rotmain Hall, Bayreuth, Sept. 2, 1953. He is accompanied by his mother. Rudel was forbidden to address the meeting by the Bavarian Ministry for the Interior, but others were permitted to read portions of his speech to the assembly.

his participation with the Third Reich by saying it was not for Germany but for Europe that he fought. He criticized the political climate in the Federal Republic, saying:

"I think our democracy has not yet reached the level of the U.S.A. There, you can openly say what you think. You cannot do it here, unless you express the opinion of the ruling political parties. When I express my opinion, I am right away disparaged and called a Nazi colonel. All I dared to say after the war was frank words to those people who insulted me and offended the soldiers. Since then, they called me a 'radical right-winger.'"[8]

In 1976, the "Rudel Scandal" brought about the early retirement of two *Bundeswehr* [former *Luftwaffe*] generals and the Social Democrat Defense Minister Georg Leber.

[Read about it at https://en.wikipedia.org/wiki/Rudel_Scandal.]

Rudel suffered a stroke in 1970, but his fighting spirit enabled him to recover sufficiently to be able to swim, hike and even ski again. But 12 years later, on Dec. 18, 1982, at the age of 66, Hans Ulrich Rudel, the "Eagle of the Eastern Front;" the man of whom the last chief of the *Wehrmacht* in 1945, Field Marshal Schoerner, said "Rudel alone is worth an entire division"—and the man Adolf Hitler wanted to succeed him as Fuehrer of the German Reich— died of heart failure in Rosenheim, Upper Bavaria. He left behind three sons, and an unprecedented record of achievement that will probably never be matched, let alone surpassed. This record includes:

- Missions flown against the enemy: 2,530 (a world record);
- Ground targets destroyed: 2,000 (including 519 tanks, 70 assault craft/landing boats, including a Soviet battleship, two cruisers and a destroyer, 150 self-propelled guns, four armored trains and 800 other vehicles);
- Air victories: nine (two Il-2s and seven fighters];
- Rescue missions behind enemy lines: six;
- Shot down/crash landings: 32 (He was never shot down by another aircraft even though Stalin had placed a 100,000-ruble bounty on his head.);
- Wounded: five times; and
- Decorations for bravery: 12 plus two foreign. He was the most decorated serviceman of all the branches of the German armed forces [apart from Hermann Goering, who was awarded the Grand Cross of the Iron Cross].

During his funeral service at Dornhausen, two Bundeswehr Phantom jet planes circled low over the gravesite[9] where most of his *Alte Kameraden*, his WWII comrades, were in attendance to bid him farewell with the familiar Nazi salute. ✦

ENDNOTES:

1 Guenther Fraschka, *Mit Schwertern und Brillanten*, 1989, Universitas Verlag, Munich, p 119.
2 Guenther Just, *Stuka-Pilot Hans Ulrich Rudel*, 1990, Schiffer Publishing, 277 pp, p 10.
3 *Ibid.*, p 11.
4 *Ibid.*, p 14
5 *Ibid.*, p 32
6 Hans Ulrich Rudel, *Stuka Pilot*, Ballantine Books, New York, 1958, p 267.

7 An organization that was purported to facilitate secret escape routes for SS members out of Germany and Austria to South America and the Middle East.

8 *Mit Schwertern und Brillanten*, ibid, p 125

9 *Der Spiegel*, "Letzer Flug" [Last Flight], Jan. 1, 1983. "Two days before the holy evening (December 24) last year... around noontime a funeral began at the village cemetery. Two Phantom jet planes circled in a strange looking pattern in the sky, crossing and bending in a way that with a little imagination one could recognize as a swastika, as one observer thought. A little later one Phantom dived in the direction of the village church, waggled with its wings and skyrocketed 300 feet above the village.... the *Deutschlandlied* was intoned in all three verses.... It did not take the Federal Ministry of Defense long to end the investigations about the ominous Phantom's low-level flight, with the result it found the *Bundesluftwaffe* did "neither on the ground nor in the air participate" at Rudel's funeral.

DEFENSE OF THE CAPITAL

Tiergarten "Zoo" Tower, where Col. Rudel was recovering from his amputation wound at the hospital inside. After the RAF raid on Berlin in 1940, Adolf Hitler ordered the construction of three massive flak towers to defend the capital from air attack. He personally made sketches which he turned over to Albert Speer, who completed the work in only six months. With concrete walls up to 11 feet thick, they were considered invulnerable to attack with the usual ordnance carried by Allied bombers, and each provided shelter for 15,000 comfortably.

CHAPTER 13

FAREWELL BERLIN

Translators' Introduction: Giesler's last days and hours with Hitler in the Berlin bunker in February 1945. Allied bombers dominated the skies everywhere in Germany and Europe, and the retreating *Wehrmacht* was assisting in the task of bringing as many Germans from their home provinces in the east farther westward, away from the advancing Soviet Red Army with its raping, murdering and pillaging. In the bunker under the Chancellery, Giesler installed the completed Linz model in a cellar room, giving Hitler many enjoyable hours studying it. We have come full-circle from Chapter One, back to Hitler's primary love for art, architecture and building. His reaction to the Dresden terror bombing is observed; Giesler visits Ley and Rudel; finally the dramatic leave-taking between Hitler and Giesler after a telephone call brings him bad news.

CREATIVE TASKS OF THE FUTURE

"Again and again the Fuehrer talks about your Linz plans and about the model of the Danube river bank reconstruction. When will your model be ready to show to the Fuehrer?"
Such calls arrived from the last Fuehrer Headquarters—the command bunker at the *Reichskanzlei* (office of the federal chancellor in Berlin), from the adjutant's office, and from Bormann during the depressing weeks of January.
The Battle of the Bulge failed. It did not lead to the strategic success hoped for and earned by our hard fighting, sacrificing divisions. In the

east, the front was weakening under the forward-storming Russian armies, and day by day the threat, not only around but also above us, increased.

The Bavarian and Danube districts[1] that were under my jurisdiction as an OT [Organization Todt] leader, were under increased bomber attacks. At that time of deadly worries and pressure, how contrary to my sisyphean work of removing the damages from the attacks was this question: "How long till the model of Linz is finished? . . . When can you present it to the Fuehrer?"

Could one understand that? I, at least, could. In autumn 1940, Adolf Hitler gave an additional task and introduced me to the new layout of Linz. His idea given to me at that time in Linz indicated that he had been thinking for a long time—maybe even since his youth—of a renovation of the city, changing its orientation toward the Danube.

Later, in the war years, whenever there was a chance, the Linz plans were a theme of our discussion. Linz was also the only peace-task dealt with, on his order, during the last war years. Often he visited my studio and discussed partial plans and part models with me, and then gave his instructions. For weeks at a time, he asked me to his headquarters in Winniza and *Wolfsschanze*.

Between military meetings, we were drawing together just like colleagues on the details of the plans. And at the hours when he was waiting for the front reports, we were talking about city reconstruction and architecture. That often took place during tension and bitter disappointments.

It seemed to me always, at the planning sessions or at the discussions, he was primarily concerned about performance—to get his mind off his concerns, maybe—but more so, he wanted to obtain a clear mind for his military decisions by concentrating on creative work.

Even during the most desperate days, he did not separate his thoughts from tasks of the future, binding them to peace beyond the war. He wanted to dedicate his time to work on the basic ideas of a new social structure, to shape the environment according to the requirements of the present time, thereby to solve the problems of city

CHAPTER 13 | 221

Hitler often stopped by Giesler's office in Munich to see how the Linz redevelopment project was coming along. He was a hands-on participant in the designing, always "full of ideas and enthusiasm" according to Giesler, as seen in this photo.

PHOTO: PERSONAL FILES OF HERMANN GIESLER

building. When he said we will win the war regardless of all the problems, he was very much convinced of it—even though he fully recognized the reality contradicted it. And that conviction had its roots in his unshakable belief in his mission.

Therefore, I understood his wish to see the model of the new creation of his hometown Linz, the architectural version of the Danube Bank reconstruction.

LINZ MODEL PRESENTED TO HITLER

Finally the Linz model was ready. The remaining model builders had worked tirelessly, often deep into night hours. It was an exceptionally high-class, professional job. The large model-structure now stood in one of the light-colored cellar rooms of the New Chancellery.

222 | THE ARTIST WITHIN THE WARLORD

A DREAM REALIZED

After five years of designing and planning, and nearly a lifetime of thought, Adolf Hitler finally sees the finished scale model of the reconstructed Linz Danube river bank. He did not let the approaching disaster in February 1945 detract from the intellectual and aesthetic pleasure it gave him. Giesler wrote: "I switched the lighting to 'midday light' to avoid blinding him. He asked for a chair. Bending forward, he looked across the river at the vertical rhythm of the housing blocks."   PHOTO: FILES OF HERMANN GIESLER

When I took Hitler to that room he stood for a long time, overwhelmed by the impression, just looking. I had positioned the searchlight like the rays of the afternoon sun; the significant Urfahr structure at the river, across from the Linz site, stood picturesque and impressive in the light. It was just as he described his architectural vision to me in autumn 1940. Now his view was just as he would see his "city on the Danube" from his planned retirement home.

With a somber face he looked at me, stepped toward my coworker, the model-builder Mehringer, still busy with the last additions, and thanked him for the wonderful achievement.

We switched the lighting to "morning light," and again he was completely engrossed, deeply sunk into the overall impression of the model. Now he looked at the Linz Danube bank construction from the Urfahr side.

What might be going on inside him? What thoughts moved him? I never saw him so serious in front of a model—so far away and so moved at the same time. I stood aside, depressed by the war events, overtired, and, looking at the model, I could not get rid of the thought: architecture never built.

Slowly, while continuing to look, he now stepped along the Urfahr side of the model toward the top side, where the Danube flows right from the natural landscape of the wooded mountains through the newly planned city district. He bent slightly to look downriver. I switched the lighting to "midday light" to avoid blinding him. He asked for a chair. Bending forward, he looked across the river at the vertical rhythm of the housing blocks. He nodded to me. Then followed the checking of the intervals and the proportions of the groups of buildings vis-à-vis the domineering verticals.

Regrettably, I was distracted by questions from the men accompanying him until Bormann sent them off with a handshake and "Later," giving me a chance to watch Hitler again. He was now sitting at the Linz side and looking across the river toward the "Great Hall" with the Danube tower and, inside, the planned gravesite for his parents marked by a bronze cenotaph.[2] Hitler observed it all attentively, awake and yet distantly dreaming, as if he would hear from the tower Bruckner's bell-tower motif[3] he was so fond of.

The escort left us alone; only Bormann stood aside in his typical pose with arms crossed, watching quietly.

The following day and during my stay at the command bunker of the Reich Chancellery, I accompanied Hitler mostly twice a day to the Linz model—in the afternoon, when lunch was often delayed because of the *Lage*, and then again in the night hours. It was nearly always the same: a long, deep, dream-like observation, followed by a discussion about details of the buildings and bridges appearing in the model.

Visitors participated, often requested by him, like Dr. Goebbels or military—if they, as he said, are open-minded. He showed the model to them as if it were the Promised Land into which we would find entrance.

One afternoon Hitler said Dr. [Robert] Ley married; he would like to know something about his wife. Then, after a short pause, to Schaub:[4] He should see that Dr. Ley sends me [Giesler] an invitation, so that I meet Mrs. Ley and could tell him [Hitler] all about her.

So one evening I was a guest at Ley's house, at their bomb shelter as it turned out. With some flowers, I conveyed to him Hitler's regards. The main theme of our discussion was Linz and Hitler's interest in the architectural model.

For various reasons, Ley was rather impressed: The Fuehrer knows how much he is interested and all that he is involved in and busy with. He knows, also, his interest in architecture; he certainly will show him the Linz model soon—more so since he [Ley] is responsible for some of the buildings at the Danube bank.

At the nightly tea hour, I told Hitler of the evening at the Leys' house. Dr. Ley met his young wife when helping a rescue party after a bombing attack. She was from the Baltics and had run away from the Russians. When I was alone with Dr. Ley he told me, "I saw her in the glow of the fiery blaze—she looked to me like the reincarnation of my wife that I lost. Giesler, you knew her—isn't there a similarity?"

Mrs. Ley, I said at the end, is a harmonious person, attentive and modest. With her intelligent eyes she carries a nice, quiet appearance. I had

Entrance lobby of the Führerhotel in Linz. Photo of the entrance hall of a scale model of the proposed five-story Adolf Hitler Hotel, which was part of the Linz Danube river bank reconstruction plan. The spacious, dignified feeling is typical of Third Reich design, which aimed to transmit a sense of clarity, cleanliness and strength. If you're surprised this is a model and not a real building interior, realize that Germans have always been exceptional model builders.

the impression Hitler was happy with my report. A few days later he showed Dr. Ley the Linz model.

DIFFICULTIES WITH ALBERT SPEER

With Bormann, I had detailed discussions about the tunnel shelter system at the Obersalzberg [Hitler's mountain retreat]. The scale of this installation for the headquarters and staff of OKW demanded and obviously justified a large labor force and rationed building materials. Speer caused problems; dissonance occurred that was out of proportion to the importance of my building requests at that time.[5]

I was the one compromised when we could not then meet urgent deadlines. I asked Bormann to understand my situation. I pointed out that even the *Jaegerbauten* (fighter program), an exclusive responsibility of Speer and Dorsch, was already delayed by three months even though they were privileged with special allocation quotas.

Those two were present when I expressed my and my brother's doubts about the location of those building sites, the use of concrete and steel, the necessary labor force, and the fixed deadlines assured by [Xaver] Dorsch. I said at that time, those steps were taken too late. The Fuehrer was annoyed: "Speer and Dorsch are responsible for that," and he gave me the order, "Giesler, you will not be concerned with that anymore. You remain with your tasks."

I stuck to that order. Now, after the deadline debacle, co-workers of Speer and Dorsch visited with me, asking if I might order the shutdown of the *Jaegerbauten* at Landsberg and Muehldorf.

"Unbelievable," Bormann remarked. "And what did you say?"

"What's that all about?—I neither proposed those super structures, nor did I plan them, and they do not fall under my supervision. The ones responsible for those buildings are—and you know it well enough—Dorsch and Speer, and a decision about the shutdown can only be made by the Fuehrer."

"They want to put the blame on you." Bormann meant: in order to weasel themselves out of the deadline problems. "Stay out of it!"

GÖTTERDÄMMERUNG AT HEADQUARTERS

The Yalta conference was on. Reports reached Hitler even before the Linz model arrived, which should have given him—if even for a short time only—some relief.

[Helmut] Suendermann, the deputy press chief, himself brought the reports in, written with large letters, and explained them. The Fuehrer dictated further directions and orders for the press, decided on meetings with the foreign secretary [Joachim von Ribbentrop] and Dr. Goebbels, and all that without taking his eyes off the model.

During the hours of the *Lage* and the other meetings, I talked to the men of Hitler's inner circle about the results we had to expect from Yalta. Apparently, they agreed again on points like in Wilson's time, only now

Dresden following the four separate bombing raids that took place on Feb. 13-15, 1945. The firestorms created by British and American planes destroyed over 1,600 acres of the undefended city center and killed up to 100,000 citizens and refugees under horrific conditions, making it the worst war crime of WWII. GERMAN FEDERAL ARCHIVES

without unholy pretensions, but with all the frank, brutal decision of the total destruction of Germany. Germany was divided into occupied zones, but they did not know yet how many National Socialists should be shot. They talked about peace-loving nations, meaning only their own, chatted about the highest ideals for mankind and sacred duties, about a secured and lasting peace and a life free of worries and misery for all people and nations; everything will be good, peaceful and glorious as soon as Germany is shattered. A courageous soldier of WWI said cynically: "Well, it seems to me the peace will be terrible!"

Did he have any idea what was approaching him? After a heavy wound in Berlin—the Lubyanka Prison in Moscow and 10 years in Siberia.

Next evening, I found a deeply shattered Hitler: Dresden. As a horrifying signal notifying the world, the great European, Churchill, dreamed up and ordered that terror attack against the refugee and hospital city, as a present to Josef Stalin.

According to the reports, far more than 1 million people were in the city, among them a half million refugees from Silesia. In a night attack of countless British bombers approaching in waves, the city was helpless, without anti-aircraft defense, hailed down upon by exploding and incendiary bombs. Then the last bomber wave arrived and unloaded phosphorus bombs on the tortured people who had survived the previous attacks.

With a stony face, Hitler listened to the reports. Standing erect, he read the messages, finally bending over the table, the crammed papers in his clenched fist. He remained shut off. Only late at night, after the second attack at the edge of the burning city of Dresden, he spoke: "This renewed attack was meant for those who were able to escape hell—that depressing day was followed by a night of recognition: the threat of relentless annihilation!

"What was possible after the terror attack at Hamburg, Cologne, Berlin and wherever else—to trace the victims—at Dresden is impossible. We do not know how many refugees were in the city. The estimates differ by hundreds of thousands.

"Whatever happened, one still could imagine Europe—after Dresden, however, it is hardly possible anymore. Now, again, like after the attack at Hamburg, I think back at the situation in 1940. The defeated French and English forces were encircled at Dunkirk. At that time I was pondering, realistic and responsible, as a soldier and politician. Should I admit that an ethical thought might have been involved in my deliberating? It is not easy to order the annihilation of hundreds of thousands.

"Today, my decision is considered a mistake, stupidity or weakness. Naturally, after the years of armed clashes degenerating into actions of terrible destruction—today, after Dresden, I would react differently.

"During the lucky, but also during the hard, unlucky battles of those war years, I tried to be sensible. I made the effort to hold on to some kind of humanity—if one could react that way responsibly in the middle of a relentless war. I did not lead a war of destruction against cities and cultural institutions, neither when occupying a place nor moving out—Rome, Florence or Paris. They should not pretend keeping Paris undamaged was the merit of the resistance or even the Allied forces. If I would have thought that the defense of the city would have been necessary, then that would have happened. And if I wanted the destruction of Paris, a battle-experienced commander with a division would have been enough."

That terror attack at Dresden can by no means be militarily justified—it was wanton murder, and destruction of a culturally prominent city.

A remark of Dr. Goebbels refers to it also: "That is the raging of a follower of Herostratus,[6] the deed of a madman knowing that he is unable to build a temple and trying to prove to the world he is at least able to burn it."

To me, those words were too one-sided, referring to Dresden as a city of historical culture. My thoughts were with the victims. Those people were fleeing the horror of war, the rape and murder by Asiatic bolshevists, and then met relentless death by explosive and fire bombs, and the phosphorus of Winston Churchill.

Later—after the devaluation of all values—pompous non-historians celebrated Churchill as the great European and awarded him, at Aachen, the *Karlspreis*.[7]

RUDEL GETS PERSONAL ATTENTION

During my further stay at the chancellery, Hitler again took officers and men he held in high esteem to see the Linz model, and explained his city planning. Everybody was impressed, be it only because they experienced the Fuehrer at a level they had been excluded from until now.

I saw my task fulfilled. My discussions with Bormann and the military at the OKW about the protective system at the Berghof, and the area for the alternative headquarters at the Obersalzberg, were completed. At the late afternoon tea, I reported my departure to Hitler.

No, he decided he would ask me to stay. He still has to talk with me about many matters. Did I know that Col. Rudel lies at the Zoo bunker with an amputated leg?

"Yes," I said, "Col. [Nicolaus] von Below told me so."

"Visit with him tomorrow, give him my regards, talk with him! Get personally acquainted with him, and report to me."

Rudel rested at the hospital of the gigantic shelter bunker at the Zoo.[8] He was surrounded by *Luftwaffe* comrades and young ladies. I gave him Hitler's greetings and congratulations for receiving the highest military award. Then I was only a listener to a very lively conversation with a very attentive Rudel until the doctor entered and the visiting hour closed.

After the busy saying of goodbyes, I could talk with him for a short while and ask him a few questions undisturbed. "What should I report to the Fuehrer? How are you—peppery and confident as I've seen you during this conversation?"

"Confident, yes! But still with some worries. I hope to fly again soon."

"With one leg?"

"I will manage that! My place is now at the front line. Especially now, when we have to defend German soil, I cannot leave my wing and my comrades alone."

I asked another question: Does he know in the meantime what task is awaiting him from the Fuehrer? No, Rudel thought the Fuehrer understands him very well: he will not deny him his further front mission.

When I reported to Hitler in the evening, he shook his head thoughtfully and said, looking at me, "There is no time now. I will give Col. Rudel a very important task within the *Luftwaffe*. I am certain he will master it."

In the evening and night hours, Hitler talked about political, social, military and world affairs. He was concentrated, spirited, often visionary and promethean.[9] During the war years, especially at his solitary times, I was his talking partner—mostly, however, about space configuration, environment, architecture and city building. Now, I was surprised about these themes and how he summarized them; I was fascinated by the richness of his thoughts and his creative power.

During one interruption—he was called to the telephone—I whispered to Bormann, "That should be recorded; that is of great importance!" Bormann answered. "I've tried it for quite awhile."[10]

CHAPTER 13 | 231

Hitler's last visit to the front, March 11, 1945, at the headquarters of the 9th Army, Oderfront. Behind him, from left: *General der Artillerie* Wilhelm Berlin; *Generaloberst* Robert Ritter von Greim (promoted to *feldmarschall* on April 19-20); *Generalmajor* Franz Reuss; *General der Flakartillerie* Job Odebrecht; *General der Infanterie* Theodor Busse, commander of the 9th army.   PHOTO: GERMAN FEDERAL ARCHIVES

AFTER TERRIBLE NEWS, GIESLER BIDS FAREWELL

The tension-rich hours at the command bunker at the old *Reichskanzlei* piled up to days and nights without any transitions. The timetable was marked only by the military *Lage* talks, but even they were rather fluctuating, like the interruptions by the short and very simple meals. No hectic atmosphere existed at the bunker; just the continuous coming and going by generals and officers of the armed forces. Everything was strictly organized by short orders and attentive adjutants.

On Feb. 23, my brother called me from Munich: "I bring you bad news. Get hold of yourself. Sit down and listen. Our dear mother was seriously wounded by a low-flying American fighter plane. No, no hope anymore. Our aunt was with her and died right away. Come as soon as possible, please."

Our mother was with her sister on the way to us, her sons, after her house was bombed out. I needed a long time to regain my composure, then I said goodbye to my comrades at the Fuehrer Headquarters and walked to the *Lage* room at the new *Reichskanzlei* to report my departure to Hitler.

I stood in the big hall; beneath me was the cellar with the Linz model. It got dark; candlelight was brought in after the electricity went out. The big door opened and Hitler saw me. He came toward me and gave me his hand. "I know, Giesler, your mother."

"I would like to report my departure, my Fuehrer. I take the next train to Munich."

"No, I will not allow you to be alone. Come on." He led me to the *Lage* room. I saw and heard, and then again I did not. What has remained in my mind was the unreal room, what I saw by the candlelight—the Fuehrer, the table with the maps, the tense faces, the officers' epaulettes, the crosses of their awards, hands pointing out, voices, reports, harsh ordering words.

All that, I saw and heard; it was the now, the present. And behind lay the dark room, uncertain like the future. It seemed to me as if I had lived through all that already, or dreamed about it, deeply depressed. I remembered the evening at the Berghof, in February 1941. Instead of the hoped-for peace, there stood the threatening danger from the east. Also at that time there was the flickering light from the fireplace in the dim room when Lizst's *préludes* resounded as a fateful preamble—I was thinking about my mother.

The *Lage* ended. At the Fuehrer's side, I went back to the bunker. Hitler said, "Kaltenbrunner[11] takes the train to south Germany tonight; he will bring you safely to Munich. Your brother will be informed."

"After all that's happened, I would now like to become a soldier, and I ask you for it."

"No, you did your duty as a young volunteer in World War I. You remain as my architect. I have enough soldiers, if they and their leaders only stand up steadfast and fight."

A little later Kaltenbrunner arrived. I said goodbye. Adolf Hitler gave his hand and, as so often, he laid his left hand on my arm, wordlessly. I looked into Hitler's eyes for the last time.

Before the Allied tribunal at Nuremberg in 1946, Col. Gen. Alfred Jodl said this about Hitler: "He acted like all heroes in history act, and they will continue to act that way. He let himself be buried in the ruins of his Reich and his hopes. Condemn him, ye who may. I cannot." ✦

CHAPTER NOTES:
1 These were the Gaus, the administrative districts in Germany at the time.
2 A cenotaph is, of course, a monument erected in honor of a dead person or persons whose remains lie elsewhere.
3 A motif from Bruckner's Fourth Symphony, on special occasions, chimed from a bell tower in Linz.
4 Julius Schaub was Hitler's personal adjutant since 1925.
5 Albert Speer, Hitler's chief architect, was in charge of all building material allocation at that time.
6 Herostratos was an ancient Greek who set fire to the temple in Ephesus, one of the most beautiful buildings in the world. He is said to have destroyed that which he was unable to build.
7 The *Karlspreis* is given annually to an "outstanding European" by the German city of Aachen.
8 "The Zoo" refers to the Zoological Gardens district in Berlin where a five-story, super-strong bunker, with anti-aircraft batteries on top, had been built. Inside the bunker were shelters and a hospital.
9 Promethean, in the sense of one who is boldly creative or defiantly original in behavior or actions. The talks Giesler is referring to are the supper-time and late night talks Hitler conducted with his entire inner circle.
10 This appears to be a reference to what has come to be known as "Hitler's Table Talk," notes taken by Bormann's adjutants Heim and Picker during mealtimes, with Hitler's approval.
11 Ernst Kaltenbrunner was head of the RSHA, the Reich Main Security Office.

A Letter from Breker

This appeared in an appendix in the original edition of *Ein Anderer Hitler*. Arno Breker was Hitler's favorite sculptor and also highly admired throughout Europe, especially in France.

Professor Arno Breker
29 November 1977

Dear Hermann Giesler:

Last night I finished reading the final chapter of your book; it is also truly shattering. Your book brought many things to light I did not know; above all, the scope of the unbelievable treason. That up to this time one does not know who was behind it, baffles me anew.

Your writing covers by far the most essential, most true and realistic reporting that has been written about the immense tragedy of that epoch. Specifically concerning the field of architecture, one has to go far back in history to meet a similar situation. Our epoch proves anew that the powerful documents of architecture, lasting beyond all time, derive from a lonely personality coined by fate for a specific period.

I am convinced that today's media is helpless when confronting what you've written. Thanks to your extensive documentation, historiography is faced with a new task. In your report, the fateful events roll on like a natural phenomenon.

Hitler is the consequence of the Versailles treaty. The whole drama fell upon an anonymous man and providence destined him to break the fateful situation. Hitler's primitive, dazzled enemies were not aware that there stood a man who wanted to create a new epoch —also [in] architectural [terms]. That could only happen during a quiet, peaceful period. Your book clearly demonstrates it.

The prologue already makes one prick up his ear. It is a masterful work. How blindfolded the world still is today is proved by the trouble you had to go through before you found a publisher for your manuscript.

Arno Breker in front of a version of his famous relief Apollo and Daphne. The most significant neo-classic sculptor of the 20th century, Breker (1900-1991) placed the image of man in the center of his creative work. Like his patron Adolf Hitler, who named him "official state sculptor" and gave him a large property, studio and many assistants, Breker thought in historical dimensions. After the war, the Allies destroyed over 90% of his public works.

Nobly, you treated your adversaries with your critique, above all Mr. Reeps.[1] Cool and collected, you can look your opponents in the eye. Max Liebermann[2] would say: *Mir kann keener* ("nobody can touch me"). Everything is said by that. Either your book launches an avalanche of comments, or it will be silenced to death. We face that alternative. For now, my dearest regards,

Always yours,
—Arno Breker

ENDNOTES:

1 Reeps is Speer spelled backwards. A long chapter in Giesler's book is devoted to his oftentimes difficult relationship with fellow architect Albert Speer, both during and after the Third Reich period.

2 Max Liebermann was a prominent Jewish impressionistic painter of the Weimar period who associated with anti-Nazi elements and the Stauffenberg circle. He remained unmolested up to his death in 1935.

A Reich of Art & Culture

By Carolyn Yeager

The effort to "explain" the phenomenon of Adolf Hitler is made impossible for mainstream writers by their obligatory need to portray him as a perpetrator of genocide, war atrocities and "the murderer of millions."

Frederic Spotts, in his informative though biased book *Hitler and the Power of Aesthetics*, obligingly writes that it was Hitler who "turn[ed] Europe upside down and nearly destroy[ed] it."[1] Yet he also wrote in the preface that, "After being appointed chancellor in 1933 the first building he had erected was not a monument to his own triumph but a massive art gallery."[2] Hitler's complaint to his field commanders after Winston Churchill refused peace terms in 1940 was, "It is a pity that I have to wage war on account of that drunk instead of serving the works of peace."

The tasks of peace—grand architectural renovations and the promotion of German culture—were uppermost in Hitler's mind, as Hermann Giesler has shown us throughout his memoir. But not only Giesler. After pondering the matter for 20 years in Spandau Prison, Hitler's other architect, Albert Speer, concluded that Hitler was always, and with his

The Fuehrer Art Museum for Linz designed by architect Hermann Giesler. Linz was to become a cultural mecca, with a large theater, a concert hall devoted to Anton Bruckner, a special operetta theater and an opera house with 2,000 seats, along with the art museum —all placed along a grand boulevard. Most of the buildings were based on Hitler's own sketches.

1937: Hitler works on a sketch for the facade of a massive domed structure. This was intended to be the Great Hall in Berlin. The sketch ended up in the possession of Albert Speer.
GERMAN FEDERAL ARCHIVES

whole heart, an artist.[3]

Hitler's secretary Christa Schroeder recalled that his non-military conversation turned more and more to the arts.[4] Josef Goebbels provides numerous examples in his diaries. In January 1942, after a long discussion with Hitler, he wrote: "The intensity of the Fuehrer's longing for music, theater and cultural relaxation is enormous." The life he was then leading was "culturally empty," the Fuehrer had told him, and he looked forward to the war's end when he would "compensate for this by a dedication stronger than ever to the more beautiful sides of life."

Giesler, in charge of designing Hitler's retirement home overlooking

Hitler sketches out an architectural idea or detail for Albert Speer (right) in Nuremberg while longtime aide Julius Schaub looks on.

Adolf Hitler's study at the Berghof, where every detail was carried out to his exact specifications. A 1938 *British Homes & Gardens* magazine pictorial lay out on Hitler's home described him as "his own decorator, designer and furnisher, as well as architect." The furniture was made of maple, and over the fireplace (not seen) hung a portrait of Helmuth von Moltke the Elder, the brilliant 19th century Prussian field marshal and strategist. A telephone switchboard room was directly off the study.

Linz, was told by him, "The great hall with the terrace [is] the right room for an 'Artus Runde' [Round Table, in King Arthur's style].... You, as my architect, will be a member." Hitler envisioned discussion of art, philosophy and matters of importance to the future of Europe by those invited to his home. "Ms. Braun," whom he would marry when he retired after the war, would be the lady of the house.[5]

Hitler was no dilettante. His knowledge of architecture was enormous, along with many other subjects. He had supported himself from 1909-1913 in Vienna and Munich by drawing and painting architectural landmarks in watercolor and oil, selling his works through dealers. His Munich landlord, Herr Popp, said he often found his lodger reading the works of Schopenhauer and Plato, along with war histories. Throughout World War I, Hitler carried with him a pocket edition of *The World as Will and Idea*.[6]

His enthusiasm for Richard Wagner's music began as a 12-year-old boy attending a performance of *Lohengrin* in Linz. He's said to have seen *Tristan und Isolde* up to 40 times and *Der Meistersinger* 100 times. He could hum or whistle all its themes.[7]

In 1942, Hitler became equally enthused about Austrian-born composer Anton Bruckner. He considered Bruckner's Seventh Symphony the equivalent of Beethoven's Ninth. Always generous with his own funds, Hitler personally financed a center of Bruckner studies, had his organ repaired and added to his library; he also designed a monument in Bruckner's honor in Linz; endowed a Bruckner Orchestra and subsidized the publication of the composer's original scores.[8]

No other leader of the time came close to that dedication. Stalin, Lenin, Mao Tse-tung, even Mussolini, had hardly set foot in an art gallery.[9] While ostensibly better educated, Churchill, Roosevelt and Wilson were far below Hitler's level of cultural awareness. It turns out, by a close study of Adolf Hitler's biographers, memoirists, associates and the record itself, that his idea of national greatness was only fulfilled in a true national art and culture—reminiscent of the ancient Greeks he admired, wherein physical beauty combines with a brilliant mind and noble soul. ◆

ENDNOTES:
 1 Frederick Spotts, *Hitler and the Power of Aesthetics*, Overlook Press, Woodstock and New York, 2002, p. 8 (456 pp, #377; available from TBR BOOK CLUB for $22).
 2 *Ibid.*, p xi.
 3 *Ibid.*, p 3.
 4 Christa Schroeder, *He was my Chief*, Frontline Books, 2009, p 226.
 5 According to Hermann Giesler, Chapter 7 this book, p. 123.
 6 Werner Maser, *Hitler: Legend, Myth & Reality*, Harper & Row, 1973, p 124.
 7 Spotts, op cit., p. 235.
 8 *Ibid.*, p. 233
 9 *Ibid.*, p. 10.

GLOSSARY OF GERMAN WORDS

Alte Kameraden: Old Comrades. Usually used among war veterans.
Aufschneider: Austrian dialect describing a person who boasts or "shows off", but also refers to "cutting," thereby a name for a surgeon.
Bauleitung: Building construction management.
Bekennende Kirche: Confessional or Confessing Church. A Protestant schismatic church founded in 1934 in opposition to German government-organized church commissions.
Bendlerstrasse: Street on which the building housing the Ministry of Defense in Berlin stood. Used as the headquarters of the *Wehrmacht* officers who carried out the July 20th assassination plot.
Bundeswehr: Federal Defense Force of Germany since 1955
Fallschirmjaeger: Paratrooper. German elite troops engaged in special aerial operations.
Festung Europa: Fortress Europe. Refers to the fortification of Europe to prevent invasion from the British Isles and/or the Soviet Union.
Fliegerabwehrkanone: (FLAK) Anti-aircraft gun.
Flakturm: Anti-aircraft defense tower. Three were built in Berlin with big guns on the roof and shelter, medical and other facilities inside.
Gau: A regional administrative district of the NSDAP (National Socialist German Worker's Party).
Geheimrat: Privy Councillor. A title reserved for the highest official at the German court; also used in the First Republic and during the Third Reich.
Götterdämmerung: Twilight of the Gods. Specifically, the turbulent ending of the Teutonic house of the gods in Asen.
Grossdeutschland: Greater Germany after1938. Included Austria, Sudetenland, Eupen-Malmedy, Untersteiermark, Wartheland.
Haftladung: A magnetic hollow charge used against tanks, ships and fortifications.
Hochverrat: High treason. Acts to destroy the existence of the state or constitution; for instance by killing the head of state.
Karlspreis: International Charlemagne Prize given by the city of Aachen.
Kaiserpfalz: Emperor's palace. Temporary residence of the Holy Roman Emperors of the German Nation since the early medieval time; 60 in all.

Kapuzinergruft: Crypt of the Capuchins. Imperial tomb for most of the Habsburg rulers, located in Vienna.
Kessel: Cauldron. In military language, a pocket or salient encircling enemy forces.
Kriegsmarine: Navy. The naval part of the German Forces.
Kriegstagebuch: War diary; daily log of military events.
Lage: Daily military situation meeting held at command headquarters.
Landesverrat: Treason against your country. For example, informing foreign governments about secret affairs of state.
Lebensraum: Living space. The territory deemed necessary for a nation's continued existence and well being.
Luftlandetruppen: Airborne troops. A special wing of the German military forces for transportation and landing of infantry units.
Luftwaffe: Air Force.
Machtuebernahme: Accession to power
Nahkampfspange: Close Combat Bar. A military decoration for hand to hand combat.
Odessa: O/rganisation D/er E/hemaligen SS/A/ngehoerigen. Organization to help former SS members leave Germany (where they were viewed as criminals after 1945) via the Alps and Italy.
OrganisationTodt (OT): Construction monolith founded by Dr. Fritz R. Todt.
Panzer: Tank
Panzergrenadier: Motorizedinfantryman, fighting in combination with tanks.
Reichskanzlei: Federal Chancellery; seat or home of the head of the government, the Reichskanzler.
Reichstag: German parliament
Reichsmarschall: Highest rank in the German *Wehrmacht*. Hermann Goering was the only Reichsmarschall.
Rote Kapelle: Red Orchestra. Code name for an underground spy organization working out of France, Belgium and Switzerland, helped by well-placed German communist traitors.
Ritterkreuz: Knights Cross. High German decoration for bravery and leadership in war.
Sperrkreis: Security zone, usually barricaded.
Staubmantel: Dust coat. A lightweight, often light-colored coat.
Schnellboot: Fast boat. Small and quick, they were equipped with guns and/or torpedos.
Staffel: Squadron. The smallest unit of the *Luftwaffe* with 12 airplanes.
Stuka: Dive bomber. Full name: Sturzkampfflieger. Aircraft type: JU 87 and JU 88.
Tauchpanzer: Dipping tank. Amphibious vehicle designed to be driven under water. Planned for Operation Sea Lion, it's only action was crossing the river Bug in Russia in 1941.
Tiergarten: A large green space in central Berlin, with the Reichstag at one end facing the more centrally located Victory Column.

GLOSSARY | 243

Untersberg: High mountain peak near Salzburg, Austria visible from Hitler's Berghof residence.
Vierkanter: Four-sided. Vierkanterhof: Four cornered farm house, a traditional Upper Austrian architectural style.
Volksgemeinschaft: People's community. Hitler envisioned the ideal German society as a racially unified "Volksgemeinschaft" where national interests overrode individual interests.
Valkyrie (Walküre in German): In Nordic mythology, young women who acted as battle and shield carriers. In the Third Reich, the code name for emergency military alerts. Used by the Stauffenberg conspiracy in their attempt to bring about a *coup d'état*.
Völkischer Beobachter: NSDAP Party newspaper, edited by Josef Goebbels.
Wehrmacht: Armed forces. The three branches were *Heer* (Army), *Kriegsmarine* (Navy), *Luftwaffe* (Air Force). The Waffen SS is considered by some historians as a late 4th branch.
Weltanschauung: Comprehensive world view.
Werwolf: The name for Hitler's farthest east military headquarters, in Ukraine. Wehr equates to Defense.
Wolfsschanze: Wolf's lair. Hitler's heavily camouflaged headquarters located near the East Prussian town Rastenburg.
Zoo: Area near the Zoological Gardens in the Tiergarten. One of three FLAK towers was built there and colloquially called "The Zoo."

About the Translators

WILHELM L. KRIESSMANN was born in 1919 in Klagenfurt, Carinthia, Austria. "Willi" grew up in turbulent nationalist times. In school, he loved and excelled in history and geography and became a follower of Adolf Hitler. "Called to the colors" in 1938, accepted in the Luftwaffe as a pilot-cadet, his war service included 93 missions on the Eastern Front as a bomber pilot. After the war, Willi earned a Ph.D. from Gratz University, married, and secured a coveted position in the Austrian Trade Ministry in Vienna. Following a promotion to Trade Commissioner for the U.S. West Coast, he moved his growing family to California in 1953. Always an avid reader as well as sports enthusiast (skiing, biking, hiking and tennis his favorites), in retirement he took up writing for German-American periodicals and generously offered his services for translation. For more about Wilhelm's life, please take a look at the WLKriessmann Archive at http://kriessmann.carolynyeager.net/.

CAROLYN YEAGER is a published author, writer and podcaster. Since 2007, she has specialized in 20th-century German and European history and related subjects. Her active websites include www.carolynyeager.net and www.eliewieseltattoo.com. Carolyn began producing weekly Internet radio programs on March 1, 2010 and is the founder of The White Network, which flourished for two years (2012-2014) before being forcibly shut down by her partner. She has been responsible for getting a number of important German documents translated into English, including hard-to-find speeches by Adolf Hitler and Heinrich Himmler, which you will find archived on her personal website, along with her entire body of work.

Meet an Adolf Hitler you never knew in the pages of this truly extraordinary book . . .

Wilhelm Kriessmann and Carolyn Yeager, working as a team, translated sections from the German *Ein Anderer Hitler* ("Another Hitler"), the memoir of architect Hermann Giesler . . . and the result has become this volume which they titled *The Artist Within The Warlord—An Adolf Hitler You've Never Known.*

This is not the usual copy-cat "history" by another "historian" who tries to find some angle to make his or her book stand out from the hundreds of other books already on the shelves about the most misunderstood man in history.

This book is genuinely unique—taken from the account given by an intimate of Adolf Hitler who was privileged to enjoy many private talks with him during the time of some of the most momentous events of contemporary world history. Munich architect Hermann Giesler became from 1938 on not only Hitler's favored architect for the renovation of Munich and Linz, but also an agreeable confidant to whom the Supreme Commander felt comfortable unburdening himself as they spent many hours together drafting city-wide building ideas. Hitler's artist nature needed such a creative outlet, leading Giesler to become a more frequent guest at the Berghof and the two secret military headquarters *Wolfsschanze* and *Werwolf* for this very purpose. You will gain insight into how the artist and humanist in Hitler revealed itself in his character and his world view (*Weltanschauung*).

Of Giesler's book, Arno Breker, the great sculptor who also knew Hitler very well, wrote that it was "by far the most essential, most true and realistic reporting that has been written about the tragedy of that epoch." Gerard Menuhin—son of famed Jewish-American violinist Yehudi Menuhin and the author of *Tell the Truth and Shame the Devil*—called Giesler's book "wonderful" and "one of the main books to read about Hitler" in July 2017. That Giesler had so much trouble finding a publisher for his book tells the true tale of the value of this volume.

Surely, there has been no offering like this one, in English, of a more authentic Adolf Hitler. Now you have available the sections of Hermann Giesler's memoir dealing with the Fuehrer in a well organized, easy to follow format, featuring a generous number of illustrations and helpful commentary from the translators. It's a book you will treasure. Softcover, 244 pages.

www.ingramcontent.com/pod-product-compliance
Lightning Source LLC
Chambersburg PA
CBHW032032290426
44110CB00012B/772